RELIGION IN HISTORY, SOCIETY, AND CULTURE

Edited by
Frank Reynolds
and
Winnifred Fallers Sullivan
The University of Chicago, Divinity School

A ROUTLEDGE SERIES

RELIGION IN HISTORY, SOCIETY, AND CULTURE:
edited by Frank Reynolds and Winnifred Fallers Sullivan

LITURGY WARS

RITUAL THEORY AND PROTESTANT REFORM IN NINETEENTH-CENTURY ZURICH

Theodore M. Vial

Routledge
New York and London

Published in 2004 by
Routledge
29 West 35th Street
New York, NY 10001
www.routledge-ny.com

Published in Great Britain by
Routledge
11 New Fetter Lane
London EC4P 4EE
www.routledge.co.uk

Routledge is an imprint of the Taylor & Francis Group
Printed in the United States of America on acid-free paper.

10 9 8 7 6 5 4 3 2 1

Library of Congress Cataloging-in-Publication Data

Liturgy wars : ritual theory and Protestant reform in nineteenth-century
Zurich / [edited] by Theodore M. Vial.
        p. cm. -- (Religion in history, society & culture ; 4)
Includes bibliographical references and index.
    ISBN 0-415-96698-1 (alk. paper)
 1. Biedermann, Alois Emanuel, 1819-1885. 2. Baptism
(Liturgy)--History--19th century. 3. Zurich (Switzerland)--Church
history--19th century. 4. Reformed
Church--Switzerland--Zurich--Liturgy--Theology--History--19th century.
I. Vial, Theodore, M., 1962-   II. Series
    BX9427.5.B36L58 2003
    264'.042494572--dc22

                                        2003015565

For Nancy

Contents

Contents   ix

Series Editors' Foreword

Religion in History, Society and Culture brings to a wider audience work by out-standing young scholars who are forging new agendas for the study of religion in the twenty-first century. As editors, we have two specific goals in mind.

First, volumes in this series illumine theoretical understandings of religion as a dimension of human culture and society. Understanding religion has never been a more pressing need. Longstanding academic habits of either compartmentalizing or ignoring religion are breaking down. With the entry of religion into the academy, however, must come a fully realized conversation about what religion is and how it interacts with history, society, and culture. Each book in this series employs and refines categories and methods of analysis that are intrinsic to the study of religion, while simultaneously advancing our knowledge of the character and impact of particular religious beliefs and practices in a specific historical, social, or cultural context.

Second, this series is interdisciplinary. The academic study of religion is conducted by historians, sociologists, political scientists, anthropologists, psychologists, and others. Books in the series bring before the reader an array of disciplinary lenses through which religion can be creatively and critically viewed. Based on the conviction that the instability of the category itself generates important insights, "religion" in these works encompasses and/or informs a wide range of religious phenomena, including myths, rituals, ways of thought, institutions, communities, legal traditions, texts, political movements, artistic production, gender roles, and identity formation.

In the present volume (the fourth in the series) Theodore Vial explores crucial aspects of the intense struggle that occurred within Protestant Christianity as it actively participated in the highly disruptive processes of modernization that were transforming European life in the late nineteenth century. He focuses his attention on the dramatic struggles that occurred within the Protestant community in Zurich, Switzerland–struggles that pitted "liberal" reformers who supported the changes that were occurring against "orthodox" conservatives who mobilized a powerful resistance. In Vial's narrative he adopts an unusual strategy by placing in the foreground the character and significance of battles concerning religious practice.

In order to accomplish the task that Vial sets for himself he turns to the field of ritual theory and develops a highly sophisticated and innovative approach that enables him to identify intrinsic correlations between the conflicting theological positions that separated the two Protestant groups and the conflicting liturgical practices to which they were committed. He also explores the fascinating interactions between the theologically charged liturgical battles that constitute his special concern and other battles (political, social, cultural, etc.) in which the same groups were simultaneously engaged.

Vial's book demonstrates the creative possibilities that can be generated through an engagement between approaches to the theory and practice of ritual on the one hand and approaches to the study of mainstream Protestant communities on the other. We hope that *Liturgy Wars* will stimulate others to carry forward the process that Vial has initiated.

WINNIFRED FALLERS SULLIVAN
The University of Chicago
Divinity School

FRANK REYNOLDS
The University of Chicago
Divinity School

Preface

This book began its life a long time ago as a dissertation. Generous research support was provided by the Overseas Dissertation Research Committee of The University of Chicago, and Agnes K. Smith, a family friend.

Though I had no official status in Zurich I was welcomed by Professors Eduard Schweizer (emeritus), Fritz Büsser (emeritus), and Fritz Stolz (emeritus). Without their good will I would not have been able to gather the material I needed, or think it through adequately. I was particularly impressed when Professor Stolz named a key article in an obscure Festschrift in a field far from his own, and walked me to the library shelf where it was located, saving me roughly a month's worth of work. This was typical of the generosity and erudition I found so wonderfully combined in all three at the University of Zurich.

The argument I make here does not fall neatly into traditional disciplinary categories, and this work would not have been possible without the flexibility and open-mindedness of my dissertation committee, chaired by B. A. Gerrish and including Frank Reynolds and Daniel Brudney (of the Philosophy Department), all of the University of Chicago. It is no coincidence that each is unusually dedicated to the vocation of graduate teaching. My greatest hope is that the high standards for historical theology and scholarly writing set by Brian Gerrish, the encyclopedic knowledge of theory and unfailing good judgment embodied in Frank Reynolds, and the passion for ideas of all three are reflected in some small way in this book. Frank also read drafts as the manuscript made the long journey from one genre (dissertation) to another (book that more than three people would want to read). He is an extraordinarily good and supportive critic. David Chidester also read the entire manuscript and made generous suggestions, enough to have created three books instead of one. He taught me a lot about how to tell stories about religion. Those familiar with the scholars mentioned above will know that errors and inadequacies that remain could be my responsibility alone.

For the past six years it has been my privilege to teach at Virginia Wesleyan College. Although it sees itself as a teaching college, the administration understands that this noble endeavor is greatly enhanced by research, and has given generous support to my scholarly projects. Coupled with the freedom to teach whatever I want, up to and including completely revising the program in Religious Studies, this has made it a rewarding place to work. I am grateful to President William T. "Billy" Greer, Dean Stephen Mansfield, and Craig Wansink, colleague extraordinaire. I especially want to thank my students in Religious Studies 340, "Ritual Studies," whose astute comments and probing questions have greatly clarified my own thinking on ritual.

In the end this book is about how people look at and act in the world. I have the fabulous good fortune that Nancy Walsh shares her world with me, and I dedicate the book to her.

Acknowledgments

Portions of "Opposites Attract: The Body and Cognition in a Debate over Baptism," *Numen* (1999): 121-45 ended up, in a very different format, in the Introduction and chapters five and six.

Portions of chapters one, two, and three, again in a very different format, appeared in "A. E. Biedermann's Filial Christology in Its Political Context," *Zeitschrift für neuere Theologiegeschichte/Journal for the History of Modern Theology 3* (1996).

I am grateful to Brill and de Gruyter for permission to re-use this material.

I am particularly grateful to Friedrich Wilhelm Graf for permission to quote from a working draft, "Making Sense of the New Empire: Protestant University Theology in Germany, 1870-1918," in *Papers of the Nineteenth Century Theology Group: AAR Annual Meeting, Philadelphia 1995,* ed. by James C. Livingston and Francis Schüssler Fiorenza, 5-18 (Colorado Springs: The Colorado College, 1995); and to Bob McCauley and Tom Lawson for sharing with me the manuscript of their book, *Bringing Ritual to Mind: Psychological Foundations of Cultural Forms,* and allowing me to cite the manuscript. It will be in print before this book.

INTRODUCTION

Between 1864 and 1868 the Reformed Church in Zurich threatened to split in two in a battle over how to baptize. On one side was the conservative faction (they called themselves "positives"), on the other the liberal faction *(freisinnige* in German) headed by Alois Emanuel Biedermann. The debate began in 1864 when Zurich's Great Council asked the Synod to consider a revised liturgy at their next annual meeting, and ended in 1868 with the adoption of a revised liturgy.

Biedermann had come to the University of Zurich in 1850 after his 1844 book, *Free Theology, Or Philosophy and Christianity in Conflict and in Peace,*[1] skyrocketed him from obscure parish ministry in the rural Swiss village of Mönchenstein to dominance of the Swiss theological scene. In the 1880s the head of the Zurich church, Georg Finsler, recalled the book as "a mounting rocket, which heralded the deployment of a new armed force–speculative theology."[2] From 1844 until his death in 1885 Biedermann was the leader of the speculative or Young-Hegelian theological movement in Switzerland.

So what? In the scheme of world history, and in the scheme of the study of religion, these events are relatively overlooked. But they raise questions crucial to the way we understand religion, and perhaps more importantly to the way we think about the study of religion. What precisely is the relationship of theory and praxis? In other words, why did a certain theological movement effect certain specific changes in the liturgy? Further, what is at stake for a civic government in the public practices of a religion? Though we often modify the word "ritual" with the adjective "mere," this displays a bias which certainly did not obtain in nineteenth-century Zurich. If my analysis of this liturgy war is correct, it is a bias which we maintain in our contemporary world only at the risk of misunderstanding our world and our study of that world. By focusing on the ceremony of baptism, which for every citizen of Zurich was a rite of passage into the civic as well as into the religious community, I show the connections between Biedermann's theology and a change in ritual practice, and I show what is at stake for the hierarchical power arrangements in Zurich as people squared off in this fight over ritual, this liturgy war.

The savvy reader will be asking, Why Biedermann? (Or, Who is Biedermann?) Why Zurich? There are a number of reasons having to do with theoretical considerations in the study of religions and with theological issues. I list four here:

First, Biedermann provides a marvelous case study. The modern world we inhabit was constructed by the Enlightenment and the arrangements, social and intellectual, that were fought out in its wake in the nineteenth century. Our world is still constituted by clashes between modernity and "traditional" religion and culture. Most of the conflicts–religious, political, economic, and educational–I describe in this book will have a very familiar feel to twenty-first-century readers. Biedermann was a prominent member of one of the most important vanguards of modernity, the Young Hegelians. More familiar names in this movement include David Friedrich Strauss, Ludwig Feuerbach, Bruno Bauer, and eventually the young Karl Marx. Whereas other Young Hegelians (Strauss, Feuerbach, Bauer) finally felt compelled to leave the church, Biedermann's philosophy of language allowed him to share their modern worldview, yet remain a preacher, theologian, and ritual specialist. He thus offers an opportunity to see how this modern worldview, shared by some of the thinkers who shaped modernity in Germany and beyond, cashes out in theology, preaching, and liturgy.

Second, Biedermann's theology deserves a second look. Because the nineteenth century's debates and issues are still with us, Biedermann's theological strategies have not lost their relevance.[3] Biedermann remained faithful to traditional Christian symbols and language, while at the same time wholeheartedly endorsing a modern worldview. He is an exceptionally clear thinking and courageous theologian, about whom very little has appeared in English.[4]

Third, the case provided by Zurich's liturgy change and its relation to Biedermann's theology forces several key issues in contemporary ritual studies. A recent trajectory in ritual studies focuses on the body as the central category of analysis. Lawrence Sullivan, for example, writes that "the body is constructed, dismembered, or repaired in ritual." According to Theodore Jennings, "ritual knowledge is gained by and through the body." For Pierre Bourdieu, "[M]ythically or ritually defined objects . . . almost all prove to be based on movements or postures of the human body, such as going up and coming down . . . ." Catherine Bell agrees that "the implicit and dynamic 'end' of ritualization . . . can be said to be the production of a 'ritualized body.'"[5]

This focus on the body tends towards a view that the analysis of ritual is largely the analysis of social power relations. Thus Sullivan writes, commenting on the work of López Austin, that focus on the body "can bring to light the coherence and power of ideological systems associated with the body." For Jennings ritual is "bodily action which alters the world or the place of the ritual participant in the world." For Bourdieu, mastery of ritual can "transform ritualized exchange into a confrontation of strategies." A "skilled strategist" can turn ritualized exchanges "into an instrument of power." Bell, who, to date offers the most fully worked out analysis of ritual using the categories of body and power, claims that, "[r]itualization always aligns one within a series of relationship (sic) linked to the ultimate sources of power." "[R]itualization is a strategic arena for the embodiment of power relations."[6]

Another development in ritual studies seems, at first glance, to stand in opposition to this focus on the body. Frits Staal, Dan Sperber, Pascal Boyer, Caroline Humphrey and James Laidlaw, Ilkka Pyysiäinen, E. Thomas Lawson and Robert McCauley, Harvey Whitehouse, and others, focus on the cognitive aspect of ritual.[7] They would not be inclined to agree with Jennings's assertion that ritual is "primarily corporeal rather than cerebral."[8] Is ritual fundamentally a matter of the body or of the mind? Is it best analyzed through the concept of power or as a cognitive activity whose structure looks something like the deep grammar of human language? In my analysis of ritual change in Zurich I offer a taxonomy of ritual studies that helps sort out some of these issues, points out weaknesses of both trajectories, and allows us to make use of their insights.

Fourth, the book on ritual theory that takes Protestantism as data is rare. I do not think that the lacuna is accidental. The study of religion, as Jonathan Z. Smith writes, "has been by no means an innocent endeavor."[9] David Chidester has shown how the standard histories of the study of religion "have been almost exclusively preoccupied with the questions, issues, or modes of analysis that were internal to the development of a set of European academic disciplines."[10] In telling the story of religious studies as a story of European debates (mostly located in Protestant universities) that drove developments in theory, these standard histories inadvertently replicate a colonial economic model, in which raw materials (data) are extracted from places like South Africa, transported to theory production centers of Europe, and then exported as intellectual manufactured goods.[11] Chidester shows that here was a lot of theorizing about religion going on on the South African frontier, and that this theorizing was intimately linked to changing power relations between native

South Africans and pioneers, colonialists, imperialists, and the structures of apartheid.[12] European scholars worked not with raw materials but with post-consumer products. In doing so more or less unawares they contributed, perhaps dangerously and culpably, to the various political and colonial projects of their states.

By showing that there is theory as well as data on the "margins," Chidester has provided an important corrective in the study of religion. The other half of this move is to begin to see that there is data as well as theory in the "center." A quick survey of books in the field of ritual studies turns up none that focus on Protestantism.[13] This is to repeat the pattern J. Z. Smith points out in *Drudgery Divine* in which comparative religions developed as one of the pieces in the theological game between Protestant and Catholic polemicists. "They" have rituals. "We" are justified by faith. Huldrych Zwingli founded the Reformed church in Zurich almost contemporaneously with Luther's movement in Germany. With Wittenberg and Geneva, Zurich is as close to the center of Protestant Europe as you can get. To analyze ritual there is to begin to take seriously the turn in comparative studies initiated by scholars such as Smith and Chidester.

The issue is not merely one of fairness, but of the accuracy begotten of self-awareness in the study of religion. Karl Popper took for the epigraph of *The Logic of Scientific Discovery* Novalis's dictum that "theories are nets: Only he who casts will catch." To push the metaphor perhaps too far, if fish are like data, my own belief is that the nets we cast are largely shaped by local species of fish, and to be ignorant of this is dangerous when we set off fishing around the world. As we pursue our etic (or scholarly) work on ritual theory we must not buy uncritically the emic (or insider) claim that Protestantism is a matter of faith not ritual. Otherwise unconscious assumptions will slip into our work and skew our analyses. Ironically, these assumptions pose the greatest threat to the very scholars who most fear a theological agenda in religious studies and so run from theology as hard as they can.

The category "religion" that shapes our work is in turn shaped by the cultural context of our schools and our lives. While it will probably be clear that I am partly in sympathy with the arguments of scholars such as Timothy Fitzgerald and Russell McCutcheon that "social formation" is a key aspect of the analysis of religions[14]–this book, I think, is an example of just such an analysis–I cannot agree that we are better off replacing traditional categories such as "ritual" and "religion" with "social formation." Religions and rituals do support, contest, and construct social arrangements. That does not mean we should assume that they can be analyzed and understood in the same way that other social arrangements can, such as politics or economics or the military. Cars and horses both can provide transportation, but we use different tools to understand them, and a veterinarian may not be your first choice to analyze and fix your car.

Benson Saler's approach is more subtle and, finally, more practical. He argues that "religion" is a folk category appropriated by scholars.[15] Against the argument that it is not a "native" category, he argues that it is, in the West.[16] It is a category defined not by essences but by prototypes, "cases that best fit."[17] For Western scholars the prototypes of "religion" are Christianity, Judaism, and Islam. Whether we acknowledge it or not, we fish with Protestant nets.

There are a growing number of books and articles at this meta-theoretical level of the construction of religious studies, and the issues are far more complex than I can take up here. Too many of these books are all theory, no data. Since God and the devil both dwell in the details, their promise is unfulfilled unless, through painstaking analyses of messy historical cases, we can show that our theoretical work illuminates the religious thought and behavior of the very real people we are trying to understand (ourselves included). I intend this latter kind of book, and simply wish to point out that our best strategy will be to analyze our prototypes (our nets) as thoroughly as possible, to take them self-consciously as data. Protestant Christianity tends to be taken as more a matter of belief than ritual, and so it is especially important to correct this view as we lean on Christianity to underpin the category "religion."

The first three issues are the explicit subject matter of the book, and the reader will find them discussed on almost every page. The fourth set of issues would require a whole separate treatment, and I will not tackle them explicitly in the course of the book's argument. But it is important to see that my analysis of ritual change in Zurich is, in fact, situated in broader theoretical debates that extend its significance beyond Zurich, and beyond a specific moment in nineteenth-century theology.

When the Zurich government called Biedermann to the University, the choice was controversial. While conservative ministers could do nothing about his appointment to the University, they tried unsuccessfully to block his admission into the Zurich Synod. Biedermann himself acknowledged that his appointment was part of the political backlash of the liberal government against their conservative political opponents.[18] Clearly, then, in the minds of the politicians, theologians, and, as we will see, the public at large, a link existed between a particular standpoint in the political and social struggles of the day and a particular theological movement. This link could almost intuitively be mapped onto a position in the liturgy struggle.[19] But the nature of these links between theology and ritual and between religion and other contested sites in Zurich society were largely taken for granted.[20] Similarly, in the contemporary United States no one is surprised that conservative Christians by and large are also political conservatives. But it is difficult to say why this is the case. An attempt to read the New Testament "literally," as conservative Christians are most likely to claim to do, could just as plausibly result in political radicalism. One goal of this study is to explain the relationship of Young-Hegelian theology, represented by the work of Biedermann, to the liberal social and political movement in Zurich in the mid-nineteenth century. Another is to show how this relationship plays out in ritual. *I argue that the worldviews of Young-Hegelian theology and liberal politics share a sense of the dynamics driving history forward, a sense that emerges in the rapidly modernizing Canton of Zurich, as in other areas of Europe, in the mid-nineteenth century. This sense of history's dynamics contrasts markedly from the historical assumptions of preceding religious, social, and political structures.*

While I discuss the sense of history's dynamics presupposed by the liberals in terms of politics, economics, education, theology, and ritual, I believe that this same sense of history is increasingly presupposed across all aspects of Zurich society and culture. I hope to hint at the wider cultural shift by taking for the epigraphs to each chapter quotes from Gottfried Keller's autobiographical novel, *Green Henry*.[21] The critic Georg Lukács calls Keller "one of the greatest narrative writers of the nineteenth century," one of the leading authors in world literature.[22] Lukács describes the novel as follows:

> *Green Henry*, the great autobiographical novel of his younger years, takes as its basic theme a multi-talented and problematical person growing up to occupy his place in public and political life. Here, as in the greater part of his writings, Keller portrays the positive and negative human characteristics which determine whether or not one is suited for public office. Education for public activity: this is the basic notion underlying all of Keller's work as a writer.[23]

Keller, like Biedermann, served in an official capacity in the Zurich government. "The spirit of democracy pervades the whole of Keller's thought and work."[24] It is, therefore, not surprising to see the same themes, manifested in a different genre, that we find in Biedermann's theology, and in the liturgy struggle.

In showing the relationship of Young-Hegelian theology and the liberal political movement, I address a major concern in the study of historical theology: the social context in which theology takes place. Historians have long done an admirable job of showing the way theological traditions unfold–the influences and innovations of predecessors and successors in a particular, self-conscious theological tradition. I call this style of historical theology a horizontal intellectual history. Were this book a horizontal history of theology, it would focus on the influences of G. W. F. Hegel, D. F. Strauss, F. Schleiermacher, and others on Biedermann, and in turn Biedermann's influence on L. Ragaz, etc.

Instead, I undertake a vertical history, one that emphasizes the local political, social, and economic context over transnational intellectual movements. Of course Zurich's local history is profoundly tied to wider movements in Switzerland and Europe, and I will not overlook these. Nonetheless, my focus is always the relevance of the time and place Biedermann lived, his theology, and the Reformed liturgy, for one another. Friedrich Wilhelm Graf calls this kind of history "*neue Geistesgeschichte.*" For him, as for other younger historians in Germany over the past ten years, "[t]he reciprocal determinedness of social structures and *gedachte Ordnungen* [conceptual or symbolized orders] is . . . the main issue."[25] Such an approach, while not ignoring intellectual predecessors and successors of a theologian, will ask: "In which networks was he involved? Was it more likely for him to define (sic) by a local milieu or by a national level of communication? Did he have many contacts with foreign countries? Did he have many relations with people outside the university? In short: what was his world?"[26]

The need for such vertical intellectual history has been pointed out by Claude Welch, among others. Reflecting on his classic own book, *Protestant Thought in the Nineteenth Century*, Welch writes:

> Though I sought always to have in mind the social, economic, and political context, as I hope is evident, . . . the lack of explicit attention to how the developments in theology were responses to the relevant social changes is a real problem.[27]

Welch cites, as one of the few examples of attempts to show the relation of theology and political context, Marilyn Chapin Massey's book on the prominent Young-Hegelian D. F. Strauss.[28] Massey, using literary critical theory to compare Strauss's famous book to a contemporary novel, explains the social and political storm unleashed by Strauss's theological work. While I think that Massey makes her case successfully, it is important to note that her analysis extends only to the university-trained elite of Germany. Left unexplained is the reaction of other classes of society, those less likely to read novels or theological treatises or participate actively in politics. In other words, Massey's use of literature does ground Strauss's work in its social context, but her vertical history plumbs only so deep.

In order to show the relation of theology and society in the broadest context possible, I examine as a historian of religions the religious reforms undertaken by Biedermann and his allies. The events in Zurich at this time offer an excellent opportunity to undertake such a history of religions analysis. The intersection of theology with the life of every citizen of Zurich, university trained or not, took place in the liturgy. Liturgy controlled the public religious lives of all levels of society. This was especially true of Zurich at the time, since the Reformed church was a state church. Church rituals played a civic as well as religious function. For example, the roll of people eligible to participate in communion, kept in each community by the minister, was the same roll used by the state for the military draft, and was used to determine the distribution of social services. In such an environment, liturgy is where the theological rubber meets the road.

This work, then, stands at the intersection of ritual studies by bridging the gap between thought and action, and a kind of intellectual history that connects a theological and ritual movement to other social and political arenas. It will be necessary to spend a great deal of time in ritual theory, and the book in fact is divided about in half between analyses of nineteenth-century intellectual and theological movements, and contemporary work in ritual studies. Readers with a strong theology phobia can focus on chapters one, two, five, and six and understand all the claims I make about ritual, as long as they are willing to accept on faith my argument that Biedermann's theology presupposes an immanent view of historical dynamics. But I believe that, specific arguments aside, one of the true contributions of this book is taking Protestant Christianity (including theology) as data for theorizing in ritual studies. Thus Durkheim describes "the principle totemic beliefs," including cosmology, of Australians before explaining the Intichiuma (an annual ritual) of the Witchetty Grub clan.[29]

Historical theologians might be tempted to concentrate on chapters one, three, and four. But they will miss one of the most important points demonstrated here, the value *for theology* of using the kind of work that is typically called science of religion or religious studies or history of religions (in the sense it is used in Chicago, not in Göttingen). In bringing together these dual foci, I hope to give a specific instance of what I believe to be a general principle, namely the usefulness for both the history of theology and the history of religions of examining Christianity, and Protestantism in particular, from the perspective of the history of religions.

Chapter one recounts the key conflicts in an ongoing religious struggle in Zurich in the mid-nineteenth century. When the liberal government tried to appoint David Friedrich Strauss to a chair of theology at the University of Zurich in 1839, it set off a series of violent confrontations that kept Strauss out of the city and finally resulted in a coup. A conservative government took over from 1839 to 1846. Upon regaining power in 1846 liberals took the first opportunity to call Biedermann, Strauss's theological ally, to the University in 1850, setting off further struggles. Biedermann did join the faculty, and in 1864 he led a movement to revise the Zurich liturgy. It is this fight over baptism that I analyze in the rest of the book.

I describe the revised ceremony of baptism, adopted in 1868, and compare it with the previous ceremony of baptism. Both ceremonies, old and new, are contained in the 1868 Zurich liturgy. Each minister could decide which to use. This was the compromise solution which made possible its adoption. In laying out the debate surrounding the liturgy revision, two things become apparent. First, the participants in the debate framed their arguments largely in terms of church and state relations. Second, they simply took for granted that the new ceremony of baptism was firmly associated with liberal politics and Young Hegelian theology, while the older ceremony was linked to conservative politics and theology. But why do religious conservatives tend to be political conservatives and religious liberals political liberals? Precisely what the connections were was never stated explicitly.

We must, therefore, look beyond the record left of the debate, and analyze the ritual itself, in order to understand why the Young Hegelians felt compelled to demand the specific changes in the ceremony they did demand, why the conservatives felt compelled to defend certain parts of the liturgy, and what stake the government had in a revised liturgy. The changes made in the 1868 liturgy are all linguistic. That is, the church calendar did not change, nor did the specific physical motions (eating, drinking, pouring water). What changed were the words spoken.

Not all the words changed, however. At first glance it appears that the Young Hegelians wanted to remove overly "supernatural" language. But they did not find all language that we might consider supernatural in the baptism ceremony offensive. Further, there are some instances (preaching, for example) in which Biedermann argued that such language, which he calls representational, was required.

Chapter two describes the political, economic, and educational fights in Zurich that were concurrent with the struggles over the theological leadership of the church and the baptism ceremony. All of these conflicts can be seen as the convulsions associated with Zurich's entrance into (or construction of) the modern world. I argue that the liberals' specific policies in the areas of politics, the economy, and education are united by an immanent sense of history's dynamics. What causes historical change? Great men? New ideas? Class struggles? Technological innovations? *Women, Work, and Family?*[30] One's views of who should participate in political decision making, and what the political structures should look like, will depend on one's sense of these dynamics. The liberal policies stemmed from a view of where the dynamic of history is located, that is, how history moves forward, and who the agents responsible for its motion are. The views of their conservative opponents also presuppose a sense of history, but a different one. In each policy pursued–replacing a patrician oligarchy with a representative democracy, replacing a guild system with a free market economy, and setting up a system of elementary schools independent of the church–the liberal agenda reflects a view that the power to act significantly in history is located immanently, that is, in each citizen by virtue of his or her human nature.[31]

Although we take for granted the cohabitation of conservative religion with what we identify as conservative positions in politics, economics, and education, and liberal religion with liberal politics, economics, and education, the question is Why? Why this cohabitation? Chapter three introduces Biedermann's theology by analyzing a fight over the personality of God. I show that the same sense of history that drove liberals in their other social battles is also present in Biedermann's epistemology and doctrine of God.

In Chapter four I move on to Biedermann's stance in christological battles. It is christology that most clearly distinguishes Biedermann's Young-Hegelian theology from that of right-wing Hegelians such as P. Marheineke, "positive" (conservative) theological opponents in Switzerland such as A. Ebrard, and even other Young Hegelians. Further, in christology we see the sense of history presupposed by Biedermann most explicitly expressed. For it is in christology that Biedermann describes the kind of significant historical action possible for any historical figure, including Jesus.

Biedermann, like other Young Hegelians, defined God as the creative essence of humans. He argued that Jesus is not the Savior because of any one-time historical act. Such an act would lie beyond the possible agency of any truly historical figure. Jesus, for him, was the Savior because his religious self-consciousness is present and made available to his followers in the Christian community. In principle anyone, at any time, is capable of such a religious self-consciousness. Thus, Jesus did not transcend history, and the Christian principle (Jesus' religious self-consciousness) is located immanently, in the creative essence of humans as such. Biedermann's immanent christology will have ramifications for the ceremony of baptism, a rite held to be instituted by Jesus for initiation into the Christian community.

The baptism fight in Zurich was over the words spoken during the ceremony. To understand the connection between theology and ritual practice, and between the liturgy wars and the culture wars in Zurich, we have to be able to categorize different kinds of speech and characterize the kinds of force that different utterances can have. In chapter five I rely on the work of speech act theorists to help provide just such a taxonomy.

Most of the recent work in ritual studies that focuses on ritual as a negotiation of social power (something that is clearly going on in Zurich) has overlooked language as a ritual act. So it is also necessary in chapter five for me to give an overview of the current field of ritual studies, and locate my work on that map. This dominant movement in contemporary work on ritual, ritual as embodied power negotiations, is best exemplified by Catherine Bell. The other growth industry in recent ritual studies does take language seriously. In fact it is modeled on linguistics and sees ritual as a rule-governed, cognitively structured activity. This movement has been spearheaded by E. Thomas Lawson and Robert N. McCauley. These two theoretical trends (body/power and cognitive) appear to be antithetical. But a proper understanding of ritual shows that a complete theory must include: 1) ethnographic data; 2) a structural analysis of ritual form (something the cognitivists are good at); and 3) social power negotiations. Most contemporary work shorts one of these necessary moments. (Unfortunately both movements in ritual studies tend to short the first, which strikes me as very dangerous when one is theorizing, no matter what the theory is. Hence I hope readers will appreciate the detailed historical analyses that always underpin my theorizing in this book.)

If we are to understand why certain speech acts are appropriate in one context but not another we must understand the structure of ritual. The very language that liberals like Biedermann could not in good conscience say as they baptized babies was required by Biedermann in other contexts, such as sermons. What is it about ritual that affects the kind of language one may use in it? We must have something like a grammar of ritual. Chapter six sketches out the structure, or grammar, of the baptism ceremony, and shows why certain speech acts are appropriate in ritual while others are not.

As a result of these analyses of the baptism ceremony it then becomes clear that the major changes demanded by the Young Hegelians in effect remove sentences in certain "grammatical" contexts that describe historical acts in violation of the immanent sense of history's dynamics we found in Biedermann's christology and in the political, social, and economic reforms sweeping Zurich.

The liturgy wars were one important front in the culture wars in Zurich that pitted liberal against conservative in church, at home, at work, and at school. But ritual is judged primarily in terms of orthopraxy, not orthodoxy. It is notoriously difficult to unearth what rituals mean to individual participants. As long as the participants perform their appointed actions correctly the ritual is successful. Did they perform their actions grudgingly, defiantly, ironically, absent-mindedly, joyfully, etc.? There is no real historical fieldwork. So how can we say that something in this structured, prescribed, group activity is similar to what is going on in the un-prescribed political, economic, and educational actions taken by individuals? Our lack of access to the inner lives of ritual participants does not, however, cut off our analyses. As Roy Rappaport argues, regardless of the ritual participants' attitudes towards their rituals, their very participation is a (perhaps the) most significant fact about the ritual. It signals acceptance. One can still lie after having sworn an oath in court, but one is nevertheless submitting to the social conventions and institutions that condemn and punish perjury.[32] Furthermore, this acceptance need not follow belief or commitment to social norms–it often precedes them.[33] That is one of the reasons people fight about ritual change. A change in ritual can produce change in other social arrangements. As we analyze this ritual fight and the connections between theology and ritual and between religion and other cultural arenas, we must remember that the stakes were high.

CHAPTER ONE

RELIGIOUS CONFLICT IN ZURICH

Therefore we want absolute freedom of conscience in all directions. But the world must get to the point where it can with the same fine calm with which it discovers an unknown natural law or a new star in the heavens, accept and contemplate the occurrences and consequences of intellectual life, prepared for everything and always its own self, erect in the sunlight and saying: Here I stand!

–Gottfried Keller, *Green Henry*

Madame de Staël, in her analysis of nineteenth-century German society, pointed out that "the educated people of Germany argue amongst themselves with the greatest vivacity in the sphere of Theories, and as a result are fairly keen to leave the whole reality of life to their earthly rulers."[1] If cultural battles in the contemporary United States tend to be fought out in legal arenas, in nineteenth-century German lands they were often fought out or negotiated in theological or philosophical arenas. This is an oversimplification, and applies still less to German-speaking Switzerland which, while on the margins of the German cultural world, had a very different political traditions (different enough to make it a popular haven for German refugees who ran too far afoul of their governments). Still, religion touches on every other aspect of society and culture, and one can inquire to what extent religious conflicts are "also" or in some cases "really" about these other aspects, and vice versa.

Within our category of religion itself there are parallel questions. Let Durkheim stand for a moment as one familiar way of defining the category. His definition, "A religion is a unified system of beliefs and practices relative to sacred things," captures one common dichotomy within the category "religion" that divides it into belief and practice.[2] Standard histories of the Reformation explain iconoclasm and differences over how to celebrate the Lord's Supper as expressions of different underlying theologies. But as David Parkin has shown, in ritual participants can quite literally position themselves over against one another.[3] In such cases theological differences can flow from these ritualized distinctions.

This book establishes such connections between theory and praxis within the category of religion and between religion and other categories in our taxonomies of culture. I propose no general ritual theory to explain these relationships, rather I propose to explain them in this specific case, and in so doing offer a general strategy rather than a general theory. Each historical case must be taken in all its messy historical glory on its own terms. As Van Harvey has pointed out, to speak of historical methods in general leads only to confusion. "[I]t is not conducive to clarity to talk about presuppositions in general; rather, one must ask in each particular case what the warrant is and to what degree it has adequate backing."[4]

This chapter begins the detailed historical task. The fight over the baptismal liturgy in Zurich was one round in a more encompassing series of religious conflicts. There were, of course, other conflicts that we would not classify at first glance as religious in Zurich at the same time, and these will be described in chapter two. Here I describe the attempt to bring David Friedrich Strauss to the University of Zurich in 1839, an attempt that not only was unsuccessful but which led to the overthrow of the Zurich government. A similar struggle (though with less dramatic results) was waged over the call of Biedermann to the University in 1850. Biedermann was a friend and close theological ally of Strauss, and his call was an explicit attempt by a certain faction in Zurich to do what they had tried to do eleven years earlier. Once at the University and prominent in church affairs in Zurich, the theological and clerical group led by Biedermann played the leading role in the fight over baptism. It is these three fights, or better three rounds in a greater ongoing war, that I describe in turn in this chapter.

Round One: David Friedrich Strauss and the Overthrow of the Zurich Government

On the morning of September 6, 1839, several thousand hymn-singing citizens of the Canton (State) of Zurich, carrying scythes, pitchforks, and guns, marched from the countryside into the city. They were led by Bernhard Hirzel, a local pastor and instructor (*Privatdozent*) at the University of Zurich. They headed for the post office building where the Great Council, the legislative branch of the government, was meeting. Their confrontation with the government was sparked by the call of David Friedrich Strauss to the position of Dogmatic Theology at the University.

This call, among other things, had made the government wildly unpopular among the citizens of Zurich. The protest, which developed into a march and then into a riot and then into a coup, had been coordinated by a group called the "Faith Committee," twenty-two representatives of churches and conservative Christians that had formed to try to overturn Strauss's call. Some soldiers who had remained loyal to the government were gathered at the post office on September 6 to protect Council members. When the horse was shot out from under the military commander who rode up to meet Hirzel, the soldiers opened fire on the crowd. One of the popular members of the Great Council, Dr. Hegetschwyler, himself a supporter of the Faith Committee, stepped onto the balcony of the post office to order the soldiers to stop shooting, but was himself laid low by a shot from the crowd. The remaining council members fled the city, and the Faith Committee ruled Zurich informally for ten days until it could hold elections on September 16 and 17 to replace the Great Council with a new Council.

Although the call of academic theologians does not often occasion coups, Strauss had been a lightning rod for religious controversy since the publication in 1835 of his book, *The Life of Jesus Critically Examined.* The then twenty seven year old, a so-called Young Hegelian, was teaching at a college preparatory seminary in Tübingen, and had hoped that *The Life of Jesus* would win him a university position. Instead, he was immediately removed from his teaching position and barred from holding any church position in the state of Württemberg until he publicly recanted. The leading Protestant newspaper, the *Evangelische Kirchenzeitung,* pronounced his book a "triumph of Satan," and called Strauss and all who agreed with him "the vile products of carnal unions between unclean spirits and whores."[5] One of his former teachers at Tübingen denounced him as the anti-Christ, and another wrote a book in response to *The Life of Jesus* entitled *The Iscariotism of Our Days.*[6] Colleagues wrote to Strauss begging him not to review their books, for fear that a favorable review might jeopardize their jobs.[7]

Strauss had tried twice in 1836 to get an appointment to the University of Zurich, where he had some support from the rationalist theologian Ferdinand Hitzig and the prominent philologist J. K. Orelli. Finally on January 26, 1839 the Education Council recommended to the Great Council that they call him. The vote on the Education Council was tied at seven for his appointment and seven against. The tie was broken by the mayor of Zurich, K. M. Hirzel, who stated quite openly during the discussion that in bringing Strauss to the University faculty what was at stake was a reform of the Zurich church. Strauss was to open up an academic and theological front in the campaign to extend political, economic, and educational reforms already undertaken by the government. The effort to undertake religious reform through the call of Strauss clearly backfired, with Council members fleeing for their lives, replaced by a group of anti-reform Council members. This round of religious conflict in Zurich went to the conservatives.

Rounds Two and Three: Biedermann and the Fight over Baptism

The conservative government stayed in power in Zurich from 1830 to 1846. After liberals regained control in 1846 the Board of Education took the first opportunity offered by an opening on the theological faculty to call Biedermann, the most prominent Swiss Young Hegelian, to the University.[8] Again, the explicit goal of the government in calling Biedermann was to enlist his aid in reforming the Zurich church.[9] The government hoped not only that he would have great influence in the theological faculty and beyond at the University of Zurich, but that he would be a force in the Zurich Synod of the Reformed Church. The government's choice was again controversial, but this time conservative ministers were unable to rally enough popular support to block his academic appointment. They then tried unsuccessfully to block his admission into the Zurich Synod. Biedermann himself acknowledged that his appointment was part of the political backlash of the liberal government against their conservative political opponents.[10] Round Two went to the liberals.

The set of issues that concern us in this book surround ritual change in Zurich.[11] What is the relationship between these fights over orthodox versus Young-Hegelian theology and fights over revision of the baptism liturgy? What is the link between theology and ritual? Furthermore, as we will see in chapter two, these religious battles are related to political, economic, and educational struggles in the mid-nineteenth century. To understand how these issues play out in a ritual arena, and what the links are between baptism and other social and cultural arenas, we need a detailed report on the "liturgy struggle" ("*Liturgiestreit*"), as the combatants themselves referred to it. This round (Round Three) in Zurich's religious conflict ended in a draw. The rest of this chapter is devoted to this struggle.

The fight was largely framed by the participants in terms of the relationship of the church to authority, both the authority of tradition and the authority of the civic government. Left unstated in these struggles is why the participants focus on the specific components of the liturgy that they do. That certain changes were required was apparently self-evident to the proponents of change, and that these changes were precisely the ones that must not be made was equally self-evident to the defenders of the existing liturgy. Laying bare the implicit reasons for these explicit stances will be the task of chapters five and six.

The liturgy which was in use in the Zurich church had been adopted in 1854. The 1854 revision was, however, minor, and stood in substantial unity with the Zurich liturgies stretching back to Zwingli.

The initial formal proposal to undertake a more sweeping revision came from the Cantonal government, not from the Church Council or Synod or any organization of clergymen. This fact is significant for the Synod, whose discussions on the liturgy question were then framed in part in terms of the relationship of church to state authority. It also indicates that the liturgy revision was to be part of a larger scheme of church reform undertaken by the liberal politicians controlling Zurich's government.

Article 10 of the ecclesiastical law passed by the Great Council in 1861 required that the Great Council appoint each year a special commission to review the annual reports and minutes prepared by the Church Council and the Synod.[12] This commission was to alert the Great Council to any problems or abuses discovered in the church.[13] At the winter meeting of the Great Council in 1863 this special commission proposed that "the Church Council be invited, in conjunction with the Synod, to consider whether the current liturgy of the established church ought not to be expanded into a church book."[14] The Great Council approved this motion on January 27, 1864.[15] The Great Council's motion was sent to the Church Council, via the Small Council, on January 30.[16] The Church Council decided that, given the short time since the adoption of the current liturgy, and given the "still growing tension of two still unreconciled orientations among the clergy and other members of the community,"[17] the time was not opportune for a major revision along the lines of a church book. Still, the Church Council agreed that the present liturgy was lacking in certain respects, and they proposed to the Synod that it consider taking the following four steps (which do not fall far short of the revision into a church book requested by the Great Council): (1) The liturgy used in Sunday services ought to offer a wider variety of prayers according to the seasons of the church calendar; (2) The formulas not revised in the 1854 liturgy ought to be reworked; (3) A second formula for the sacraments ought to be offered;[18] (4) The Synod should appoint a commission to examine these proposals.[19]

The Great Council's special commission gave as a reason for their proposal the meagerness of the 1854 liturgy, which had as a consequence the constant repetition of the same prayers, leading to the possible lessening of devotion during worship services.[20] But Heinrich Lang, a close ally of Biedermann's, reported in *Zeitstimmen aus der reformirten Kirche der Schweiz*, the organ of the Zurich theological liberals, that it was an "open secret" that the Great Council, in asking for an expanded liturgy, in fact wanted a freer liturgy more in line with the needs and views of the present.[21]

At the meeting of the Zurich Synod on September 27-28, 1864, the Synod debated the motion presented by the Church Council until late in the night of the first day, and took up the discussion again on the second day.[22] Somewhat to everyone's surprise, the motion to form a thirteen member commission to examine the question was passed unanimously.[23] The membership on the Liturgy Commission included Professor Kesselring and Heinrich Hirzel, minister of Zurich's St. Peter's Church as leading spokesmen for the liberal theological point of view; Rudolf Wolfensberger[24] and George Rudolf

Zimmermann, minister of Zurich's Fraumünster Church, representing the conservatives; and Professor Alexander Schweizer and Church Councilman Georg Finsler, who in 1866 became Antistes, as proponents of mediating theology (Schweizer is often referred to in the secondary literature as "Schleiermacher's most faithful student").[25]

The Commission was unable to complete its report in time for the 1865 annual meeting. At the Synod meeting of October 2-4, 1866, having decided that a discussion of a possible liturgy revision in the abstract would be fruitless, the commission presented a proposed draft of a new liturgy.[26]

The major changes proposed in this 1866 draft are as follows. (1) A number of new prayers, with the "same contents" as the extant ones, but addressed solely to God and not to Christ, were added.[27] (2) The Apostles' Creed was removed from the liturgy for the Lord's Supper. (3) The Apostles' Creed was retained in the ceremony of baptism, but was now introduced with the following words: "So runs the confession in which the Christian church has expressed its faith from time immemorial."[28] (4) The "creed" according to which the child was now baptized ran:

> Accordingly the child shall be baptized and instructed in belief in God the Father who calls us to be his children, in Jesus Christ, the son of God who redeems us from sin and death, and in the Holy Ghost, who leads us to rebirth and sanctification.[29]

The Commission felt it was important to the unity of the church to have just one formula for each of the sacraments, and so they devised what they thought would be a compromise acceptable to both the conservatives and the liberals.[30] The Commission argued that, since many churches did not use the Apostles' Creed for the eucharist, it was not essential here and could be omitted. The Creed was, however, thought to be crucial to baptism. The new introduction to the Creed was intended to preserve continuity with tradition, but to alleviate the burden of conscience on those who could not, in an unqualified manner, subscribe to each article. Technically, the introduction to the Apostles' Creed requires not commitment to each of the Creed's articles, but merely acknowledgment that the Creed has been the traditional expression of Christian faith. The new statement upon which the child was to be baptized does require a commitment of belief, but one that is quite in line with the theology of the liberal party, as we will see in chapter five on the implications of different speech acts in the baptism ceremony.[31]

The compromise liturgy satisfied neither party. For the conservatives, the creed on which the child was now to be baptized, if not itself interpreted by means of the Apostles' Creed, was unacceptable. The conservatives pointed out that nowhere in the draft was the Fall mentioned. Nor did the liturgy make clear that Christ was "with God from the beginning," that is, that he was one of the persons of the Trinity, if and when he became God's son, and how redemption was effected. They protested that this was "general Christianity."[32] Even a minority within the commission itself rejected the proposed revision. Their minority report recommended retaining the current liturgy rather than adopting the proposed revision.[33]

The liberals were also dissatisfied with the proposed liturgy. They were still unable, in good conscience, to use the Apostles' Creed, in spite of the new historical introduction. In any case the proposed draft did no better than the 1854 liturgy in making baptism reflect biblical rebirth and entrance into the community.[34]

Antistes Finsler (a member of the Liturgy Commission) proposed remanding the proposal to the liturgy commission, and to ask them to examine the question of whether two formulas for each of the sacraments might not be better. They were instructed to solicit the views of local churches until Easter 1867. This motion passed by a vote of 91 to 40.[35]

Once again the Synod had to wait two years for the work of the commission to be completed. At the Synod meeting of October 27-28, 1868 the Liturgy Commission offered its second draft. For both the Lord's Supper and baptism there were two formulas, one with the Apostles' Creed and one without. The Creed was removed from the confirmation ceremony. Alongside prayers which included addresses to Christ were others that addressed themselves exclusively to God. G. Schmid writes of this revised liturgy, "the draft made allowances for the theology and the piety of a free understanding of the Christian faith."[36] After a debate of this proposal that lasted another two full days, it was finally adopted by a vote of 68 to 55.[37]

What reasons did the participants in the debate give for their positions? As will become clear, the debate is quite articulate insofar as it concerns the meaning of the proposed changes for each of the parties. It is, however, silent on the issue of why these changes were the ones at issue in the first place. In other words, the participants are theologically very articulate, but unable to state the connection between theology and ritual. The changes simply did (or did not, depending on your side) make perfect sense, in much the same way that people can produce and recognize grammatically correct sentences, but may not be able to articulate why they sense them to be correct or incorrect. This analogy is not coincidental, as will become clear in the following chapters. Unpacking this 'subtext,' articulating why the changes seemed obviously required (or obviously heretical) is the job taken up in chapters five and six.

Much of the debate stems from two principles voiced in the 1831 Zurich Constitution. The Constitution both guarantees freedom of belief, and also establishes the Reformed church.[38] Thus, the two main arguments running through the liturgy debate are (1) what do we believe, and (2) where does the authority to establish this lie?

It is not clear the extent to which either the Great Council, which proposed consideration of a church book, or the Church Council, which suggested merely adding more variation to the extant liturgy, intended the liturgy to have not simply more variety, but also to represent a greater diversity of theological positions. Whatever the original intent, the discussion of revision quickly became focused on changes to make the liturgy acceptable to the liberal theological party. From the start the two central issues were the Apostles' Creed and direct address to Christ in prayers and sacramental formulas.[39]

The conservative representatives adduced three kinds of arguments for retaining the current liturgy: (1) practical concerns, (2) an argument from tradition, and (3) theological concerns. On the practical side, they argued that the current liturgy was only adopted in 1854, and that after more than twenty years of controversy.[40] A liturgy ought not to change too often. Further, in the current context a debate over the liturgy would cause unrest in many congregations.[41] Offering ministers a choice of prayers and formulas representing theological views would put their congregations at the mercy of the minister's theology, rather than making the minister the servant of the community.[42] The conservatives claimed that the majority of the citizens of Zurich liked the 1854 liturgy, and that it was improper to undertake a revision from the top down, that is, to attempt a reformation without the people.[43] Finally, the conservatives pointed out that the current liturgy was already a compromise, since in 1854 some of the stronger direct addresses to Christ were toned down, and any reference to the literal inspiration of the Bible were removed.[44]

Second, the conservatives argued from tradition. The 1854 liturgy was still largely influenced by the Reformation liturgies worked out by Leo Jud and Huldrych Zwingli. The Apostles' Creed, though clearly not penned by the apostles, had nonetheless been the traditional interpretation of the Christian faith since the church fathers. What is more, Zwingli included it in the first Reformed Zurich liturgy.[45]

Third, the conservatives offered theological arguments in support of the current liturgy. These arguments largely come down to the view that the Apostles' Creed interprets scripture appropriately, and so in removing the Creed what is really at stake is God's word.[46] The correspondent for the *Evangelisches Wochenblatt* expressed this as follows:

> Where faith in the personality of God is placed in question, where the divine essence and dignity of the Son is challenged, his resurrection, his ascension, his coming again at judgement denied, eternal existence rejected–that is not a theological orientation, that is unfaith, that is anti-Christianity, there is lacking the primary requisites for a revision of a liturgy of a church that still stands on the rock foundations of God's word.[47]

The main argument for retaining the Apostles' Creed had a christological emphasis. For the conservatives, unless one can have the kind of Christ confessed to in the Apostles' Creed, one does not have the kind of Christ who can act as a savior. "Not only is Jesus Christ pulled down to the dust of the earth, but also in the filth of our sin; his work of redemption is denied him."[48] On the subject of direct address to Christ in the liturgy, the conservatives saw giving this up as a step from the Holy of Holies to the forecourt of the gentiles.[49]

The liberals also had a great deal at stake. They argued (1) that the current liturgy was a burden to their consciences; (2) that it was unnecessary to agree on a single creed in order to maintain church unity; and (3) that no one had the authority to mandate how one must pray to be a Christian. Heinrich Lang, a close associate of Biedermann's and editor of Zeitstimmen, wrote that,

> the fight against the Apostles' Creed, insofar as it is supposed to be the correct expression of the religious convictions of the present church and a necessary component of the holiest sacraments of the church, is, for the liberal orientation, a matter of heart and conscience.[50]

In particular the liberals were troubled by four articles of the Apostles' Creed, those professing belief in the conception by the Holy Ghost, Jesus' descent into hell, his physical ascent into heaven, and the resurrection of the body.[51] Many liberals, having expressed their discomfort at the Creed, further found themselves in the uncomfortable position of being called hypocrites by conservatives when they did in fact abide by the established liturgy and utter the Creed.[52]

Second, the liberals argued that the unity of the church was not dependent on agreeing on a single creed. Biedermann expressed this view as early as 1845 at a meeting of the Swiss Preacher's Society:

> The proposition 'Without a creed, no church' is not true. We are certainly unified at an innermost point, but that point cannot be based on the form of the creed, for that would be a unity only of words, not in accordance with the meaning. . . . Certainly there is a church without a creed. This is attested by its present situation. As a society the church can erect creeds; but it is no longer a society, rather it is a state institution, to which we belong already by virtue of our birth. Therefore no creed is necessary anymore, and none is possible; the Apostles' [Creed] should be for us a relic, but not worshiped as such. The church proceeds historically from Christ, and in it lives the one spirit of Christ that is expressed, but that divides itself into different factions.[53]

Here Biedermann combines two different arguments for the point of view that the unity of the church needs no creed. The first is that the church in Zurich is no longer a separate society, but a state institution into which everyone is born. Presumably, it no longer needs a statement defining itself over-against the rest of society. Second, the unity of the church is based not on a statement

of belief, an external set of claims to which one assents. Rather it is based on
the spirit of Christ that founded the church and lives in it.[54]

The second of Biedermann's arguments was echoed in the speech given by
Antistes Finsler at the opening of the 1867 Synod meetings:

> A definitely formulated, binding confession is not compatible with a true
> freedom of belief. So, a church without a confession? No, gentlemen. A
> church without a creed is also, I am convinced, an impossibility, and if our
> church really were without a creed it would not be able to exist any longer.
> So, a creed that hovers in the air? Yes, if you like. The conviction that no-one
> can lay another foundation than that which is laid, which is Jesus Christ, faith
> in the salvation revealed in him, is still the faith of our church today.[55]

A similar point of view was expressed by Lang, who argued that there has
been no unity of belief in the Protestant church since the Reformed creeds.
The only fundamental that binds the Reformed church together is the Gospel,
and each has the right to interpret this for him or herself. As far as the sacraments are concerned, should they begin to give offense to any large portion of
the church the only solution is to return to them as instituted by Jesus.[56]

Third, the liberals argued that a liturgy which not all could pray freely goes
against the tenets of Christianity. A liturgy must express the beliefs of the community. If it does not, no one has the right to impose it on the community.[57]

Antistes Finsler, in his speech to the Synod in 1867 in which he summed
up the history of the liturgy struggle and laid the groundwork for its resolution the following year, touched on most of the main themes of the discussions: individualism, the location of authority, and the nature of the "spirit"
that unifies the church. To Finsler the debate was a question of balance
between religious freedom and a state church. The problem was particularly
acute in the Reformed church because, since the teachings on predestination
of Calvin and Zwingli, the Reformed tradition has had a strong individualistic
bent. This led Finsler to conclude that external, "theocratic" measures must
not be taken to maintain church unity. Rather, belief in Christ as the one
ground of the church is the only "creed" necessary. Exactly how "belief in
Christ" cashes out theologically Finsler left open, thus opening the way to a
compromise in which both conservative an liberal orientations were represented in the sacraments of the Zurich liturgy.[58]

Beneath these issues of authority and freedom lies a changing conception
of historical agency. Where does authority lay? Who has the freedom to effect
historical change, that is, to act as agents of history? What role does ritual play
in the negotiation over historical agency? How is the baptism ceremony in
Zurich shaped by these changing ideas, and what role does it play in shaping
them? As it turns out, a seemingly esoteric debate about relatively minor
changes in the ceremony became one of the most contentious issues in Zurich,

which, as we will see in the next chapter, had many other things to worry about. This suggests that ritual is an important arena of negotiation, and a potent means of constructing identity.

CHAPTER TWO

CONTESTING HUMANITY AND CONTESTING HISTORY

I believed that everything which men accomplished had its importance solely in the fact that they had been able to accomplish it and that it was the work of reason and freewill.

–Gottfried Keller, *Green Henry*

Mircea Eliade argued in *The Myth of the Eternal Return* that the study of the myths, rites, and symbols of "premodern" or "traditional" societies could teach us their metaphysics, metaphysics which they themselves could not put into words.

> Obviously, the metaphysical concepts of the archaic world were not always formulated in theoretical language; but the symbol, the myth, the rite, express, on different planes and through the means proper to them, a complex system of coherent affirmations about the ultimate reality of *things*. . . . [I]f the word is lacking, the thing is present; only it is 'said'–that is, revealed in a coherent fashion–through symbols and myths.[1]

Eliade is of course wrong and right about this. And he is wrong and right for the very same reason. The idea that ideas are "said" in rites smacks of a symbolist model that has been justly criticized in recent scholarship. Why "say" ideas in rituals when they can be much more easily and clearly said in words? Ritual is a notoriously thorny and expensive avenue of communication. Nevertheless, human action–political, economic, ritual–is revealing. Analysis of human action can yield a construction of what the world looks like to the actors. This is true whether or not the social group under consideration has a "metaphysics," is "modern" or "premodern," because none of us is very good at perceiving and articulating the base assumptions from which we construct our worlds. The notion that we need to examine "others'" religions while "we" can articulate our own worldview or metaphysics ourselves in different ways is the notion this book most fights to overcome. There's just "we," all in the same boat (or, if you feel alienated, there's just "others," yourself included), and "our" actions can and should be revealing. I will have more to say about the relationship of thought and action, and about whether it is revealing or distorting to *talk* about the meaning of nonlinguistic actions, in chapter five.

The nineteenth century in Europe is a breaking point between fundamentally different ways of constructing the world. These ways are not compatible and so are at odds in every societal and cultural venue. The fights are not only religious but also political, economic, and educational. One of the ways of understanding these culture wars in Zurich and elsewhere is as a conflict over human agency, and how that agency effects historical change. In this chapter I begin to sketch out several of the battlefields. In describing the battles over politics, economics, and the school system I begin to get at some of the assumptions, perhaps not conscious, of the combatants. Briefly, conservatives in Zurich saw human agency located hierarchically, whereas liberals saw it as located broadly and immanently. I will not be able to make my case in its strongest form that the culture wars are wars over human historical agency until I can unpack the baptism struggle in chapters five and six, which at base was a fight over what kind of historical figure Jesus was. But human agency was contested in other spheres as well, and in this chapter I begin to show that the same issues of agency so hotly contested in the liturgy struggle had ramifications throughout all aspects of life in nineteenth-century Zurich.

Biedermann lived and worked in Zurich during a period of Swiss history known as the Regeneration.[2] For the majority of the years between 1830 and 1870 the Canton's political and cultural life was led by a group of people sharing a liberal worldview.[3] I argue that this liberal worldview is best characterized as a changing conception of who acts as an effective historical agent, and how. Liberals located historical agency immanently and broadly. In other words, one of the characteristics of the liberal period of Regeneration in Zurich is a changing view of the location of history's dynamic.

One historian of Zurich claims of the Regeneration that "in little more than two generations Zürich essentially made the transition from a medieval to a modern city."[4] While it is perhaps a bit of an exaggeration to call the Zurich of 1820 a medieval city, it is nonetheless true that during this time period the aristocratic oligarchy was replaced by a representative democracy, the guild system was torn down and replaced with a system of free enterprise, and a system of universal education was instituted.[5] Even the appearance of the city underwent a great change. In 1833 the seventeenth-century ramparts surrounding the city were torn down to improve transportation.[6] By the end of the period of Regeneration Zurich had left the *ancien régime* behind and entered the modern world.

These changes in Zurich's public life were undertaken systematically beginning in the early 1830s when the liberals won control of the cantonal government. The liberal period is commonly divided into two parts, the first lasting from the accession of the liberals to power in the Great Council (the Canton's highest legislative body) in 1831 until they were overthrown in the Strauss affair of 1839, and the second dating from their re-ascent to control of the government in 1846 until the adoption of a new, radically democratic constitution in 1869. During the intervening years of 1839 to 1846 the government was run by a group of conservatives. While certain changes in governing were inevitable under the conservatives, by and large the fundamental course of the Regeneration was not changed.[7]

The uprising in 1839 was sparked by the call of David Friedrich Strauss, but that call was a match thrown into a tinderbox. The traditional lifestyle of many in the Zurich countryside, one of agriculture supplemented by participation in the cottage industry, had been rocked by rapid mechanization and economic fluctuations in the textile industry. Strauss's call infuriated the conservative element of the church, already made to feel insecure by the recent separation of the schools from church control, and by the arrival in many villages of well educated and modern-thinking teachers.[8]

Liberal Politics during the Regeneration

The push in Zurich for liberal government began with the revolution in Paris in 1830 and led up to a new Zurich constitution in 1831. But the roots of this process go deep into Swiss history.[9] Zurich was one of the free cities in Europe during the Middle Ages, most of which were located in South Germany.[10] In the 1330s Rudolf Braun, Bürgermeister for life of Zurich and longtime enemy of Austria, banned nobility from Zurich and placed control of government into the hands of the guilds.[11] Zurich thus became one of the cities offering a third option of rule, alongside cities and territories under the protection of a king, and those under protection of nobles.[12]

The banning of nobles from cities like Zurich resulted in the first association in Europe of self-rule with a productive labor class. This social pattern was nowhere stronger than in Switzerland.[13] The reaction of outsiders to this development was to see all Swiss as peasants, and they often mocked the Swiss with the claim that "only a wall separates the burgher from the peasant."[14]

In the absence of nobility, the Small and Great Councils took on the role of lords, buying for the city the feudal rights of nobles who had controlled the Zurich countryside.[15] "The city ruled the country, and the guilds ruled the city."[16] This arrangement, referred to as "turning Swiss [*Sweytzer werden*],"[17] was a pre-condition of the military and political alliances of urban centers with rural districts unique to Switzerland. While the process of "turning Swiss" was based on the principle of self-rule, the councils soon came to see themselves "less as servants of the communes than as 'lords' who ruled over 'subjects.'"[18]

In 1830 the Great Council, the Canton's highest legislative body, was still elected by educated male property owners. Participation in the election was through electoral councils (themselves appointed by the Great Council) or through guilds.[19] The Great Council in turn selected the members of the Small Council, the Canton's executive branch.[20] The Great Council also selected all judges, as well as members of the Church Council and School Board. The City of Zurich was represented disproportionately in the Great Council, at the expense of the Zurich countryside.

Following the revolution in Paris in 1830 great popular pressure began to build in Zurich, especially in the countryside, to revise the constitution. On November 22, 1830, about 10,000 citizens gathered in a field in the village of Uster to demonstrate for political change.[21] This event is known as the *Ustertag*. The discussions of this meeting were formalized in writing in a pamphlet entitled the *Uster Resolution* ("*Das Memorial von Uster*"). The major demands of this petition included a new election for the Great Council, two thirds representation in the Great Council for the Zurich countryside, a requirement that the meetings of the Great Council be open to the public, separation of powers, freedom of the press, and the doing away of several of the more onerous feudal taxes.[22]

On December 6, 1830, a new Great Council was elected, and on March 30, 1831 the Canton of Zurich adopted a new constitution by a popular vote of 40,503 to 1,721. The new constitution was based on the principle of the people's sovereignty.[23] One concrete manifestation of this principle was that the franchise was extended to all adult males, without property or educational restrictions.[24]

In the years following the adoption of the 1831 Constitution the Great Council of the Canton of Zurich embarked on an aggressive program of reform legislation.[25] The common thread running through the legislative program is characterized by Largiadèr as follows:

> The years around 1830 are in our cantons the starting point for the fact that finally the masses enter into political life as a decisive factor. The entire subsequent development is the logical application of this principle.[26]

This principle is clearly stated in the first paragraph of the constitution adopted by the Canton of Zurich in 1831:

> The Canton of Zurich is a republic with a representative constitution, and as such a member of the Swiss Confederacy. Sovereignty is based on the totality of the people. It is exercised in accordance with the Constitution by the Great Council as representative of the people.[27]

We must examine more precisely what it means for "the masses [to enter] into political life as a decisive factor."[28]

The principle of the people's sovereignty in Swiss liberalism was, in part, determined by the influence of the idealistic philosophies and worldviews of Immanuel Kant and Johann Gottlieb Fichte on the leaders of the movement.[29] Very generally, two fundamental assumptions in particular of the Swiss liberals find resonance in idealistic philosophy. The first is a view of anthropology: the liberals saw humans as living in two worlds, the physical world and a higher, eternal, moral world.[30] They claimed, secondly, that access to and participation in the moral world was guaranteed not by revelation, but by reason.

These two presuppositions, influenced by idealism, manifested themselves in what Wolfgang von Wartburg isolates as the three central ideas that characterize the worldview of early Swiss liberalism. The way these three ideas played themselves out in practical politics determined the development of the principle of mass political participation which, Largiadèr claims, characterized the Regeneration (or, period of liberalism). The first idea was freedom. The liberals defined freedom not as arbitrary will, but as the ability to follow the moral law.[31] The second was justice. Because humans were essentially rational, that is, because they had the capacity to follow the moral law, they were to be respected by virtue of their rational human nature, rather than by virtue of non-essential characteristics such as the station to which they were born.[32] The third principle of liberalism was a desire for a state authority to attempt to formulate political law expressive of the moral law.[33]

These views influenced the ways in which "sovereignty . . . based on the totality of the people" was realized. The conception of popular sovereignty at this time rested not so much on the sum of public opinion, but on the nature of all human beings as rational beings. The government represented above all reason, regardless of whether this agreed with majority opinion.[34] Reason was located broadly in the sense that every person was to be regarded as essentially rational. The location of reason, while broad, was also individualistic. Each human was a rational being, and this rationality had nothing to do with belonging to a majority, a class, or a collective.

The way the liberals conceived of the location of political power paralleled (and relied on) their anthropology, that is, how they conceived of the location of reason. The political system constructed by the liberals to bring the moral law to expression in civic law reflected their view of the broad, individualistic location of reason. The constitution of 1831, while basing sovereignty on the people, also took steps to insure that the government would be able to pursue rational legislation buffered and protected from the very masses it represented. For example, the Great Council selected thirty-three of its own members.[35] Citizens elected neither the Small Council (the highest executive power in the

Canton) nor members of the judiciary. Both were selected by the Great Council.[36]

This characterization of the liberal worldview helps explain some of the positions adopted by liberal standard bearers at the end of the 1860s *vis-à-vis* proposals that, to us, seem to be the logical extension of popular sovereignty. The liberals were strident opponents of proposals for constitutional changes in the late 1860s, some of which can be classified as proposals for radical democracy, others as socialist proposals.

For example, the liberals did not want to institute the power of petitioning the legislative branch in such a way that a certain number of signatures on a petition would obligate the Great Council to consider it. The number of signatories in no way increased the rationality of the proposal. Further, the liberals opposed submitting all legislation to the power of popular veto, for, despite their efforts at universal education, and the fact that "sovereignty is based on the totality of the people," they still feared mob rule.[37]

So we must refine Largiadèr's characterization of this period as the one in which "the masses enter into political life as a decisive factor." Reason, and therefore political power, and therefore the ability to act as an agent in history (at least as far as the political realm was concerned) was conceived by the liberals to be located immanently, that is, within human nature, and broadly, that is, in every human.

Biedermann shared these liberal political commitments. Shortly before arriving at his new post in Zurich, he wrote:

> We too believe in the principle of the sovereignty of the people, not in the crude materialistic, atomistic sense, . . . rather, in the only rational sense: that the highest authority of the public life should originate from the rationally and morally conditioned whole of the people as a spiritual unity, which brings about in an organic way its ethical self-consciousness, not of what the individual arbitrarily covets, but rather what is right and rational for the whole.[38]

The location of this rationality that brings about what is best for the whole, however, is located neither "merely in the individual" as it is for the radical democrats, nor as an "abstract universal" as for the socialists.[39] Rather, rationality is located as a "concrete universal" in each individual:

> The human individual . . . has its absolute determination and thereby its absolute human right only in that its inner essential unity with the absolute is set in motion concretely on the basis of its sphere of existence, determined in the general natural context of the world process.[40]

The absolute is located in individuals as microcosms.

The political reforms undertaken during the Regeneration presupposed a changing view of historical agency, one that saw humans as essentially rational, and that located this rationality immanently and broadly. I turn now to economic struggles and battles over the educational system. I will argue that liberal reforms in these arenas can also be seen as being based on this view of historical agency.

Economics in Zurich during the Regeneration

In 1832 the Corrodi & Pfister textile factory in Uster was burned to the ground. Roughly fifty participants were jailed. Far from being looked down upon or seen as dangerous, the ringleaders of this attack were local heroes, and the fact that they were still in prison in 1839 was one of the aggravating factors that led to the coup in the Strauss affair. One of the demands of the Faith Committee to the Great Council was their release.

The Canton of Zurich was one of the areas in Europe to undergo an early and intensive industrialization.[41] Corrodi & Pfister was the first firm to introduce mechanical looms. The Uster fire enjoyed such popular support because for many in the Zurich countryside rapid industrialization was yanking the economic carpet and traditional means of livelihood from under their feet.

Textiles was Zurich's most important industry, especially the spinning and weaving of cotton, but also including silk, wool, and linen. The textile industry was based in the countryside. The first mechanical spinning mills were introduced into Zurich in 1805 by Escher, Wyss & Company.[42] Corrodi & Pfister attached the first mechanical looms to a spinning mill in Zurich in 1832. By 1827 there were 106 spinning mills containing a total of 180,000 to 200,000 spindles. The number of mills dropped to sixty-nine by 1843 as a result of the rapid growth of larger concerns at the expense of smaller firms. In 1843 the number of mechanical spindles had grown to 300,000.[43] Other industries, including communications, railroads, and banking experienced similar expansion.[44]

Due to this rapid industrialization in Zurich, the percentage of the Zurich population engaged primarily in agriculture dropped from 70% in the 1830s to 40% by the 1860s.[45] In addition to separating work and domestic space, mechanization entailed a total shift in the ownership of the means of production. Workers involved in the cottage industry almost always owned their own hand spindles and looms. They could not, however, afford the investment in factories and mechanical spindles and looms, and so ownership of the means of production passed into the hands of a small class of industrialists.[46]

In the face of such rapid development and massive shifts in the traditional order of ownership, wealth, and power, new sets of rights and duties were hotly contested.[47] This contentious history left a record in which we see the same re-construction of the location of history's dynamic that we saw in Zurich's political life.

The Regeneration conception of economic rights and freedoms under-mined the traditional guild system. Control of the Great and Small Councils, which once had been based on birth, had, since the 1400s begun to be based more and more on the economic success of guild masters.[48] This class of eco-nomic patricians, for all practical purposes, played the same role in Zurich that the noble class played in the rest of Europe.[49] While the strength of the guild system had originated in the principle of self-rule, by the 1800s the patrician class had indeed become quite a small elite in Zurich.[50]

Economic reforms thus went hand in hand with political reforms. Freedom of trade became a central tenet of the law, depriving the guilds of their almost absolute control over access to various professions. The Constitution of 1831 states:

> The freedom of trade and industry is expressly ensured, to the extent that it
> is consistent with the well being of the entire citizenry, and the well being of
> the trade, business, and artisan classes. In this spirit shall the trade regulations
> be revised through legislation as quickly as possible.[51]

The legislative task prescribed by the 1831 Constitution came to fruition in 1837 in an act legislating occupational freedom.[52] A revision of the Constitution adopted in 1838 incorporated these more stringent guidelines decreeing freedom of trade into the Constitution.[53]

As their power to regulate the economy eroded, the political power of the guilds was persistently reduced. Their clout was lessened significantly in 1831 when more seats in the Great Council were allocated to the countryside than to the city of Zurich.[54] In 1838 the guilds were stripped of all official political power when a revision of the Constitution established electoral districts to replace the guilds as the vehicle through which citizens expressed their fran-chise.[55]

The reduction of guild control over the economic and political life of Zurich went hand in hand with the process of industrialization. These legal changes freed the industrialists to pursue their own modes of production and seek their own markets independently of guild restrictions.[56]

There was, of course, a downside to the principle of freedom of trade.[57] While the dismantling of the guild system removed artificial restraints on freedom and on economic expansion, it also removed the traditional means of regulating and protecting the living and working conditions of the wage laborers. Thus, in addition to promoting a legislative agenda of occupational freedom, the liberal government also got involved in efforts to regulate working conditions.[58]

At particular risk during the heyday of industrialization were children. A Local Council report from Wiedikon, a community adjacent to the city of

Zurich, described the children working in the Escher Wyss spinning mill as follows:

> These children belong to the poorest class of people. In no respect do they receive sufficient nourishment appropriate to their growth and effort, especially not in times of inflation. Half naked they are already underway in the winter at five in the morning in the ice cold. Winter storms lash them along the snowy pathless road. Thus–shivering and wet through and through–they enter the damp, unclean, work-place smokey from steam and dust. This offers them 14 full hours of heavy labor, with only one hour of rest, from 12 to 1 o'clock. Thus it is, year in and year out. The development of their physical strength is never fostered through careful cultivation, rather it is inhibited and tormented from excessive strain. Violence is done to their youthful nature and development. Exhaustion follows on exhaustion. Their appearance, earlier glowing, soon changes into a pale yellow, dull, emaciated complexion. The gay liveliness of their first years of life is devoured by a sluggish, shuffling, letting-themselves-go-to-sleep. The strength of their outward vitality is visibly broken by the time their development ought just to be beginning; but with it snaps as well the internal love of life, the moral courage to face life.[59]

Though children had contributed to their family incomes under the previous cottage industry system, that system allowed for their work to be regulated and supervised by the head of the family. The system centered on mechanized factories which overtook the economic landscape in Zurich beginning in the 1820s placed all working family members in factories under the supervision of non-family members.[60]

In 1837 the Ruling Council adopted a regulation forbidding the employment of children younger than twelve. This regulation was confirmed and strengthened by a more comprehensive "factory law" passed in 1859 by the Great Council. The 1859 law limited the daily work hours of workers younger than sixteen to thirteen hours.[61] Children were also banned from night labor, and forbidden to work on Sundays and religious holidays. In tandem with the factory law, a law obligating school attendance and Sunday school attendance was passed in 1859.[62]

It is not surprising that the industrialists who saw their profit margins affected by these regulations on child labor and on work conditions fought against their adoption. A district representative, himself an investor in industrial enterprises, summed up the basis of their argument in a petition to the Great Council:

> We hope and desire that each citizen of the Canton can ply his trade according to his desires freely and unrestrained (within the boundaries of the laws).[63]

Perhaps more surprising is that laws restricting children's labor were also, by and large, unpopular with the workers. While considering the legislation (eventually passed) requiring school attendance, and forbidding school aged children from working in factories, the Great Council received a petition signed by forty-four "heads of households" objecting to the proposed legislation. In addition to noting the loss of income they would sustain, as well as their opinion that it is good for children to begin to work at a young age, the petitioners appealed twice to their rights:

> We are of the opinion that each citizen, who stands under the same government, must also have equal rights and freedom. . . . We conclude with the most heartfelt wish that the Great Council might grant our urgent request to provide employees of spinning mills the same rights as those in other trades.[64]

All parties involved, the government, the industrialists, and the workers presented their arguments in the same terms. The government was concerned to provide all people, and especially children, with the conditions necessary for the exercise of their rights. Above all, the education of children could not be sacrificed to their labor in factories. The industrialists, of course, saw any intervention by the government as meddling in their recently earned rights to undertake their business in a free market, which included the buying and selling of labor, until recently a guild monopoly.

The workers used the same rights-based vocabulary to express themselves. The basis of the argument in their petition is their right to control their own labor and that of their children. They argue that it is in their own best interests to enter the free market of labor as individuals with the same rights as anyone else, whether they be workers in other trades, or the factory investors themselves. Thus, they see themselves (1) as the legal equals of every other citizen in the economic sphere, and (2) not as a class or proletariat, but as individuals. All involved claim personal freedom, equality, and self-determination.[65]

Both industrialists and workers adopted the same rhetoric in their conflicts before and with the government. In so doing, though they were often enemies, they stood together over against the traditional economic system. They took for granted a sense of agency in history. Their ability to influence legislation, or to buy and sell labor on an open market, was located in them by virtue of their rights as rational beings. Furthermore, rights were located broadly across all levels of the community (member of government, industrialist, worker), though not collectively.

School Reform in the Regeneration

Modern industrial nations require a "level of literacy and technical competence, . . . a common conceptual currency," that can only be provided by a school system. Ernest Gellner argues that the minimum size for a viable national political unit is the size required to support primary schools, secondary schools to train primary teachers, and universities to train secondary teachers.[66] As Zurich struggled into the modern world, school reform was one of the most contested sites.[67] Before 1831 most children in Zurich received a minimal education from the local minister. Ignaz Thomas Scherr, the man hired by Zurich's Board of Education to reform their schools, instituted examinations to see which instructors had the proper qualifications to teach. He immediately fired 104 teachers who failed the exams, a move that was seen as anti-religious and arrogant. One of the first acts of the conservative government established after the coup in 1839 was to fire Scherr and close down the teacher's college he had established. In these battles over the education of Zurich's children we also get a sense of worldviews and fundamental assumptions that divided the contestants.

For the leaders of the Regeneration education was a priority.[68] The 1831 Constitution, in establishing a new School Board (*Erziehungsrath*), stated the goals and commitment of the liberal government:

> The supervision of all the Canton's institutions of learning, the promotion of higher as well as popular education is to be provided by a School Board. . . .
> The organization of the school system, and especially the establishment of a school synod, is reserved to the issuing of laws upon obtaining the expert opinion of the School Board.[69]

Prior to the founding of a school board and school synod, education had been the responsibility of the church. In most villages lessons were taught either by the minister or by someone under the minister's supervision.

> These [pre-1831] elementary schools cannot bring about much more than a little bit of reading, the beginnings of writing, as well as a satchel of religious aphorisms learned completely by rote. . . . Nothing much changes [in this state of affairs] until the Ustertag of 1830. School remains largely under the tutelage of the church, and the subjects of instruction and corresponding educational material are essentially the same.[70]

After receiving the report of the School Board, the Great Council, as instructed by the 1831 Constitution, passed a comprehensive education law in 1832.[71] It removed responsibility for schooling from the churches. Education for children up to twelve years of age became tax supported. The School Act of 1832 provided for the founding of a Teachers College in the town of Küsnacht to train competent teachers independent of the church. Within a decade the Canton had built 141 new schools.[72]

To serve as point man in the educational reform, the School Board appointed Ignaz Thomas Scherr as director of the Teachers College in Küsnacht. His pedagogical theories are revealing.

In an 1838 address to the Helvetic Society, Scherr linked the necessity of his school reforms to the new political situation in Zurich:

> The recognition of the people's sovereignty inevitably brings with it the necessity of the people's education to the point of citizenship [literally, "political knowledge"]. . . . Either we turn back from the path we are treading (may God prevent that), and put the people under tutelage again, or we throw off all timid hesitating and strive with all our power to raise the people to political majority.[73]

Because the schools were under the control of a school board and school synod, rather than the church, they aroused the distrust of many orthodox elements in the Canton. This mistrust was exacerbated by the introduction of new school materials, many of which written by Scherr, to replace the traditional emphasis on the catechism, religious songs, and aphorisms.[74] It is not surprising, then, that Scherr has been painted as an anti-religious reformer.

But a closer look at Scherr's theory of human development, on which he based his pedagogy, shows him to be concerned to the utmost with the creation of religious citizens. The battle over school reform is a battle between two profoundly incompatible religious worldviews.

Scherr divided human development into three psychological stages. It is not until the third and final stage of development that the child achieves self-consciousness and becomes capable of the "nobler feelings."[75] Thinking and feeling reach their highest power at this stage, and elevate the person to rationality. At the third stage reason first reveals,

> the ideas of a most perfect essence, that is, of God, of immortality, of perfection, and of otherworldly reward. . . . [T]he longing for a higher relationship to God and to eternity, for religion, that lies in human nature, forms. . . . Religion appears, in this development, as a fruit of the highest blooming of the spirit.[76]

Thus, the goal of Scherr's entire system is to make people religious.[77]

Although conservative groups in the Canton understood the turmoil surrounding the schools as a conflict between religion and anti-religion, it is better understood as a clash of religious pedagogies. At the center of Scherr's system stands a fully developed, reasonable human. The methods and materials used to attain this fully developed result follow strict levels of epistemological development. The goal is a reasonable (and reasonably religious) citizen on the one hand, and the progress of humanity as a whole towards perfection on the other.

That Scherr saw the progress of both history and of individuals towards reason as a religious progress is expressed clearly by a close associate of his:

> Thus, I find the holy spirit where I meet it itself, [where I meet] freedom, truth, love, [in the] crusades, the Swiss liberty of 1315, the spiritual struggles

in the church in 1414 and 1431, the driving apart of the elements in 1519, the bursting of chains in Switzerland in 1649, 1700, in America and in the whole western world in 1765 and 1789 and 1830.[78]

But that Scherr's religious view of history must conflict with more conservative views is also clear. In a letter to a friend expressing his relationship to Christianity, Scherr sought to find the "rational kernel" within the shell. It is a shell the orthodox were unwilling to discard.

> As regards my feelings, I experience profoundly an inner religious need. I find the precepts for the satisfaction of the same in the Christian teaching. But there, to be sure, you must make a distinction: in that which is given to us as Christian revelation I find very much that is false, Jewish, superfluous–in short, a mixture of ingredients of human error and ignoble strivings. But for the sake of the kernel I will never contemptuously throw out these husks and shells, although they have for me become inessential. That which is contained purely and clearly in the Christian teaching about the moral and eternal world order, about a highest governing being, about *spiritual* life everlasting, and spiritual reward; that constitutes my religion.[79]

Insofar as Scherr's religious views influenced his pedagogical views, those pedagogical views cannot help but clash with those of traditional Christianity. In Scherr's opinion, at the center of the traditional Christianity's pedagogy stands a person sharing in the resurrection of Jesus Christ. While one can develop intellectually and grow in knowledge, one must finally turn to grace as pedagogy. The idea that an individual, or humanity in general, can make steady progress toward the goal of humanity, salvation, is foreign to traditional Christianity. Scherr's brother Johannes wrote, in justification of Scherr's pedagogical activity in Zurich, that Christian

> textbooks can merely present the contents of faith, and always only of faith, in more or less detail (small fragments of questions, master, catechism, testament). And the church subject matter can only be arranged and treated according to the peculiar relationship of the dogmas among themselves, not according to the requirements of the developing soul. Inquiring after the apprehension of the articles of faith, of catechization, cannot have the end of making the incomprehensible clear, but only to discover if the contents of the teaching, the total material of faith has come to a complete breakthrough. Church catechization cannot, therefore, develop, but can merely listen.[80]

Scherr's brother was arguing that the schools, under the control of the church, had focused not on developing the innate reasoning ability in each student, but on presenting a set of dogmas. The pedagogy was controlled by the needs of dogma, not the needs of the students. This may or may not be an accurate description of the pedagogical epistemology of the schools under orthodox Christianity, but in any case it does allow us a glimpse of the issues at stake in the fight over school curriculum and leadership, as they were perceived by the participants. For Scherr history proceeds towards a fully developed human. The history of politics and the history of religion play roles in bringing this about. The goal of education, as well as the goal of Christianity, is a rational human.[81]

Scherr's "reason" is wholly individualistic. Each individual child is, in principle, capable of achieving it, if it is taught at each stage of its development in a way appropriate to that stage. There was no talk of educating a class of people, rather only of making full development available to each individual of all classes. History, then, progresses towards the realization of the rational nature that is the essential goal of each individual. The goal of the schools, in service of the goals of the state in general, is to bring every person to the realization of this essential nature.[82]

Wegmann makes the link between Scherr's pedagogy and Young-Hegelian Theology explicit:

> But to the degree that the Zurich church, not the least because of reaction to the theories of religion of Hegel and Strauss, abandoned the hitherto at least partially philosophical starting point, the rift between the theory of development that the school had need of, and Christian psychology, had to become obvious.[83]

In this chapter I have narrated a series of battles in Zurich–political, economic, and educational. One plausible account of these fights is the differing assumptions about anthropology, about the nature of human agency and the role that that agency plays in historical change. This account, though plausible, is not one that the participants articulated themselves, but that is not surprising given the rarity of that level of self-awareness.

That these conflicts were sometimes violent struggles over human agency and historical dynamics can be shown more clearly on another battlefield, where the link to historical conceptions is closer to the surface. That battlefield is the one we categorize as religious. In the final two chapters of this book I will argue that the liturgy struggle, the fight over how to baptize babies, was essentially a struggle over historical agency in which the historical agency of Jesus was the unavoidable flashpoint. Before turning to baptism, however, we must look closely at Biedermann's christology to see what is at stake. The next chapter (chapter three) introduces his theology so that his role in Switzerland's christological controversies can be grasped (chapter four).

THE PERSONALITY OF GOD AND OTHER CONTRADICTIONS

> In a republic, said I, the greatest and best is demanded of every citizen, without requiting him by bringing about the downfall of the republic, by setting up his name above all others and raising him to the rank of a prince. In the same way, I regarded the world of the spirit as a republic, which had God above as its sole protector, whose majesty, in complete freedom, kept holy the law that He had given, and this freedom was our freedom too, and ours was His!
>
> –Gottfried Keller, *Green Henry*

Contemporary churches define themselves, or divide themselves, along fairly predictable lines. A few key issues stand in for a host of positions. If you know where someone stands on biblical inerrancy or the expectation of an imminent and literal rapture, for example, you can infer with reasonable accuracy a slew of his or her other theological positions and probably even political and social views such as abortion and the ordination of gay clergy.

In the nineteenth century the two theological litmus tests were the personality of God and the life everlasting. In showing the position Biedermann staked out in the first of these two theological controversies, I lay out his basic theological moves.[1] This will begin to show what it looks like in the realm of theology when one takes one's bearings from an assumption that historical dynamics are driven by agency located both immanently and broadly, and make possible a clear exposition of his christology in chapter four.

For Biedermann, as a theologian, the question of history could also be phrased as the question of the relationship of God to creation. History progresses the way it does, and has meaning, because of the ways God is present in history (or, for Biedermann, because of the relationship of absolute and finite spirit).[2] Through the analysis of Biedermann's theology in this chapter I will arrive at a precise meaning of the word "immanent" in this context. First, for Biedermann all humans (as finite spirit) have God (absolute spirit) as their ground, goal, and essence. That is to say, God is defined as the universal creative essence of humans. God is present in us. Second, this is true of all humans as such, including Jesus. According to Biedermann, we all participate in precisely the same filial relationship with God as did Jesus; he is not qualitatively unique.[3] In other words, not only is God present *in us*, but God is present *broadly* across the human community. Locating the relationship of all humans with God equally across the entire human community will have links with the kind of government one sets up over any specific community, and, as we will see, it has implications for the way in which that community baptizes its infants (that is, initiates children into the community).

Point/Counterpoint: Was Biedermann a Christian?

Soon after the appearance of Biedermann's *Die freie Theologie* in 1844, Johannes Heinrich August Ebrard[4] launched an attack against the Young Hegelians in an article entitled "Five Articles of Christian Faith and Five Articles of Hegelian Knowledge."[5] Ebrard was a professor at the University of Zurich from 1844 to 1847, when he was called to the University of Erlangen. He founded and edited the journal *Die Zukunft der Kirche* [*The Future of the Church*] in 1845, at the same time that Biedermann and D. Fries founded *Die Kirche der Gegenwart* [*The Church of the Present*]. Ebrard's attack on "Hegelian knowledge" was the first public, written attack in Switzerland against the Young Hegelians and Biedermann. The debate between Biedermann and Ebrard in these two journals in 1845 was the first extended written debate, and set the terms for much of the conflict to follow.

Ebrard's initial attack on Biedermann juxtaposed five articles of Christian faith and five articles of (Young) Hegelian knowledge, and under each pair added "a number of short sentences giving a summary of the contents of the articles for the uneducated, for whom the academic jargon is less understandable."[6]

It is these summaries for the uneducated that caused the controversy. Ebrard's juxtaposition of sentences from Christian faith and sentences from Hegelian knowledge were intentionally provocative. His juxtapositions included such statements as: Christianity: "God is in himself eternally personal;" Hegelianism: "God is not eternally personal, rather is thought of only as eternal, that is, infinite." Christianity: "Reconciliation must be as much a fact as sin is a fact;" Hegelianism: "Reconciliation of this contradiction [the opposition of the divine and the human, which is sin] consists in the sublation of this opposition, that is, in the surpassing of religion." Christianity: "Jesus is the Christ," "Christ has redeemed us from the debt of sin through his death;" Hegelianism: "Jesus is not the Christ," "The community has redeemed itself from the representation of a difference between divinity and humanity, through the development of the idea of Christ."[7]

The Biedermann/Ebrard debate quickly became polemical, and the two never achieved an understanding. But at least two significant points of disagreement emerged that manifest the distinct views of history presupposed by both theologians. First, they fought over whether or not it makes sense to speak of the personality of God. Second, while both agreed that reconciliation was a historical fact in some way effected by Jesus, they fought over exactly what kind of historical fact this was. The first fight is sorted out in this chapter, the second in the next.

Epistemology

"Nearly all the wisdom we possess, that is to say, true and sound wisdom, consists of two parts: the knowledge of God and of ourselves."[8] So begins Calvin's *Institutes*, the touchstone of the Reformed tradition. For Calvin neither part of true and sound knowledge is possible without the other, to the extent that there is no systematic way of deciding which topic one should take up first. Calvin opts to discuss knowledge of God first because "the order of right teaching requires" it, by which I presume he means that because some glory is associated with chronological priority, to do otherwise would be arrogant.[9] In a sense that would perhaps surprise Calvin, but in a very real sense nonetheless, the same link between epistemology and the doctrine of God is found in Biedermann's systematic theology.

Biedermann described the ultimate goal (*der Endzweck*) of the unending process of nature, and of humans who are the "peak and conclusion" of the natural order, as a return to absolute spirit.[10] The key to this return (or reconciliation) is found in Biedermann's christology, the centerpiece of his theological system. As with all good systematic theologians, however, the shape of Biedermann's theology pervades his entire system. In order to understand what is at stake in Biedermann's christology we must first discuss some other aspects of his theology, specifically his theory of our knowledge of God, which begins with his theory of knowledge in general (epistemology). Discussing these will serve to introduce the terms and concepts important for a clear understanding of Biedermann's christology, as well as show that an immanent sense of history is presupposed throughout his entire theological system.

Perhaps Biedermann's most noted contribution to intellectual history is the way in which his epistemology (which includes his theory of language) allowed him to construe the relationship of philosophy and religion. This relationship was one of the issues that split the Hegelian school after Hegel's death. The debate in part originated in Hegel's own ambivalence on the subject. He affirmed that in religion the true content of philosophy is already found.[11] Yet he also identified religion with representational language

(*Vorstellung*), which seems, finally, to be limited in its capacity to express the unity of finite and infinite spirit (God is represented as "over-against," as a character in a story).[12] Hegel seemed to hold that this unity can be more clearly expressed by philosophy, which he identified with conceptual language (*Begriff*). Thinkers normally classified as Young Hegelians (e.g., David Friedrich Strauss, Ludwig Feuerbach, the later Bruno Bauer) generally concluded that the time had come when whatever truth might be expressed in religion was more adequately expressed in philosophy, and that therefore religion ought to pass over into philosophy.

Biedermann, who in almost every other respect was close to the Young Hegelians, argued that this was not the case. The way in which Biedermann related representational language (*Vorstellung*) and conceptual language (*Begriff*) in his epistemology allowed him to share a worldview with Young Hegelians and yet remain a Reformed pastor. This makes him an ideal test case. He offers us the chance to examine the way the worldview of the thinkers most closely associated with the political and social upheavals of German speaking countries as they entered modernity (and surely among the Young Hegelians we must include the young Karl Marx) plays itself out in a religious system, specifically the effect of theory on praxis (in this case, on liturgy).

Biedermann argued that epistemology has three stages, the latter two of which receive their objects solely from the immediately preceding stage.

> The process of consciousness has . . . three stages to be differentiated essentially, each of which continually hands over its specifically befitting content of consciousness to the succeeding [stage] as the object of consciousness.[13]

The relationship between the second and third stages of epistemology, representing (*das Vorstellen*) and conceiving (*das Denken* or *das Begriffen*) in Biedermann's epistemology has received much of the attention given to his work in the secondary literature.[14] Equally important for this discussion is the relation of the first stage of epistemology, perceiving, to the succeeding two stages.[15] I begin with this relationship before moving on to the relationship of representation and concept, and the relationship of religion and philosophy.

The relationship of perceiving to the other two stages of the epistemological process led Biedermann to identify his position as one of "pure realism."[16] I will define some terms within Biedermann's system which should make clear what he means by this.

Biedermann defined humans as finite spirit. By spirit he meant "the principle of rational thought and free will."[17] Humans are spiritual beings existing in the natural world (hence our finitude). As such we are conscious beings. Biedermann defined consciousness (*das Bewusstsein*) as "nothing other than a relationship between subject and object."[18] The ego is the subject of this consciousness, which as we have seen was divided by Biedermann into the three stages of perceiving, representing, and thinking.[19] The second and third stages are each based entirely on the respective preceding one. Since representing and conceiving are operations of the spirit based entirely on the preceding stage of consciousness, it follows that all knowledge originates in perceiving.

Given that consciousness entails a relationship with an object, and we are only in relationship with the things we perceive, Biedermann defines the world as follows:

> The object of possible perceiving is all ideal [*ideell*] and material being that itself stands in a real relationship of being with the appropriate moment of being in the subject, and therefore constitutes for the latter the available world.[20]

Biedermann argued that we have real knowledge of ideal being, pace Kant, because we perceive ideal being, and the ideal aspect of material beings (which is their law-abiding existence in time and space) in the world.[21] Hegel, by contrast, correctly gave us epistemological access to ideal being, but he erred in proceeding as though we ourselves could deduce a priori knowledge of ideal being.[22]

For Biedermann, we cannot know anything we have not first perceived, and then represented to ourselves. The task of the activity of conceptual thought is simply to judge the adequacy of our representations to our perceptions, that is, to differentiate the ideal and sensible aspects of our representations. Biedermann described his position *vis-à-vis* Kant and Hegel as follows:

> Surely Kant correctly placed the subject of consciousness epistemologically on its real ground, but from the outset [he] displaced from him [the subject] abstractly-dualistically the object of consciousness. Hegel, by contrast, correctly fixed the object of consciousness, but carried away the subject of consciousness from its real ground. The former sends us into the water, but keeps us from learning to swim; the latter wants to teach us to swim in the air.[23]

Biedermann argued that skepticism regarding perceiving is misplaced. Even imagined perceptions exist as perception for the subject.[24] Errors in knowledge occur not because of misperception, but because of inadequate representation. For example, a perception that is the product of the imagination might be mistaken for one that is a product of the world. A drunk person might see a pink elephant. The root of the problem of error is not misperception, but an inadequate representation, and the failure of conceiving to identify what is ideal and what is material. If the drunk person were a theology student trained by Biedermann he (not she in that day) would understand that the elephant does exist, but ideally, in his representation, not as a material object in the world.

Representations make perceptions available to the consciousness as pictures and word signs. They are always in need of purification. Representations of material objects are obviously not themselves the objects; rather they are images of these objects. Representations of ideal objects, as images, represent these immaterial objects in material form. Therefore every representation contains within itself a contradiction between the content of the representation and the form. There is no representation which is not in need of conceptual thinking in order to isolate the sensible from the ideal in the representation so that the adequacy of the representation to our perception is apparent.

Conceptual thought (or philosophy) serves the useful function of clarifying or purifying our representations. Biedermann defined conceiving as "the subjective differentiation of the ideal content of representation from representation of sensible existence."[25] Conceiving, therefore, does not determine truth a priori. Rather, in isolating the sensorial from the ideal in the subject's representations, conceiving merely determines the extent to which representations are adequate to the subject's perceptions.

Biedermann argued that philosophy cannot replace or surpass religion for two reasons. First, it is never possible for conceptual thought to replace the representational thought associated with religion.[26] Conceptual thought is in fact completely dependent on representational thought, parasitic on it. Conceptual thinking is never independent of representation, for conceptual thinking has only the contents of representational thinking as its object. Even the very words that the philosopher uses in conceptual thought are a product of representation.[27] Thus after doing the work that Biedermann called "critical-speculative processing" the philosopher or theologian returns to his or her representations, but with a firmer grasp on their truth (that is, their adequacy).[28]

Second, not only will conceptual thought never completely be able to turn its back on representational thought, but Biedermann did not associate religion with representation as strongly as did many in the Hegelian school.[29] Biedermann defined religion as:

> the whole personal relation of the ego to God . . . which is carried out in man's thinking, feeling, and willing as a unity, and which for this reason is not at all based on the representational form in terms of content, and is not dependent on it [the representational form], rather for which this form [representational] psychologically merely presents itself naturally, as everywhere where our consciousness is concerned only in content and not in form.[30]

Religion is a relationship with the absolute rather than representational thought about the absolute.

Biedermann defined philosophy, in contrast, as "nothing other than reflection of consciousness on its own essence."[31]

> When one does philosophy, as a philosopher he concerns himself with his relation to the object of philosophy only according to the universality of his thought, not according to his individuality.[32]

While religion is the relation of the whole subject to the absolute, philosophy (insofar as it is philosophy) is the conceptual stage of the ego reflecting on the absolute (which, as we will see, is the same thing as its own essence).

One begins to see how his epistemology dissolved the tension between religion and philosophy that pushed many Young Hegelians out of the church. Religion is a relationship of finite and infinite spirit (most often, but not necessarily expressed in representational language); philosophy is the activity in which the philosopher, as a conceptual thinker rather than as an individual, considers the object of thought. Both religion and philosophy share the same object (the absolute), but religion is the relation of the whole individual to the object, philosophy is conceptual reflection on the object. Philosophy is practiced by a person, to be sure, but insofar as someone philosophizes he or she abstracts all aspects of individuality as much as possible (conceiving, after all, is "universal," i.e. it does not vary from individual to individual). To think that the two come into conflict is to confuse two distinct activities of the human spirit. Biedermann identified the "true kernel" of Hegel's philosophy as its demonstration

> that everything that is and that happens contains reason, but through our own reasonable, strictly logical thought this reason in things is discerned, as the same creative essence, as the inner ground of their appearance.[33]

In other words, conscious egos share with everything that is and that happens the same creative, reasonable ground.

Biedermann's epistemology works if one shares the assumption of idealism that we can know things because there is some relationship between the ideas in our heads and what is happening in the world outside of us. Humans share with everything we perceive an inner ground, which is a rational creative essence. Things totally unlike us would be imperceptible to us. "Like can only know like."[34] Despite Biedermann's very profound differences with Kant, he lived in the thought world of German idealism set off by Kant, and one could just as surely say of Biedermann's epistemology as Terry Pinkard says of representation in Kant's epistemology (with all the implied social and political ramifications): "[I]t was not a property only of noble or educated minds; it was a property of all *human* experience, of, as Kant put it, a 'universal self-consciousness.'"[35]

The Doctrine of God

Given Biedermann's position that the world for us consists only of the objects of our perceiving, and given that it would be impossible to perceive something totally other than ourselves, it follows that not only can like only know like, but further that like can only exist for like. Biedermann did not shy away from the conclusion to this train of thought when he turned to theology. In so far as humans know anything, including God, it must be the case that this object of our knowledge is somehow encompassed in the essence of humanity. Biedermann stated the case as follows:

> If the thinking person has acknowledged in philosophy that absolutely nothing can approach the spirit, can enter into any kind of relationship with it, can exist for it at all, that is not also encompassed by its own universality and so belongs itself to the human essence: so he must also say from the outset that the other member of the religious relationship, the divine, with which in religion the human places himself in a real relationship that penetrates and determines his whole essence, cannot be anything that lies beyond the universal essence of humans.[36]

God, for Biedermann, is the "universal creative essence of humans."[37] Our task now is to understand what Biedermann meant by this definition so that he avoided the position of a Young Hegelian like Feuerbach, for whom ultimately God is an illusory objectification of humanity, writ large.

Biedermann asserted that the most accurate and all-encompassing term for the concept of pure ideal being, or God, was "absolute spirit."[38] He was not concerned with deducing or proving to a materialistic worldview the existence, or necessity of existence, of absolute spirit. The world abounds with representations of divinity, and the thinker's (in this case the theologian's) task is not to be skeptical of the perceptions that give rise to representations, but rather to judge whether or not these representations are adequate to the perceptions, and to differentiate the ideal content of these representations from their ideal-sensible form. The way one does this is not a priori, as Hegel attempted to do, but empirically, that is, by working through the history of human representations of ideal being to discern the rational kernel expressed in the representations. In other words, one arrives at an adequate conception of God through a critical processing of the history of dogma. It is the skill with which Biedermann undertook this processing of the history of dogma in the first half of his *Christian Dogmatics* that led Emil Brunner to recommend him so highly to his students.[39]

We know from all of our perceptions that all objects in the world, ourselves included, are presented to us as a combination of material and ideal being. Even inanimate objects, as existing in space and time and acting according to the law-governed nature of the system as a whole, manifest ideal being. Representations of ideal being, like all representations, are a mixed bag of the sensible and the ideal. The conceptual task in determining the adequacy of representations of ideal being to the perception of ideal being itself is to isolate and remove all sensible aspects of the representation. The task for Biedermann in moving representations of God to the conceptual clarity of absolute spirit was to conceive of ideal being in such a way that it is freed from all traces of representation that would lead it to contradict itself.

Hegel's speculative philosophy, Biedermann believed, offered a way of conceiving of ideal being that did not lead to contradiction. The representations of absolute spirit Biedermann was most concerned with, of course, were those contained in the history of dogma. For Biedermann, then, the hermeneutical key to interpreting church doctrine was found in Hegel.[40] This is why the theological task is one of critical speculative processing. In other words, one interprets ecclesiastical dogma as representations of the relationship of finite and absolute being.

Biedermann defined his starting point in the history of church doctrine of God as follows:

> The basic ecclesiastical concept of the essence of God, in which are the *tres personae* of the *Deus unus,* consists of two moments, the grasping of which as a unity was the endeavor of all definitions of the *notio Dei:* (1) the absoluteness of the essence, and (2) the subsistence as personal spirit, on the analogy of the human personality. In the unity of both, God is the personal absolute spirit.[41]

The first of these two moments in the rubrics of traditional theology, absoluteness, is the category of the metaphysical attributes of God (eternity, omnipresence). The second of these two moments, personality, is the category of God's psychological attributes (feeling or self-consciousness, willing or omnipotence, knowing or omniscience).[42] Representational thought can give up neither of these two moments. If the first (the absoluteness of God) is surrendered, the result will be deism. If the second (personality) is surrendered, the result will be pantheism.[43]

These two moments are appropriate representations of God. When we turn to conceiving, can we isolate the material from the ideal in them? Is the representation adequate to the perception? For the first set of representations, representations of the metaphysical attributes of God, the answer is yes. The representations of metaphysical attributes can properly be conceived of by conceiving of God as pure spirit.[44] So we can purify our representations of any contradictions.

But when the thinker turns to the task of distinguishing the ideal kernel of the representations of the psychological attributes from their sensible form, the concept of personality is no longer adequate. For Biedermann, no attempt to conceive of God's attributes on the analogy of human spirit would ever escape representational contradictions. Humans are spirit in that they are knowing, willing, and feeling subjects. Any concept of knowing, willing, and feeling, however, that comes close to normal usage of these words, involves subjects that stand over-against other objects in the world. Biedermann defined knowing as passing from a state of ignorance of something to a state of awareness, just as willing involves acquiring something or altering a state of affairs. Knowing and willing necessarily involve change. Any attempt, therefore, to define God as personality, that is, God as knowing and willing, but without limit, will necessarily give up the notion of absoluteness. The task is not to try to come up with some definition of personality that fits our idea of God, but to inquire after the truth contained within this representation of personality.[45]

Again, Hegel's speculative philosophy offered a way around the problem of conceiving of the personality of God adequately. Biedermann's view was that it is only speculation's metaphysics that allowed us to conceive of God as absolute spirit in such a way that we will not be forced into a contradiction. The task is to find a conception of absolute spirit that does not involve personality, but that retains the kernels of truth contained in the traditional representations of God as feeling, willing, and knowing. For Biedermann,

> being-absolute is not abstract infinity, mere negation of all finite being–this is just nothingness–rather [being-absolute is] at the same time positing of itself and in itself of all finite being. Being-absolute is: pure being in–and through–oneself and being-in-itself-ground of all being outside of itself,–the aseitas of God in ecclesiastical doctrine.[46]

We know, according to Biedermann, that absolute being cannot be the mere infinite extension of finite being. And yet we know that absolute being cannot *not* exist, else neither would we as finite being exist.

Given this Hegelian conception of the absoluteness of absolute being, what is the kernel of truth contained in the traditional representation of God as absolute *person?* As we have seen, personality in humans involves feeling, willing, and thinking. We need not run through all of Biedermann's interpretations of the truth about the attributes of God contained in ecclesiastical dogma, but I offer as an example what Biedermann makes of the doctrine of God as knowing, or omniscient:

> Essentially the same process of the spirit, which in the finite human spiritual life constitutes the essence of objective consciousness, is in the *actus purus* of the absolute spirit on the one hand [1] the being-immanent of its spaceless and timeless absolute being-in-self in all finite moments of the natural process of existence of the world as their absolute principle, that is, as their goal as well as their ground; while at the same time on the other hand [2] all existing things in each moment of their finite process of existence reflect the eternal and omnipresent being-of-God-in-itself, that is, [they] are the subjectified object of absolute spirit.[47]

In other words, absolute spirit is not omniscient in the same way that humans are knowing, with the stipulation that absolute spirit knows absolutely everything. Even then, in the case of knowing everything, knowing as an act implies standing over-against something to be known. The omniscience of absolute spirit can be conceived of without contradiction if finite existence is conceived of as posited by absolute spirit as the moment of absolute spirit's objective consciousness. Absolute omniscience represents the perception that absolute spirit is the principle of everything that exists.

It is clear in Ebrard's summation of Hegelianism for the "unlearned" that he found the personality of God to be a critical doctrine, in part because it precluded pantheism and the divinization of humanity. Ebrard attributed to Hegelianism the knowledge that:

> God has no other existence than in the world, which is his manifestation. . . .
> Only in the human spirit does God become personal, that is, God becomes
> self-conscious when the human becomes conscious that he himself is God.[48]

In response to Biedermann's argument that it is impossible to conceive of divine personality because personality entails finitude, though personality is an appropriate representation of God, Ebrard distinguished subjectivity and personality. Ebrard defined subjectivity as the contents of the subject arising from its dependence on the world, and its existence in the world. Personality in humans, in contrast, is entelechy, the part of the subject that is a constant force, that is free self-determination rather than being-determined by the world. Subjectivity is the aspect of the subject that stands over-against objects, and therefore does entail finitude. It is what makes a human being an individual. Personality recognizes objects as the subject's own essence. It is attributable to God, who is not an individual over against objects, who never learns of objects, but rather who, in thinking objects, is the very ground of their existence.[49]

Biedermann responded that what Ebrard called personality is simply what he and other Young Hegelians call the creative essence of humans. It was the "newer philosophy" that taught Ebrard to search for what Ebrard called personality in humans in the first place.[50] Biedermann's definition of personality was far more in line with common usage of the word. For Biedermann "personality" is not the eternal moment in the human subject. Rather, it is a mode of being, that which is essentially human as opposed to animal.

> 'Person' is the free, internally and externally independent ego, who calls its
> thoughts and its willing, and therefore also a certain portion of spiritual and
> corporal goods, its own. As such it is a self-contained unity, and stands over-
> against other persons. This self-contained unity over-against others–which
> exactly constitutes the essential of the person–entails finitude and limited-

ness, because every person has its boundary, its end, in the other; each person is a unity in itself over-against others.[51]

Because "personality" denotes a mode of being that entails finitude, it is not conceptually accurate to attribute it to God.

The Knowledge of God and of Ourselves

We are now in a position to try to understand the nature of the absolute spirit's relationship to the world. Since consciousness for Biedermann by definition requires an object,[52] the self-realization (or self-consciousness) of absolute being requires positing something within absolute being which is at the same time other than absolute being, but which returns to absolute being.[53] Biedermann called the posited world of finite being "*das Andersein*" ("the being-other"). This being-other is a moment in God (self-knowledge), but it follows its own development:

> The absolute substance enters in non-spiritual existence not itself, directly in its all-oneness, but in the rationality and regularity of the world.[54]

Not only is this being-other posited, but it must in some sense return to absolute being. The possibility of this return occurs with the positing of a being both material and spiritual: finite spirit, the "peak and conclusion" ("*der Endzweck*") of the natural process. This finite spirit is capable of being conscious of its principle, and living in accord with that principle, and using each object in the world in accord with that principle.[55] Humans are the actualization of the moment of divine knowledge or self-consciousness.

The key is that neither this world, nor God, is the "really real," of which the other is a reflection or objectification. The "really real" is a unity, of which God is one moment (the abstract ideal), and humans are another moment (the individual concrete).[56]

Perhaps Biedermann's clearest statement of the relationship of absolute spirit and *das Andersein*, between God and humans, comes from a discussion of the historical task undertaken by speculative philosophy in *Die freie Theologie*:

> To ascertain scientifically such a possibility [the possibility at all of the unity of the divine and the human, the reality of which was the content of faith] only takes place if the divine and the human natures are not two different substances standing over-against one another, each having its existence for itself, but rather if they stand in and for themselves in relation to each other so that what representation casts apart into two different existences are moments of one and the same spiritual reality, the divine nature being the universal, eternal, ideal moment, the human in contrast being the moment of

the individual existence of the one actual divine-human nature mediating itself in temporal-spatial finitude.[57]

I wrote at the outset of this section that Biedermann defined God as the creative essence of humanity, and that in this sense one could say of his theology, as I have said of politics, economics, and education in the Regeneration, that it located human agency immanently and broadly. We now have a more refined vision of the nature of this immanence. Two aspects important for my argument are clear.

First, God lies within the compass of human consciousness:

> The taking over of theory is not yet completely realized so long as the content of faith is accepted as super-rational mystery, rather than recognized from the essence of the spirit as the reasonable content of the spirit.[58]

Anything "superhuman" in theology, whether it is a God standing over against humans, or a life everlasting beyond this worldly existence, merely demonstrates that theology has not completed its task of speculative processing of the representations found in dogma. For Biedermann the content of Christianity is precisely the fact that humans are not a substance separate from God, nor is God a human illusion, nor are humans themselves God. It is not that God is the absolutization of human essence. Rather, as finite spirit humans have God as their principle, that is, as their essence. This was one of Biedermann's points of contact with other Young Hegelians: God is defined as human essence.

But note the real difference between Biedermann's position and Feuerbach's. God is not humanity absolutized, rather we have God as our principle. So now we have one sense of immanence, God and humans as two moments of one unity that is reality. The "really real" is not outside us in some Platonic sense, material beings being real only to the extent that they participate in and come close to this "beyond."

The second important aspect of this immanence for my argument is that all humans as such, as finite spirit, have the same relationship to absolute spirit. The implications of this view will become clearer in looking at Biedermann's christology, but for now we can begin to draw some of the connections between theology and politics by quoting a passage from David Friedrich Strauss, whose Hegelian starting point was similar to Biedermann's. Strauss discussed the presupposition of "supernaturalists" that, at least as far as biblical history is concerned, God can act immediately in particular cases (rather than on the whole). Strauss took exception to this presupposition of the supernaturalists. For him, biblical accounts of the violation of the laws of nature indicated nothing more than an unhistorical account. Strauss noted the politically charged ramifications of this theological point of view:

To a freedom from this presupposition [the presupposition of immediate divine agency in particulars] we lay claim in the following work [*The Life of Jesus*]; in the same sense as a state might be called free from presupposition where the privileges of station, etc., were of no account. Such a state indeed has one presupposition, that of the natural equality of its citizens; and similarly do we take for granted the equal amenability to law of all events.[59]

Biedermann's discussion of the doctrine of God began with his definition of religion as a relation of finite and infinite spirit. The question then arises how one can know of one's participation in this relationship, which is to say that our discussion of Biedermann's doctrine of God has led us to the heart of his theology, christology. How is it that humans become conscious of their relationship to absolute spirit (that is, that humans are essentially a concrete moment of a unified reality, the ideal moment of which is none other than God)? What is our relationship to the revealer of this relationship, (that is, our relationship to Jesus)? The answers to these questions will bring us to the core of our discussion of historical human agency, since in discussing christology one is discussing significant historical events and our relation to them.

CHAPTER 4

WHAT WOULD JESUS DO?

> While I loved the person of Christ even if it was, as I believed, a myth as far as the perfection claimed for it went, I had yet grown hostile to all that called itself Christian.
>
> –Gottfried Keller, *Green Henry*

About once a year, one or more major weekly news magazine prints an article on the latest results from the Jesus Seminar. This allows the magazine to put Jesus on the cover, which reportedly results in more sales than the "sexiest man alive" issue, and it allows seminar members to regenerate interest in their project.

Biedermann, too, fought battles over the historical Jesus. Recall one of Ebrard's "Five Articles of Christian Faith and Five Articles of Hegelian Knowledge" that I cited at the beginning of chapter three: "Jesus is the Christ," "Christ has redeemed us from the debt of sin through his death," Hegelianism: "Jesus is not the Christ," "The community has redeemed itself from the representation of a difference between divinity and humanity, through the development of the idea of Christ."[1] In contrast to the Jesus Seminar, however, my interest in Biedermann's fights over Jesus is not what history can teach us about Jesus, but what Jesus can teach us about history. I will argue in chapters five and six that the root of the baptism struggle was unarticulated assumptions by both camps about the nature of human agency and historical dynamics. These assumptions are most easily laid bare in the controversy over what kind of historical agent Jesus was.

During the course of my exposition of Biedermann's christology I will draw a comparison between Biedermann's christology and that of David Friedrich Strauss. This comparison with a close associate of Biedermann's will highlight some of the nuances of Biedermann's position. We will then be in a good position to show the struggle between Biedermann's christology and the more conservative christologies of his opponents. This will allow us to see how theological differences and ritual controversies are part of wider culture wars in Zurich. If the way I have construed these wars is correct, that is, one can see in them different assumptions about human agency in history, then I should be able to demonstrate that other christologies entail other anthropological and historical assumptions. It will not be possible, or necessary, to sketch out the entire map of the christological options available in the mid-nineteenth century. Two comparisons, however, will be illuminating.

First, it is important to show the view of history presupposed by Biedermann's opponents in Zurich. I lump these opponents together under the term "orthodoxy." Their own chosen designation was "Positives." While they are a very rich and diverse group, they do share enough similarities, especially in their positions in the culture wars, to be grouped together responsibly. I will continue to take Ebrard as a representative of this group.

Second, I will compare Biedermann's christology with that of an Orthodox (or Right-Wing, as opposed to Young- or Left-Wing) Hegelian. On the surface it seems that anyone who begins with Hegel's view that the truth of religion is the "idea of the reconciliation of the finite with the infinite," that is, of the unity of human and divine, will have an equally immanent worldview. Therefore, I must show why it is that orthodox Hegelians were generally associated with conservative rather than liberal social and political movements. For this comparison I have chosen the theology of Philipp Konrad Marheineke, with whom Biedermann had the opportunity of studying during his stay in Berlin at the end of his days as a student.[2]

Processing Christology

Biedermann's central interpretive move in processing ecclesiastical christology was based on his Hegelian viewpoint. Biedermann's speculative christology was based on his definition of religion as "the self-conscious mediation of [humans'] two contrasting moments."[3] In the context of this philosophical view, the kernel of truth contained in the doctrine of Christ is the essential unity of the divine and the human.[4] But, as we have seen, Biedermann was not content to try to deduce this kernel of truth *a priori*. The failure, for Biedermann, of previous speculative theologies was that they did not ground themselves empirically, that is, they did not come to their conclusions by working through the history of Christian doctrine.

Biedermann framed the christological question as follows: What is the Christian principle, and what is the relationship of the man Jesus to this principle?[5] That there is a new religious principle (a new religious consciousness of the relation of finite and infinite spirit) that entered human history (and thereby also became a problem for thought) was clear to Biedermann. It was not a necessary part of a Hegelian dialectical view of history, rather it was a historical fact that a new religious community was founded, and this community left a record of its developing reflection on the religious self-consciousness present in its members. Consistent with his epistemology, the task for Biedermann at the stage of conceptual thought was neither to show why this new religious consciousness must have entered history at this point, nor even to try to grasp the conceptual content of the church's representations a priori. The dogmatic theologian's task is to work through these representations and distinguish the truth of their contents from the mixed ideal/sensible form that is appropriate to all representations. That is, the theologian must recover the rational kernel from the representation. In so doing the theologian determines in what way the representation is adequate to the perceptions of the followers of Jesus and their successors who have recorded them.

The clearest scriptural claim of the new religious self-consciousness is John's assertion that "the word became flesh."[6] The church has traditionally represented the relationship of principle and man, word and flesh, with the category of the son of God, or the God-man. Biedermann argued that there are two levels of contradiction inherent in this representation of Jesus Christ as the God-man, "psychological" and "historical."[7] The "psychological" contradiction (by which Biedermann meant the contradiction grounded in the epistemological process) is the contradiction shared by all representations. It is the contradiction of consciousness making present to itself a pure ideal reality in sensible form. A principle cannot be a man. Thus, representing the Christian principle of the unity of God and man in the form of a God-man contains a contradiction.

Second, this specific representation contains within itself an additional, historical contradiction. The new principle has been accounted for in the very forms of the religious environment through which it broke. In other words (and Biedermann singled out here Paul and the Reformers in particular), followers of Jesus have talked about the new principle using the very ideas of Jewish messianism which were overcome by the principle.

As Biedermann pointed out, if one begins by representing humanity and deity as two antithetical sorts of essences, one will never achieve an adequate conception of their unity (the Christian principle). The history of the doctrine of christology is the history of attempts to come to terms with this increasingly obvious cluster of contradictions.

I will not retrace Biedermann's critique of the entire history of the doctrine of christology here but we should take note of its conclusion. Biedermann found the logical completion of representational interpretations of the Johannine doctrine "the word became flesh" in the kenotic theologies of his Lutheran contemporaries. In trying to maintain at the same time the integrity of the divine essence, the integrity of the human essence, and their unity in the person of Jesus, kenotic theology resulted in a contradiction. This contradiction was most clearly and fully expressed in the treatment of the *communicatio idiomatum* in Wolfgang Friedrich Gess's theology. Biedermann characterized Gess's kenotic christology as follows: "The Logos so completely emptied himself of not only his divine mode of being, but also of his divine essence, that he began again to develop as a pure human soul."[8] Conceiving of the God-man as a divine essence (Logos), which begins again from the start as a human essence without, however, becoming another ego than it was as the Logos, is the logical completion of the process of increasingly obvious contradiction that began to unfold with the church's representation of the Christian principle as the God-man. Gess's kenotic theology was also, Biedermann pointed out, a "complete kenosis of reason."[9]

Biedermann versus the Liberals

Nor were other christologies on the contemporary theological map any comfort. Rationalism held fast to the human pole of the christological equation, seeing faith as a historical consequence of Jesus' personality. In doing so rationalists avoided contradiction, but also gave up the Christian principle (the unity of divine and human).[10] Speculative theologians could express the religious principle of unity, but could not prove this to be the real principle of historical Christianity.[11] That is, having deduced the unity of absolute and infinite spirit a priori, they had no way of showing that this principle was in any way related to Jesus of Nazareth. For Biedermann a religious principle is not an idea which one or another person could have had. Religion is a relationship between a whole finite human spirit and the absolute. It is the religious self-consciousness of a particular person.

Mediating theologians, following Schleiermacher, had at least two christological difficulties. First, they were no more successful than the speculative theologians in relating the Christian principle to Jesus. Even if Jesus was the first example of the complete consciousness of absolute dependence, it is this principle of absolute dependence, and not the personality of Jesus himself, which accounts for the historical effects from which Schleiermacher deduced their cause.[12] Second, Biedermann charged Schleiermacher with overstepping historical and philosophical limits in differentiating Jesus' archetypal self-activity from his appearance as a person determined by nationality, custom historical period, etc.[13]

The fundamental contradiction running through all these christologies was the identification of the Christian principle with the man Jesus. For Biedermann, the principle of Christianity was not abstract:

> The content of this principle to begin with may not be grasped universally-cosmically [Hegel], nor universally-anthropologically [Schleiermacher];

rather it must be fixed as a specifically religious principle, that is, as the specific determination of the religious inter-relation between absolute and finite
spirit that constitutes the essentially new in the religious personality of Jesus,
on which the Christian faith is based.[14]

In other words, it is not that there is some principle of which Jesus was the
first historical exemplar. The principle is not an idea thought up by Jesus, or
which finds its first or fullest expression in him. The principle is not abstract,
it is concrete. It is a relationship, not an idea; it is the awareness of the relationship of finite and absolute spirit found in Jesus' religious self-consciousness.
Biedermann's problem was not somehow to relate the principle of Christianity
to the man Jesus: the fact of Jesus' religious self-consciousness, as evidenced by
its effects on his followers, is the empirical starting point. The task rather was
to "purify" the representations of this religious self-consciousness so that we
correctly conceive of it.

> The determination of its content [Jesus' religious self-consciousness] is for
> this reason not to be grasped in such a way, that the same could have been
> realized eo ipso in human history before and apart from that fact.[15]

Jesus Christ's self-actualization of that principle was the first history has
recorded, that is, the first in a world-historical figure. Jesus is thus the historical redeemer.[16]

Biedermann's Filial Christology

What precisely are the contents of Jesus' religious self-consciousness, and of
belief in Jesus, that constitute the Christian principle? We have seen that any
attempt to identify the principle with the God-man will result in contradiction. Instead, Biedermann claimed, with the religious self-consciousness of
Jesus an essentially new consciousness of the form of the relationship of God
and humans enters into history.[17] The followers of Jesus were conscious of this
new relationship as an entrance of God into humanity, a revelation.[18] After
tracing the course of the inner mediation of the self-consciousness of the
Christian faith, we understand that the rational kernel of this representation is
that the two members of the religious relationship, the divine (pure, eternal,
universal essence) and the human (particular existence) are, in fact, both
moments of the one real free spirit.[19]

Jesus' followers were right to characterize him as the God-man, the son of
God. That representation is adequate to the perception of the unity of human
and divine, or finite and infinite spirit, with which the followers were confronted in Jesus' self-consciousness. The relationship of finite to infinite spirit
found in Jesus' self-consciousness is best represented as a filial relationship. But
the conceptual truth of this representation is the unity of finite and infinite, a

unity in which all humans, as finite spirit, participate. It is not *conceptually* accurate to state that Jesus is the God-man; rather in Jesus' religious self-consciousness the principle of God-manhood is for the first time actualized.

Biedermann described this principle of divine sonship as follows:

> The content of the human personality, that spiritual being-for-self that in [the personality] ought to come to realization, is in the first instance naturally to be described as the spiritual substance or the universal human essence of man (the *natura humana*), potentially immanent in every human ego by nature. The fact that this essence actualizes itself as the subjective spiritual life of this subjective ego by the *actus purus,* by which the ego distinguishes itself from its natural presupposition, this fact has its absolute ground, the ground of its possibility in general and the ground of its actualization in each moment, in the being of God as absolute spirit.[20]

As finite spirit, humans are determined by nature, but also able to choose freely. There is no human being who is wholly a part of nature. To the extent that we choose according to our essence as spirit, we fulfill our ultimate goal. What we learn in the Christian principle is that our essence, as spirit, is in fact the same as the ground, goal, and presupposition of existence. Choosing to live in accord with this essence, and to use the material world available to us in accord with this essence, is reconciliation, justification, and eternal life.

Given that humans, as finite spirit, bear this relationship as such to absolute spirit,[21] what is gained in the Christian revelation?

Nothing and everything. On the one hand, one's metaphysical status as finite spirit does not change. Biedermann writes that though man's reconciliation with God is revealed only with Jesus, God is always (and has always been) reconciled with man.[22] The statement that God is already reconciled with man implies that God, in the self-realization of positing *das Andersein,* stands in the same relationship to finitude and to self-consciousness regardless of our awareness of our participation in this relationship.

On the other hand, if one becomes vividly aware of one's own essence, then living in accord with that essence, i.e. true freedom from our contradictory existence (as ideal-material beings), is possible:

> This redemption of finite subject, reconciliation with God and filial relationship to God, mediated through the theoretical consciousness of the real unity with God of Christ, becomes a lively current state in the believer, a real determination of his consciousness.[23]

It is not that Christ is reconciled to God, and we through him, as the orthodox would claim. Rather we have the possibility of coming to the same religious self-consciousness of our relationship to God (a relationship that already exists).

The Christian principle is the new religious relationship in Jesus' self-consciousness. The task is not to try to deduce why the principle entered with Jesus, or if the principle could have entered history with someone else, in some other time. We only know that he is the first world-historical individual to have this religious self-consciousness, thus he is the redeemer.[24]

Jesus himself represented his religious self-consciousness in the forms of Jewish messianism. His followers recorded this representation, presenting it with the conviction that they had witnessed God born into history. The history of Christian doctrine is the history of increasingly obvious self-contradiction to which these representations lead us. But the portrayal of Jesus as the Son of God, or the God-man, is an adequate representation of the fundamental principle (relationship) of divine childhood, the awareness of which enters history with Jesus. It is the representation of the awareness in Jesus' religious self-consciousness of the unity of human and divine, finite and infinite spirit.

Before refining this discussion of Biedermann's christology by comparing it to that of Strauss, it is worth pausing to point out in general the way that history's immanent dynamics again rears its head here. Recall our two rough themes, (1) that God is present in us, and (2) that God is present broadly.

To demonstrate the first point we need do little more than re-state the Christian principle. It is

> the relationship of the two members, between which this movement of self-consciousness occurs– . . . the relationship and mediation of the pure, eternal, creative universal essence and the particular finite existence of the spirit, as they are the two moments of the one concrete unity of the one real free spirit.[25]

It is, of course, this principle that is presupposed in Biedermann's entire discussion of the doctrine of God, since it is only the historical effects of Jesus' religious self-consciousness that has made possible awareness of the filial relationship humans bear with God. It is our awareness of our relationship that makes available to us knowledge of the eternal, ideal moment of the real unity, of which humans are the concrete finite moment.

Second, we have seen in Biedermann's christology the universal nature of the filial relationship with God. This is a significant break with orthodox theology, for which our redemption is obtained on our behalf through Jesus. For Biedermann, all humans as such participate in the unity of finite and infinite. This is clear in his statement that God is always reconciled to humans, with or without the revelation of Jesus. Awareness of this relationship, of course, has a practical effect on humans (one can choose to live in accord with one's true principle), and so from the subjective side redemption constitutes a real change. The true principle, God in us, remains the same, however, and is located universally across the human community.

Biedermann versus Strauss

Of the theological views contemporary with Biedermann's, his christology was most closely linked with that of David Friedrich Strauss. Readers familiar with Strauss might, at this point, throw down the following gauntlet: the case for immanent historical agency, along with all its political implications, is an easy one to make for Strauss. His mythological christology replaces Jesus with the human race as the subject of christological claims. You can't locate agency much more broadly than that. But the case is much harder to make for Biedermann, who makes much more limited use of the mythological view, and who does not replace Jesus with humanity as the locus of revelation.

In arguing that Biedermann's christology requires an immanent view of historical agency, even where Biedermann is critical of Strauss and diverges from him, I will adopt the defense attorney's strategy: My client was not at the scene of the crime, and if he was, he did not do it. That is, I will argue that while some of Biedermann's criticisms of Strauss hit the mark, others are not justified by Biedermann's own theological system. Furthermore, I will argue that even where Biedermann diverges from Strauss's views, Biedermann's christology is at least as immanent in essentially the same sense.

It is often noted that the substance of Strauss's theology was not original. In 1825 Karl Otfried Müller had already put forward the view that myth is not the expression of a single creative mind, but of a community consciousness.[26] Irreconcilable discrepancies between the various gospel accounts of the life of Jesus, as well as the argument that events defying laws of nature could not be considered historical, had been made for years by the rationalists. The theological and political storm that broke on the publication of the first edition of Strauss's *Life of Jesus* in 1835 must therefore be accounted for on other grounds.

Marilyn Chapin Massey has shown that it was Strauss's inversion of Hegelian philosophy that led to his being branded the Iscariot of his day and dismissed from his post at the *Stift* in Tübingen.[27] Those who were trying to restore the rights of monarchs after the expulsion of Napoleon in 1814 and unify Germany under a single king thought they had found philosophical justification for the bureaucracy they headed in the Hegelianism of theologians such as the Berlin Hegelian Philipp Marheineke. The German people were to find their expression in an individual, the king. Hegelianism had therefore achieved something of the status of official state philosophy in the German states during the Restoration. Strauss's argument that the Christian myth (which represents the idea of human and divine unity) was a product not of an individual (Jesus) but the community had ramifications not only for theology but for the entire social structure of Germany, because it implied that significant historical agency is located in a community, not an individual.

Hans Frei argues, from an analysis of German literature and literary criticism, that the "failure of realism" in German letters is indicative of the "lack of ability or desire to cope realistically with contemporary historical forces."[28] In other words Germans, by and large, did not at this time see themselves as agents in history. It is in this environment that Strauss published his version of Hegelianism.

Strauss was far more concerned than Hegel to relate the idea of the Christ to the historical figure Jesus.[29] Neither the orthodox view that the Gospels were reliable eyewitness accounts, nor the rationalist views that miracle accounts were either frauds or misinterpretations of events explainable scientifically, were convincing to Strauss.

Nor was Strauss satisfied with the mediating christology of Schleiermacher. He launched a devastating attack against Schleiermacher's lectures on the life of Jesus (which had been published posthumously). Of his criticisms of Schleiermacher the most important for us is Strauss's argument that Schleiermacher erred logically in positing a greater cause than is warranted by the observable effect. That is, Schleiermacher argued back from the relative perfection of the God-consciousness found in the contemporary Christian community to the absolute perfection of its cause, Jesus' God-consciousness.[30]

Though Strauss did not deny that there may be some historically accurate accounts in the Gospels, he judged that in practice it was usually impossible to distinguish Gospel history from evangelical myths. The Gospels were neither history nor fiction; rather they were the product of "the unconscious myth-building power of the community, expressing its apprehension of the truth through the development of the stories about Jesus."[31]

For my purposes the mythological interpretation of Strauss has two important consequences. First, note that the source of christology is not Jesus but his earliest followers. Christianity's representations, from which the theologian must mine the kernel of conceptual truth, are the product not of Jesus but of the Gospel writers, whose stories express the community consciousness of Jesus' early followers. In this sense Strauss's christology appears to be more immanent than Biedermann's, since Strauss has extended the very locus of revelation from an individual (Jesus Christ) to the wider community of Jesus' earliest followers.

Second, Strauss argued that Hegel's notion that absolute spirit revealed itself completely in Jesus violates the laws of historical development. Or in Strauss's words, "the Idea is not wont to realize itself in that way, to lavish all its fullness on one exemplar and to be niggardly towards all others."[32]

> This is the key to the whole idea of Christology, that, as subject of the predicate which the church assigns to Christ, we place, instead of an individual, an idea; but an idea which has an existence in reality, not in the mind only,

like that of Kant. In an individual, a God-man, the properties and functions
which the church ascribes to Christ contradict themselves; in the idea of the
race, they perfectly agree.[33]

The church has correctly identified the predicate of christology (the unity of
God and humans). The proper subject of this predicate, however, is not an
individual, but the idea of the human race.

Biedermann had two important criticisms of his ally's christology: First,
though Strauss correctly identified the proper predicate of christology, he
failed to identify the proper subject. Second, Biedermann criticized Strauss for
applying the mythological strategy too broadly. Biedermann argued that the
gospels present enough information for contemporary Christians to draw conclusions not just about the mythological consciousness of the community
founded by Jesus, but of the consciousness of the man Jesus himself.

Biedermann's first criticism of Strauss was fairly straightforward: like other
Young Hegelians, Strauss took Hegel's definition of religion ("the representational view of the philosophical idea of the reconciliation of the finite with the
infinite") to mean "consciousness of the absolute in the form of representation."[34] Biedermann found this interpretation of Hegel too one-sided (though
it is apparently also Hegel's interpretation of Hegel), in that it tended to make
Strauss want to replace representation with conceptual thought (*Vorstellung*
with *Begriff*). As we saw in the discussion of Biedermann's epistemology, conceptual thought is required to purify representation, but religion is not identified with representation, and can never be replaced by philosophy.[35]

The result of this definition of religion, for Biedermann, is that he found
Strauss's negative critique of the church's doctrine of christology absolutely
necessary, and followed Strauss in this critique one hundred percent. But like
others, Biedermann found Strauss's positive proposals for the doctrine of
christology wanting. Strauss never fulfilled the promise of speculative construction, never overcame the tendency of speculative philosophy to make
Jesus merely accidental to the Christian principle.[36] It is to Biedermann's
assessment of Strauss's positive proposals that we now turn.

Strauss's formulation of the predicate of christology was judged by
Biedermann to be absolutely correct: the unity of the divine and the human is
an absolute truth.[37] And, as we have seen, Biedermann found Strauss's negative critique of the subject of church christology to be irrefutable: the subject
can no longer be thought of as an individual, but must be essentially universal.[38] But in defining the subject of christological claims, Strauss wavered
between an abstract generic concept (as universal essence of humanity) and a
concrete generic concept (as collective of the human race). Both concepts
failed to take the Christian principle seriously enough as a religious as opposed
to philosophical principle, and both failed to connect the principle to the man

Jesus. According to Biedermann, the subject of christology is the real unity, that is, it is the concrete unity of absolute and finite. As a concrete religious principle, it can be neither external nor accidental, that is, neither merely a doctrine newly delivered by Jesus, nor one merely receiving impetus from the person of Jesus.[39] Religion is not an idea but a relationship. A religious principle, therefore, must be the relationship of an individual to absolute spirit, the religious self-consciousness of a particular finite spirit. The Christian principle is the personal religious life of Jesus. As we have seen, the predicate of christological claims is the unity of divine and human; the subject of these claims is Jesus' religious self-consciousness:

> But Jesus' personal religious life was the first self-actualization of that principle in a world historical personality, and this fact is the source of the effect of this principle in history: Jesus, as the historical revelation of this principle of redemption, is the historical redeemer.[40]

The attractiveness of this formulation of the subject of christology is apparent on several fronts. First, it is absolutely consistent with Biedermann's definition of religion as a relation of the whole finite spirit, rather than an idea in the form of representation. Second, it ties redemption concretely to Jesus, that is it ties *concretely* as a relationship rather than (mere) idea, and it ties *to Jesus* in locating his religious self-consciousness as the seat of revelation, rather than stories about Jesus generated by his followers. Biedermann got great mileage from this point when he defends himself against the attacks of his positive opponents, who tend to lump him with Strauss, Feuerbach, and worse.

But Biedermann is in danger of losing some of the historiographical gains made by Strauss. Biedermann himself waffled a bit on the question of whether what is redemptive in the doctrine of christology is a product of the accounts left by Jesus' followers which reflect the effect of Jesus' religious self-consciousness on them, or whether what is redemptive is Jesus' self-consciousness itself. He appears to want to have it both ways: he made extensive use of Strauss's mythological view, and yet wanted to tie the Christian principle (the unity of God and humans) to the historical Jesus.[41] In the end he came down strongly on the side of Jesus as the historical redeemer. This created a historiographical problem for him, and a complication for our argument that his christology presupposes an immanent philosophy of history.

I turn first to the historiographical issue. Strauss's *Life of Jesus* is a devastatingly accurate assessment of the reliability of the gospels as historical sources for information about Jesus. For Strauss, however, the important issue was that the idea of unity has indeed entered history. He was perfectly willing to locate the entrance of this idea in the mythological products of the communal consciousness of Jesus' first followers. The Gospels do give reliable access to the representations of the community from which the gospels arise.

Biedermann, too, subscribed to the mythological view in part. He made full use of this view in treating the resurrection. Confronted both by the fact of Jesus' religious self-consciousness, and by the fact of Jesus' death, his followers took their subjective apprehension of the event (their inner experiences) for objective occurrences. Infused with "Jewish messianic expectations," Jesus' followers represented the reality of the effect of Jesus' religious self-consciousness on them as the resurrection.[42]

But the central doctrine for Biedermann was not the resurrection but the incarnation: that is, the entrance of a new religious self-consciousness into history. Biedermann was not content, like Strauss, to take the Gospels as evidence merely for the consciousness of Jesus' followers. Biedermann used this evidence, though he admitted it was fragmentary, to draw conclusions about the religious self-consciousness of Jesus himself. That an "absolute" religious self-consciousness is possible in principle, Biedermann thought he had shown in his definition of the relationship of the divine and the human. That such a self-consciousness is possible historically Biedermann thought was demonstrated through the fact of Jesus. He listed six "facts" in his dogmatics that he thought we knew about Jesus' self-consciousness that demonstrated that, while of course in a historically concrete form, Jesus' religious self-consciousness was in fact absolute. I quote the paragraph in full:

> The central moments of the religious self-consciousness of Jesus, as historical inquiry determines, the analysis of which gave rise to the preceding purely conceptually determined religious self-consciousness as the substantial contents of [Jesus'] self-consciousness–naturally in a historically determined form–are above all the following: (1) his self-consciousness of the filial relationship with God as the real relationship of the communion of love with God in him, and as the vocation of all humans; (2) his messianic self-consciousness that in his filial relation with God is fulfilled on earth the Old Testament promises of the Kingdom of God; (3) his creation of the absolute ethical commandment directly from his own self-consciousness of his filial relationship; (4) his self-consciousness of the absolute worth of the ego over-against all worldly existence, and the relative worth of the latter as means for the ego towards its absolute intended end of the Kingdom of God; (5) his self-consciousness of the love of the Father, fulfilled in him, as also the forgiving grace of God for repentant sinners; (6) and finally, his self-consciousness that with his external defeat by the world, his sacrificial death as the absolute submission of his being and life to God, he has victoriously sealed the grounding of the Kingdom of God's grace in the world.[43]

We must ask two questions about this list of historical facts about Jesus' religious self-consciousness. First, is it justified by the sources? That is, are these facts found as predicates of Jesus in the Gospels, and if so, are we to take the true subject of these predicates to be Jesus' self-consciousness, or expressions of communal consciousness of various groups of followers of Jesus? Though

Biedermann has certainly pared down the list of attributes of Jesus to include items that are only historically plausible (as opposed to some of the historical facts assigned to Jesus by orthodox doctrine), nonetheless Strauss's move to cut the link between the Jesus of history and the Christ of faith still stands, even if the Jesus of history is portrayed as a plausible historical character. The Gospels give more reliable information about the latter than the former.

More importantly, Biedermann appears to be guilty of precisely the same illegitimate historiographical procedure he and Strauss so astutely criticized in Schleiermacher. That is, Biedermann offered no evidence that anyone, Jesus himself or any members of the contemporary Christian community, had, in fact, an absolute religious self-consciousness. At most Biedermann has shown that such an absolute religious self-consciousness is possible in principle.[44] The historical facts about Jesus listed above seem to indicate at most a heightened religious self-consciousness. Biedermann need go no further in his system than to claim that this heightened religious self-consciousness had an effect on the followers of Jesus.

Biedermann appears to have gone too far beyond Strauss in at least two aspects, and posited more than is strictly necessary (and allowable) even from within his own system. In claiming that Jesus is in fact the historical redeemer Biedermann made claims about Jesus' self-consciousness that do not seem warranted by the textual sources. First, there is little evidence of an absolute religious self-consciousness, nor is such evidence necessary as a basis for Biedermann's theological system. There is only evidence for as heightened a religious self-consciousness as can plausibly account for the effects on the followers of Jesus, as attested to by the record of representations left behind by them. As Strauss wrote, "the Idea is not wont to realize itself that way."

Second, what was redemptive for Biedermann (and here his criticism of Strauss is well-taken) is not an idea but a relationship of the whole human. It is not necessary to locate precisely the entrance of this relationship into history. Biedermann's epistemological method of speculative processing allows only for a purification of the representations handed down by tradition; it does not allow for what amounts to speculation as to the origin of these representations beyond what is available in the texts. And in fact it is precisely at this point that Biedermann was reduced to rhetorical questions: "Whence should then this new faith have come . . . if it was not communicated to them from him?"[45] The point is not to deny that the historical Jesus may be the most plausible source of the early community and its religious self-consciousness, but merely that, strictly speaking, the representations that the theologian submits to speculative-critical processing are the representations of the early community, not Jesus'. In other words, Strauss is on safer ground in locating the redemptive accounts of Jesus in the community of Jesus' followers.

In light of this comparison of the christologies of Biedermann and Strauss we can refine even further the senses in which Biedermann's christology (and sense of history) is immanent. First, the unity of humans and divine: in terms of the predicates of christology, Biedermann and Strauss both located the unity of God and humans across the entire human community. Biedermann's definition of this unity as a relationship involving the whole individual (feeling, willing, and thinking) locates in a more radically immanent way the principle of unity than does Strauss's definition of the principle as (mere) idea. That is, for Biedermann the principle is not an idea but a relationship located, in the human pole, not merely cognitively but in the entire human spirit.

Second, the broad location of this unity across the entire community: in terms of the subject of christological statements, it appears that Biedermann goes beyond what is warranted by his own method in insisting on locating christology in the religious self-consciousness of an individual. In other words, Biedermann's own system allows for locating revelation (the entrance point of the religious relationship into history), as does Strauss, broadly–in the community of Jesus' earliest followers. Not that this is critical for my argument. In one way Biedermann's christology is more immanent than Strauss's, in another way less. For Biedermann we all share the same relationship to God. But on both counts it dovetails with the dynamics of history found in politics, economics, and pedagogy in Regeneration Zurich, and on both counts it will reflect (or occasion) a change in liturgy.

The Main Event: Biedermann versus the Orthodox

The Christology of Ebrard

In chapter three we saw the attack leveled on Biedermann, and we analyzed Biedermann's differences with Ebrard on the subject of the personality of God. At the beginning of this chapter we saw too Ebrard's attack on Biedermann's christology. Now it is time to see what at bottom this fight was about, and what was at stake in terms of what each christology implies about who effects significant historical change and how. I take Ebrard as a representative of the orthodox or positive group that opposed Biedermann and the liberal liturgy revisions in Zurich. That group, of course, is diverse and complex, and so I must first justify why they can be seen as a group and why Ebrard can be seen as a fair representative.

The term orthodoxy, in Switzerland, is perhaps most correctly applied to the period of the Formula of Consensus, a creed adopted by several Swiss churches to unite against heresies in 1675.[46] The orthodoxy of the early nineteenth century is more properly called a reasonable orthodoxy, and is a result of the influences of pietism and humanism on this earlier orthodoxy.[47] In the

Zurich countryside, in particular, pietism still had a strong influence.

The main characteristic of this group was their willingness to rely on human reason in explaining, and arguing for, what they regarded as the eternal truths of Christianity. They never, however, crossed the line of believing that the truths of Christianity were anything other than revealed truths. Their opinion of reason was not so high as to think that humans could ever reason their way to these truths. Once revealed, however, they believed they could show that Christian truths were not in conflict with reason, and further, they argued that it is only reasonable to assent to them.

Christianity was recommended to the reason of the listener on its reasonable grounds and practical advantages as something that, if adopted and practiced, would stand one in the best account on earth and in heaven. But strictly, it was always the revealed Christianity, not yet that of pure, healthy, human understanding.[48]

The fundamentals, for which reason can argue, but which could never be the product of human reason, can be summarized as follows:

> Baptism in the name of the father, the son, and the Holy Ghost; the baptismal creed is the Apostles' Creed; the Lord's Supper is a remembrance of the death of our Lord Jesus Christ, who shed his blood for the forgiveness of our sins. Faith in Jesus Christ, God's only-begotten son, who was crucified and resurrected, is the core of the gospel, that no Christian church may surrender.[49]

On these points the rational supernaturalists and the pietists found common ground over-against the Young Hegelians.

Ebrard's and Biedermann's disagreement over the personality of God was not merely a semantic one–whether one calls the eternal moment of a human ego "personality" or "universal creative essence"; whether one defines personality as a moment or as a finite mode of being. The term reappeared in their disagreement over the reconciliation effected by Jesus in history. For Ebrard, Jesus was the historical expression of God's personality. Ebrard argued that redemption is a one-time historical event effected by Jesus. "Guiltless, he nevertheless bore all the consequences of sin. In him sin was judged and damned, and in him . . . humanity made satisfaction."[50] But Jesus' act of reconciliation had to be appropriated by each individual. Ebrard thus indicates that there are two historical acts involved in reconciliation, an objective and a subjective act.

> All subjective reconciliation surely consists in an 'incorporation' of Christ in us, in the new life that Christ lives in us, . . . in an incorporation that is again a magnificent historical fact of humanity, and has its historical basis in the historical deed of Jesus Christ, in the objective reconciliation.[51]

Ebrard charged, in effect, that Biedermann had no doctrine of objective reconciliation. For Young Hegelians,

each individual subject executes reconciliation by becoming conscious of his
unity with the divine, that is, with the universal creative essence of humans.
Reconciliation is not a historical fact, but a fact of consciousness that con-
stantly repeats itself in each individual.[52]

Reconciliation was not an objective fact grounded in the past, but an ongoing
occurrence in the consciousnesses of individuals. Jesus was therefore not the
redeemer, but merely "the first in whom the religious idea of the unity of the
divine with the human surfaces."[53]

But while Ebrard wanted to stress the historical, factual nature of Jesus'
(objective) act of reconciliation, he tried to be careful not to make Jesus more
than human. On the one hand Ebrard argued that Jesus is not unique, that he
was like all humans (except sinless) and was a product of history.[54] On the
other hand, Jesus was more than merely the first Christian. Jesus was the historical expression of God's personality.

> In the actions and suffering of Jesus Christ the divine essence appeared in its
> entire fullness; he, his personality in its historical development, is the revela-
> tion of the father, and so, according to Christian teaching, the historical Jesus
> is at the same time true human and the eternal word of the father, become
> human and appearing in time.[55]

Biedermann, of course, would deny that Jesus, for him, is no more than the
first Christian. Biedermann argued that it is only through Jesus that reconciliation for each person, a possibility in principle, becomes a possibility in history
and in fact.

Regardless of whether or not one ultimately finds either christology, that of
Ebrard or that of Biedermann, to be persuasive, there is a real difference in the
kind of action each conceives as possible in history. The exact status of Ebrard's
objective reconciliation, which is then appropriated by Christians, is not clear.
But Ebrard did retain some aspects of the Anselmic satisfaction theory absent
in Biedermann's christology. For Ebrard, those who are reconciled are already
reconciled by the historical acts of Jesus. How one appropriates this reconciliation is another matter. "In him humanity made satisfaction." For Biedermann
it was not so much a matter of appropriating something that has already
occurred as it is a matter of effecting a new relationship, one made possible by
a previous historical act. It would not be accurate to say of Biedermann's theology that individuals reconcile themselves, as his opponents charged. It is only
in the context of the church, a community founded by Jesus, that one becomes
aware of the possibility of a new relationship to God. Still, for Biedermann the
historically significant action of Jesus was the founding of the community
through the force of his religious self-consciousness. By joining this community
one can encounter his religious self-consciousness in any age. Jesus founded the
community, and thus is the redeemer, but he does not balance the accounts.

Reconciliation is possible in history because of him, but we are not reconciled on his behalf. Though Ebrard has tried to distance himself from the supernaturalism of the past, it is not possible in Biedermann's worldview for a human to take the kind of historical action presupposed by Ebrard's christology. A human can share his or her religious self-consciousness with another, but cannot take any action which will result in another's relationship with God being counted as reconciled.

The disagreement between Biedermann and Ebrard over the personality of God and the nature of reconciliation highlights their different concepts of historical dynamics. From Biedermann's point of view, Ebrard's christology is docetic. Whether or not Ebrard's notion of personality achieves conceptual clarity, the true humanity of Jesus, which is to say, the possibility of Jesus acting in history in the same way we all do, is violated when Jesus becomes uniquely the expression of God's personality.

This violation of history's dynamics is exemplified in Ebrard's doctrine of objective reconciliation. History holds many examples of individuals founding communities, and for Biedermann such an action belongs within the capacities of historical human agency. It is possible for a human to found a community in which others become aware of a certain religious self-consciousness. In such a community one could learn of the proper relation of finite and infinite spirits. From Biedermann's point of view it is not, however, possible for a human agent to effect the reconciliation of finite and infinite spirits, and certainly it is not possible for an individual to effect this reconciliation for all others. Ebrard's theology retains a degree of supernaturalism, which is to say, from Biedermann's perspective, that it may represent the facts of history adequately, but it falls into conceptual contradiction, and must be subjected to further processing.

The Christology of Marheineke

It will also be useful to draw a distinction between the view of history presupposed by Biedermann's theology, and that presupposed by an Orthodox Hegelian. As Massey has argued, Hegelianism in Prussia provided support for the conservative monarchical government. The conservatives in Switzerland were always careful, in their attacks on Biedermann, to distinguish him from those they considered the true Hegelians, whose theology they did not oppose. While Biedermann and the other Young Hegelians were deeply implicated in the struggle towards liberalism in the German speaking world of the nineteenth century, Marheineke and the Orthodox Hegelians were as equally implicated in the conservative movement. How is this possible?

Marheineke presents himself as a good choice for comparison both because he is a good representative of Orthodox Hegelianism and because he is clearly aligned with the conservative movement in Prussia.[56] Marheineke and Biedermann shared much from their Hegelian background. Most important, they agreed that the truth of Christianity consists of the unity of the human and divine spirits. Biedermann would affirm Marheineke's statements that "the truth of human nature is the divine," and "only in this movement [the subla-tion of the contradiction of divine and human natures in unity] is God real, and only in it [the movement] does human nature become truthful."[57] Both stressed the Hegelian dictum that in Christianity is already found the truth of philosophy more than Strauss, Feuerbach, or Bauer.[58] What then distinguishes their theologies?

The most important differences come to the fore in their respective doc-trines of christology. Marheineke did not discuss Biedermann directly (he died just as Biedermann's publications began to appear), but many of his comments on Strauss's theology are instructive. He criticized Strauss's move to place the totality of humanity as the subject of christology, as did Biedermann. But Marheineke's subject of christological doctrines is not the same as Biedermann's (the religious self-consciousness of Jesus).

Although Strauss's view has the advantage of showing that Christ does not appear "ex abrupto," from a God "outside the machine," as maintained by older orthodox theology, it has several problems.

> With the thought of humanity one thinks that one stands in infinity, since [humanity] is the abstraction of an indefinite number. But as soon as one takes the thought as concrete, the inadmissability of this thought [humanity] immediately shows itself. The individual, personality, must much more be conceived of as the truly infinite.[59]

In other words, the subject of christology cannot be an abstraction, and so it must be not humanity in general, but a specific individual, a specific person-ality.

At the same time the subject of christology must be universal, that is, it must be redemptive for all individuals, all of humanity. Marheineke thought that Strauss erred again in excluding from his developmental view of history the possibility that development can reach its completion, its perfection.[60] And this is precisely the significance of Jesus Christ. Jesus' personality, in its perfec-tion, is universal.[61] In Jesus, human nature reaches its truth, and is universal. As the second Adam he is the representative and redeemer of all other individ-uals.[62] "Against Strauss we must certainly say that the idea of the unity of human and divine nature in one individual as never before became real. But on the other hand, as never again."[63]

Christ is clearly a unique individual. Such uniqueness violates a modern view of how history works. This becomes clear when we consider the criteria for "genuine historical scholarship of the present" as articulated by Ernst Troeltsch, perhaps the foremost analyst of the effects of history on theology.

Troeltsch claims that the "historical mode of thought" or the "historical sense" has three "essential aspects."[64] Of these three, Marheineke has overstepped two. Troeltsch claims that we can only make sound historical judgments if we assume the principle of analogy. "Analogous occurrences that we observe both without and within ourselves furnish us with the key to historical criticism." We have no basis to judge events that are so unique that we have no experience ourselves of something similar. Further, this principle, which "rests on the assumption of a basic consistency of the human spirit and its historical manifestations" leads to another principle that Marheineke oversteps, the principle of mutual interrelation.

> This concept implies that there can be no change at one point without some preceding and consequent change elsewhere, so that all historical happening is knit together in a permanent relationship of correlation, inevitably forming a current in which everything is interconnected and each single event is related to all others.[65]

Troeltsch's essay was written in 1898, but we see the same historical presuppositions outlined in Strauss's *Life of Jesus*. Among the criteria Strauss uses to distinguish myth from history, he writes that an account is likely myth "[w]hen the narration is irreconcilable with the known and universal laws which govern the course of events." In other words, when narrations describe events of which we have no similar experience. Strauss then states what he calls the law of succession, "in accordance with which all occurrences, not excepting the most violent convulsions and rapid changes, follow in a certain order of increase and decrease."[66]

Marheineke rejected all language of Jesus as *a* world historical individual. For Marheineke, Christ is *the* center of all world history. Such a point is qualitatively different from other moments and other individuals in history. He writes:

> If one only understands Christ as a world historical person, then one conceives of and continues to conceive of Christ in comparison to others, and each difference or precedence above others can only be a quantitative one. . . . Only when he is recognized as the center of world history has it been said that he is the one, the incomparable; for there cannot be more than one middle point of world history.[67]

While it is true, for Marheineke, that Jesus is a human person, belonging to a particular family and a particular nation, and as such a part of history, he is significant precisely because of his universal nature. "In assuming and taking in every human, he goes beyond [the given condition of his human existence]."[68]

This brief discussion of Marheineke's christology suffices to draw a clear distinction between his doctrine and that of Biedermann, as well as to show the political ramifications of the philosophy of history Marheineke's doctrine presupposes. For Biedermann, under the influence of Jesus' religious self-consciousness as it is presented in the historical community of his followers, it is possible for others to become aware of the same filial relationship to God in precisely the same way as Jesus did. For Marheineke, the unity of human and divine natures is a historical necessity, and was achieved in the life and death of Jesus Christ. Others participate in this unity insofar as Christ is their representative, that is, insofar as they believe in him.

The location of redemptive power in Marheineke's christology is not immanent in the sense in which I have described Biedermann's doctrine. While it is true that God is the truth of human nature (and in this respect Marheineke might affirm Biedermann's statement that God is the universal creative essence of humans), consciousness of this is available to us only indirectly. Only Jesus was directly conscious of this relationship, and he was a unique individual. The location of redemptive power is clear. In the context of discussing the unity of the whole race with God in Strauss's christology Marheineke wrote the following, which would apply equally well to Biedermann's christology:

> That which they are or can become only through him, through his spirit, through living in his community, they are supposed to have and show originally. Here the community of Christ is mistaken for him as its principle, the periphery mistaken for the center, or equated with it.[69]

It is not possible here to discuss in detail the connections between Marheineke's christology and the conservative Prussian monarchy. Prussian Minister of Ecclesiastical Affairs and Education Altenstein's support for Marheineke is sufficient indication that the connections existed. If Biedermann's christology entails a sense of history which locates the power to act as a historical agent immanently across the entire human community, then the sense of history presupposed by Marheineke's christology validates a view of history in which individuals, by virtue of their special characteristics rather than what they share in common with all others, are the primary historical agents. Marheineke claimed Hegel for the side of the individual as the location of the incarnation, against Strauss's claim for the community.

> Even if, according to Hegel, that God became a man is certainly the most difficult thing in religion, it is the unification of the absolute essence and the individual human subjectivity in the person of Christ. The puzzle is solved without difficulty, but superficially when, like Strauss, one gives it the sense that the God-man is thereby to be explained as humanity. Rather the true, indeed the only sense is that God appeared as an individual, as a single human, as a 'this one.'[70]

Such a view of history was comforting to a monarchy. Not only is the individual leader stressed over the community (the center over the periphery), but the community finds its essence in the leader. One is a true member of the community insofar as one believes in the leader. This sense of history's dynamics results in a "great man" theory of history. The best way to understand the causal factors of change over time in human communities is by focusing on the outstanding individuals who made that history happen. Biedermann's and Strauss's historical commitments result in a view that historical change is best understood at the community level, because each member of that community is equally a historical agent and contributes more or less to the shaping of the community's history.

The immanent philosophy of history underlying Biedermann's work is in sharp contrast to the philosophies of history of Ebrard and Marheineke. The fact that Biedermann, unlike Strauss, remained in the church, playing a prominent role in the Zurich Synod, a fact made possible by his epistemology (philosophy of language), offers an opportunity to see the impact of this modern christology on a liturgical system, the subject of the next two chapters.

CHAPTER FIVE

META FIGHTS
BATTLES IN THEORY OVER BATTLES IN PRACTICE

> There are born Protestants, and I might count myself one of these, because it was no lack of religious feeling but, though I was unconscious of it, a last, little fine curl of smoke from the faggots and stakes of past ages, hovering in the church, that made it repugnant to stay there while the monotonous, authoritative statements were being bandied to and fro.
>
> –Gottfried Keller, *Green Henry*

At one level chapter one already offers an explanation for the differences between the two ceremonies of baptism found in the 1868 Zurich liturgy. Very generally, the liberals, as a matter of conscience, protested against the obligatory use of the Apostles' Creed because they could not believe literally in some of the articles, while for the positives the issue was one of maintaining continuity with tradition, and particularly what they considered the traditional interpretation of central doctrines. The whole debate was framed in the context of church/state relations.

But at another level the explanatory puzzle still remains, for the participants in the controversy over the liturgy revision tell us very little about why the Apostles' Creed, and particular phrases within that creed, became the focus of the argument. Furthermore, the written record leaves no indication of why the liberals were adamant about removing any direct address to Christ from the prayers found in the liturgy. That is, in addition to the explicit text of the liturgy debate there is an implicit subtext. The task of chapters five and six is to make this subtext explicit, and interpret the liturgy revision at the level of subtext. Specifically, I will show that, in addition to the debates about tradition and church/state relations, the liturgy debate is also a clash of worldviews. Implied by the liberal ceremony is an immanent sense of history that corresponds to the sense of history presupposed both by the politics of the liberal government (chapter two) and by Young-Hegelian theologians like Biedermann (chapters three and four).

To explain and analyze the changes in the 1868 baptism, we will need to have some way of categorizing the various sentences in the ceremony and understanding their force, and we will need to understand the structure of the ritual. Chapter six will take up the question of ritual structure. In this chapter, after characterizing the major changes made in the ceremony of baptism, and situating my analysis on the map of other recent analyses of ritual, I classify the relevant sections of the baptism, relying on a taxonomy developed in the philosophy of language. This classification of speech acts in the ritual of baptism will show us how different kinds of speech give us access to the religious worldviews of the participants. That is, when we know how the participants intended different utterances to be understood, and what the effects of these utterances were meant to be, we will have access to what, for the participants, counted as a legitimate baptism.

The Two 1868 Ceremonies of Baptism

Unable to reach a compromise on a single form for the sacraments of the Lord's Supper and baptism, in 1868 the Zurich synod adopted a liturgy with two versions of each sacrament printed side by side. Both ceremonies of baptism retained some of the same elements from the previous liturgy. Both included the trinitarian formula ("I baptize you in the name of God the Father, Son, and Holy Ghost") and both retained the biblical texts which give scriptural support for baptism as a sacrament (and in particular which supported infant baptism).[1]

One of the baptism ceremonies (which I call Baptism I) made only minor alterations in the ceremony which had been in use prior to 1868.[2] Most important, from the positive theological viewpoint, it retained the Apostles' Creed (the child was said to be baptized "upon" the creed, and the sponsors were admonished to instruct the child "in" the creed).[3] Christ was addressed directly in prayer: "Surround it [the child], O precious Savior, with your grace."[4] Baptism I also referred several times to baptism as preparation for judgment day. God was asked to give the parents and the sponsors the grace to "raise the child in fear and knowledge" of God, so that the child might "on judgment day come forward unafraid at the universal judgment of your Son and . . . find eternal blessedness."[5] The minister said to the child, "God grant you that, as you now have been washed with pure water in holy baptism, so on judgment day you might appear before God, purified of sins, and be eternally blessed."[6]

The other ceremony (Baptism II) included all the changes for which the synod members associated with the Young-Hegelian theological viewpoint argued. It did not contain the Apostles' Creed, nor was Christ ever addressed directly. Both ceremonies admonished the adults in the community to remember and to live up to their baptism vows, but in Baptism I this was so that the adults "may be confident of it in life and in death."[7] Baptism II stated that the adults ought to live up to their vows for the sake of the children of the community, so that the adults did not become a stumbling block to the children.[8] Both ceremonies stated that the sponsors have come to "this holy place" to have the child adopted, but in Baptism I the child was adopted into "the community of our Lord Jesus Christ," whereas in Baptism II the child was adopted into "the bosom of the Christian church."[9] Finally, Baptism II appended to the phrase "this holy place," the qualification, "before the assembled congregation."[10]

A Ritual Theory Map

My analysis of the ritual change which occurred in Zurich in 1868 relies heavily both on speech act theory and on a way of describing symbolic-cultural systems that bears some resemblance to recent linguistic theory. This is not surprising, since the changes that occur with the Synod's vote in 1868 are changes in language.[11]

In order to make clear precisely what is at stake in this analysis, and also to point out the ways this approach might be useful to cases other than the specific data in question here, I offer a rough taxonomy of some of the approaches taken in the analysis of ritual, and locate my work in this taxonomy. As in linguistics, so in the analysis of ritual in general we can impose a rough organization on the various levels of analysis. We expect to find (1) historical or phenomenological studies;[12] (2) a syntax, a semantics, and a "phonology" (or some way of categorizing and analyzing ritual actions, including speech acts);[13] and (3) something analogous to sociolinguistics.[14]

My analysis focuses largely on the second, or "grammatical" level. In order to understand the implications of changing what is said in the course of a baptism, the structure of the ritual must be clear; we must have some way of knowing what role different utterances play in the ceremony as a whole.

Until recently most work in ritual theory fell into level (3) in the taxonomy above, which might be called (rather unmelodiously) socio-ritual studies. While this level of analysis is important, I believe that current studies tend to pursue sociopolitical aspects to the exclusion of structural aspects. In fact, however, an adequate analysis of ritual at this third level relies to a great extent on the structural analysis.

A third-level approach to the liturgy debate in Zurich might correlate the various positions in the specific struggles, as well as examples of particular performances of the sacrament of baptism and all the attendant observances, with what S. J. Tambiah (following Peirce) calls indexical symbols. Indexical symbols are symbols that point not only to whatever their conventional cultural understanding might be, but also "in the pragmatic direction of the social and interpersonal context of ritual action."[15] The manipulation of such symbols (physical and verbal) by ritualized agents, which constitutes baptism, would begin to reveal performances as "a strategic arena for the embodiment of power relations" within certain social orders, an approach for which Catherine Bell argues.[16]

Surely we would learn much from such an analysis of ritual, baptism, Zurich, and theologians like Biedermann who favored the use of Baptism II. But in the course of my argument that specific kinds of speech acts have a specific role in the structure of a ritual performance, I will show that the kind of valuable analysis proposed by people like Bell cannot proceed without far greater attention to the second, or grammatical level of ritual analysis.[17]

Bell begins with a critique of influential theories of ritual. She argues that many theoretical approaches to ritual argue in a circle. That is, they project an assumed, a priori dichotomy of thought/action onto the object of theoretical analysis. Approaches as diverse as those that see in ritual a means of social control, and those that see ritual as an expression of some conceptual scheme or worldview, all begin with a dichotomy of thought and action. But, Bell argues, this dichotomy seems inappropriate: First, theorists inevitably wind up showing how ritual reintegrates the very thought and action that they themselves split apart (e.g., Victor Turner's *communitas*, or Clifford Geertz's fusion of ethos and worldview). Second, this dichotomy manifests an unexamined valuation (acting is what "they" do, thinking and theorizing is what "we" do).[18] "We" sit around thinking about why "they" do what "they" do.

Bell argues that we can break out of this vicious circle by re-placing ritual on the grid of all human action or practice. What is ritual used for, and how does it accomplish this work? She focuses on strategies of ritualization that serve to distinguish ritual practice from other kinds of practice. The formalization, fixity, and repetitiveness that others have seen as the defining essence of ritual Bell sees as common but not strictly necessary strategies available to ritualized activities for setting themselves off from more quotidian activities, thereby giving them a certain prestige and authority. We can then examine the uses to which this authority is put.

Bell herself gives remarkably little attention to the structure of rituals before discussing strategies of ritualization. She analyzes the structure of rituals in terms of apparently fundamental binary oppositions such as in/out, up/down, and male/female. In *Ritual Theory, Ritual Practice* she gives just one clear example to support her argument that in the course of ritual performance certain privileged oppositions come quietly to dominate others. She argues that in the Catholic mass inner/outer oppositions (e.g., ingesting the elements) come to dominate others (the higher/lower of kneeling, raising the host, etc.).[19] Following Bell we would analyze the Reformed Zurich baptism by focusing on such oppositions as male/female (the child is handed from female midwife to male minister for baptism, then from male minister to female Godparent for re-incorporation into the family) and higher/lower (the water is poured over the back of the child's head into the baptismal font), etc.

Bell finds support in Bourdieu for the view that binary oppositions are the fundamental building blocks of ritual:

> [T]he countless oppositions observed in every area of existence can all be brought down to a small number of couples which appear as fundamental. . . . And almost all prove to be based on movements or postures of the human body, such as going up and coming down (or going forwards and going backwards), going to the left and going to the right, going in and coming out (or filling and emptying), sitting and standing (etc.).[20]

For Bell, then, ritualized movement built out of these oppositions creates ritualized agents, and constructs a physical environment that comes to be taken for granted as the way things are. Ritualized agents wield these actions sometimes in accord with, sometimes in opposition to, other ritualized agents, and in so doing negotiate the construction of their environment.

Such a view is immensely helpful in our understanding of what is at stake in the debate about baptism in Zurich. Why did the Zurich government concern themselves with infant baptism by instigating the ritual change, and why did the Synod and citizens of Zurich fight so passionately over the proposed change?

In instituting a representative democracy over an oligarchy, in erecting a free market economy in which everyone was free to buy and sell goods and labor on an open market and dismantling a tightly controlled guild system, and in creating a system of universal education to give all citizens the tools to make use of their new political and economic power, the Zurich government attempted to locate power more broadly, less hierarchically. In other words, history's dynamics for them were located in individuals qua human beings, rather than in great men or privileged social classes. All individuals were significant historical agents, and the Zurich government took steps to see that, as such, all individuals had an opportunity to participate equally in the political and economic life of Zurich.

If Bell is right that ritualized action constructs an environment that comes to be taken for granted as the way things are, and impresses this environment on the very bodies of ritualized agents, then the government was quite savvy in instigating a change in a ritual that would affect every citizen of Zurich. Bell argues that the ritual environment is a negotiated one, not under the control of any one power structure. But if an environment could be ritually constructed that was in harmony with the view that history's dynamics were located in an egalitarian rather than in a hierarchical way, then the government's controversial agenda might garner more support. Thus, to return to my taxonomy of ritual studies, at the third level of ritual analysis, socio-ritual studies, Bell has made a significant contribution to our understanding of the ritual change in Zurich.

But two problems immediately arise with Bell's mode of analysis. First, surely not any higher/lower and inner/outer oppositions will do. The significance, indexically as well as symbolically and iconically (to make use again of Peirce's language) of the fact that it is wine and bread (and not something else) that is raised by the priest (who may be only a certain kind of person) and not someone else, and that this must occur after and not before the elements have been blessed, must somehow find their way into our analysis in order to understand the full significance of raising the host, kneeling, ingesting, etc.

Second, the structural component of Bell's theory leaves us no way of analyzing the ritual change in Zurich. None of the kinds of actions looked at by Bell changed in Zurich: The baptism procession remained the same, the child was still handed from female midwife to male minister and then to female Godparent, the water was still poured over the back of the child's head into the baptismal font, the same feast took place after the ceremony, etc. The ritual change that caused such turmoil in Zurich was purely linguistic. Do we or do we not utter the Apostles' Creed as part of our sacrament of baptism? Do we address prayers to Christ? The binary oppositions Bell and Bourdieu rely on to analyze the structure of ritual do not take account of speech acts.[21] Clearly the change was significant to the ritual participants in Zurich, but focusing on binary oppositions leaves this change off the map. While I think Bell makes the right move in re-placing ritualized acts on the grid of all human action, we need an approach that can place *all* ritualized acts on this grid, including speech acts.

In other words, we need to be in a position to give a full-blown semantics and syntax of ritual performances, including speech acts, before the third level of analysis will really bear fruit. My intention is not to take away anything from the importance of the other levels of analysis, but to work towards more fully establishing the second, grammatical level which sometimes is passed by too quickly.

The root of the problem with Bell's mode of analysis is a flawed concept of human action. If we asked the priest or minister what he is doing, the answer surely would not be "raising and lowering," or "pouring from higher to lower." They are of course also doing that, but their action is to bless the elements or to baptize an infant. What is at stake is our sense of what it means to be a human agent. There is a difference to the performer of the action between kneeling and catching her or himself from stumbling, or between receiving the host and eating bread, even if these actions look identical to an observer. There

is a difference between a wink and a tic. The use of binary oppositions separates the intentional aspect of a human act from the external physical movements. In a sense, by separating the ritual participant's act from the ups/downs
and in/outs apparent to an observer, and then asserting that some of these
oppositions come to dominate others, Bell has ironically let the
thought/action dichotomy she so insightfully criticized in other theories of
ritual in again through the back door.

What is it that distinguishes a human act from all the other various events
in the world? Bell has separated the agent's intention in performing an act
from the act itself. But in understanding ourselves as agents, and in interacting
with others in the world, we could not function without being able to distinguish acts from things that just happen. What separates a tic from a wink, how
do we distinguish driving away in a car from stealing a car?[22] What distinguishes an act from a mere occurrence is the agent's intention.

Charles Taylor is perhaps the foremost recent advocate of a model of
human action that sees action as "directed," as somehow "inhabited" by intention. Whereas Bell's implicit model of human action separates intention from
actions (or, simply overlooks intentions), Taylor proposes a "qualitative" or
"directed" model that sees action and purpose as ontologically inseparable.
This model rejects dualism. The human subject is inescapably embodied.[23]
Action cannot be explained by means of an intention that is prior. Action and
intention are inseparable, and it makes just as much sense to explain an intention in terms of action as it does to explain action in terms of intention. Clearly
when I act it is sometimes (but not always) the case that I intend to do something, and then I do it. But the intention still inheres in the action. For
example, if I intend to signal someone by means of a wink, and then do it, that
intention is not separate from the act of winking. The agent would be able to
distinguish the case in which she or he intends to signal by a wink and does
from the case in which she or he intends to signal by a wink and then suffers
a tic. And action sometimes precedes intention. Sometimes we only become
aware of the fact that we are angry when we have struck out in anger, acted
angrily in some way.

Robert Schumann, when once asked to explain a difficult étude, responded
by playing it a second time.[24] While one can obviously try to interpret a piece
of music one has heard, Schumann's response seems to indicate a belief that
if one separates the musician's intention from the act or performance of music,
if one conceives of music as a message that then gets encoded, one has already
precluded the chance of true understanding.

There is something odd about analyzing a ritual in terms of ups and downs,
ins and outs, when the participants themselves think of themselves as blessing,
receiving, and baptizing. And that is because what they think they are doing

constitutes part of the act itself–their intention inheres in the act. Bell is right that strategies of ritualization separate ritual acts such as baptism from everyday acts such as rinsing a child's hair. Yet by removing intention from her analysis of ritual action, she is unable to say why there is a difference or what force it carries.

There is one more meta-theoretical point which must be raised in locating my analysis on a map of the study of ritual in general, before drawing in, in more detail, the theoretical landmarks from which I will take my bearings. In two separate articles Lawrence E. Sullivan has called into question the use of textual hermeneutics as an analogy in analyzing religious phenomena in general, and rituals in particular.[25] Since I will rely heavily on both the philosophy of language and linguistics, a brief discussion of how my study stands vis-à-vis Sullivan's arguments is in order.

Sullivan raises at least two important issues to consider when using linguistic metaphors to explain and interpret symbolic-cultural systems other than language. First, he is concerned that linguistic metaphors tend to flatten phenomena, to focus too strongly on structure at the expense the material aspect of language itself. "Lost in this overly smooth, clear and determined view is the struggle of the human imagination with the *chaos* inherent in the *matter* of speech (breath, muscles, organs, bones)."[26]

Second, Sullivan argues that the uncritical use of textual analogies obscures the use of other hermeneutics, other methods of cultural interpretation which can, in some societies, play a role at least as important as the role that language plays in Western hermeneutics.[27] This is particularly worrisome to Sullivan because of the tendency he sees in Western academic analysis to "measure out and define the difference between the 'world of the text' and the 'world of the reader'" in a way that overlooks the significance of the specific form of expression of "meaningful images expressed in modes of human action."[28] Sullivan claims that the analogies used in cultural analysis in certain South American cultures, for example, have the opposite tendency to this "measuring out" of textual analysis.

> For the cultures of South America, myth offers increasingly concrete imagery as one approaches the world of being where these two dimensions of reality [the meaning of reality expressed in one set of images, and the context of the interpreter's reality] intersect.[29]

In other words, textual analogies tend to distance "reader" and "text," whereas other analogies may be more integrative (and perhaps therefore more accurately reflective of reality). Sullivan seems here to be concerned with enlarging the number of models available at what I call the second level of ritual analysis. If we did not see rituals as texts to be interpreted we would not separate thought and action in the way that Bell criticizes in others, but cannot keep from doing herself.

Sullivan mentions several alternative metaphors used in cultural interpretation, including potting, canoe making,[30] and the view of the Yawalapati that the body is a container that carries on a series of exchanges of fluids with the world. In the Yawalapati view culture (or what separates the Yawalapati from animals, and from other humans) is the distinctive ways these interchanges are regulated. Thus each of the bodily orifices (mouth, anus, ears, vagina, eyes, penis, etc.) gives rise to symbolically heightened cultural practices: "table manners," "bathroom etiquette," sexual mores, and even language as controlled breath, etc.

> Learning to control these fluids in the manner prescribed by your culture and becoming aware of that self-control (the imposition of conscious form on matter) provokes individual growth and acculturation.[31]

Thus, Sullivan suggests that bodily functions may provide a more useful analogy than language in certain cultural analyses.

Most illuminating for locating the present study in relation to some of Sullivan's concerns is his discussion of pottery as a root metaphor used in cultural interpretation. Sullivan cites Claude Lévi-Strauss's *The Jealous Potter* with some ambivalence, for, on the one hand Lévi-Strauss has undertaken to "enter into the consciousness of the potter and the world of cultural meaning centered, through pottery, on the material involvement with clay, earth, and water."[32] At the same time, of course, Lévi-Strauss's analyses are based very strongly on the analogy of linguistic codes, in fact, on a Saussurean linguistics. Sullivan compares this to analyzing light by passing it through a prism, the result of which is to analyze not the light but the "state to which light has been reduced by the instruments of explanation."[33]

My response to these two challenges raised by Sullivan, that linguistic metaphors smooth over the living facts (and facticity) of manifestations of the human spirit, and that Western interpreters over-emphasize textual metaphors to the exclusion of many others, is that his concerns are on the mark. But I do not draw the same conclusions.

Sullivan's first challenge seems to be an attempt to swing the pendulum of interest back from a focus on systems to a focus on individual experience. Insofar as this is correct, it is a move similar to the one Pierre Bourdieu makes in attempting to recreate individual choice, action, and experience within a structural system. Any focus on the systemic level will necessarily blur, or at least gloss over, individual experience. Here it is worth remembering Robert A. Hinde's basic stance in his book *Why Gods Persist*, that "the complexities of human behavior . . . must not be underestimated . . . as resulting from the mutual influences of basic human propensities within and between individuals and with the social and physical environment."[34] In other words, we need to pay attention to both. But when people intentionally act in concert, as when they build institutions or perform rituals, we cannot understand them correctly if we slight systems for individuals.

Second, and more important, is Sullivan's specific challenge to the root metaphor we use when we get at structure or system. Does the West's preoccupation with text lead us to rely on textual metaphors which by their very nature distort the phenomena we are interested in? Concentrating the analysis of ritual on the grammar of ritual inevitably flattens the phenomena being interpreted, and Sullivan's arguments must be kept in mind here as a caveat. As I hope will be clear, however, both from the taxonomy of ritual analyses I offer above and in my explanation and interpretation of the ritual of baptism in Zurich, the structural moment is but one moment in analysis. It is, however, a crucial moment that we may not rush over.[35] Surely the power of Lévi-Strauss's work, in addition to the brilliance with which he sets out the relationship between variations of cultural terms, lies in part in his going beyond the pure structural level.[36]

Because of the importance of the structuralist moment in analysis, it is not surprising that scholars have relied on the academic fields that have pursued means of understanding structure most vigorously. Linguistics has been one of the metaphors used for these purposes, but it has not been the only one. One need only recall the heavy use of biological analogies by pioneers in the history of religions.[37] What appealed to these pioneers was biology's facility for creating taxonomies. While it is important to remember that text (or body, or pottery for that matter) is, in the end, only an analogy, short of learning to throw pots or build canoes such metaphors offer scholars the best opportunity to enter into other worlds of consciousness and translate them (another textual metaphor) into one we know well. As Jonathan Z. Smith argues, translation as the root metaphor for the academic enterprise has several advantages. It acknowledges that we gain in understanding by "bringing the unknown into relation to the known," while emphasizing the fact that a "translation is never fully adequate. . . . Indeed the cognitive power of any translation . . . is . . . a result of its *difference* from the subject matter in question and not its congruence."[38] Or, as Octavio Paz writes, "I do not mean to imply that literal translation is impossible; what I am saying is that it is not translation."[39] If we live in a text-o-centric world, perhaps our best strategy for understanding other worlds is to translate other idioms into textual ones, whiles heeding Sullivan's warning that something is always lost in translation.

I will rely on a linguistic metaphor in my structural analysis of the ritual of baptism. This is not to equate structural analysis with linguistics, but merely to claim that in analyzing the structure of both ritual and language, similar methods prove fruitful.[40]

While the use of linguistic analysis is distorting, it is also illuminating. To return to Sullivan's example of Newton's prism, he is only partly right about prisms reducing our analysis of light to an analysis of the state to which light has been reduced by our instruments of explanation. It was Newton's experiments with prisms that taught us that light is not simple but heterogenous. This knowledge helps explain the behavior of light even when it is not reduced to a spectrum by a prism.

In the end, then, while Sullivan is right that the linguistic analogy, like all structural analogies, is flattening, it is but one of the levels of analysis we need to consider in interpreting ritual. But it is an indispensable level. And we must keep in mind, as we discuss the philosophy of language and linguistics, that we are developing tools from a cognate field to help in interpreting ritual, rather than claiming that ritual is a language.

Speech Act Theory

The participants in the debate over the liturgy revision never explicitly state why the Apostles' Creed and direct address to Christ are so closely associated with the positive theological position, and why their removal was the central goal of the liberals. Because our analysis of the baptism ceremony focuses on these linguistic changes (that is, the central difference between Baptism II and Baptism I is the precise words spoken during the ceremony), we need to be able to classify and understand the different uses of language found in each ceremony. Without understanding the kinds of language being used, we have no way of understanding what is at stake in changing that language.

Speech act theory is based on the recognition that many of the utterances common in our day-to-day lives are not simply descriptive statements; rather, many utterances are themselves a kind of act used to do something.[41] While descriptive statements can be analyzed in terms of truth and falsity, it seems inappropriate to try to analyze other utterances the same way.[42] But clearly these utterances mean something, and so we need to include them in our taxonomy.

While sentences that purport to describe the world must, in part, be analyzed in terms of truth conditions (Does the description "fit" the way the world really is?), we need other ways of analyzing other kinds of speech. The first large scale attempt to analyze utterances that are not, at first glance, best analyzed in terms of truth conditions, is J. L. Austin's *How to Do Things with Words*.[43] Among the examples Austin offers of what he calls "performative" utterances[44] are ritual speech acts: uttering "I do" in the course of a wedding ceremony, uttering the words "I name this ship the *Queen Elizabeth*" while smashing a bottle across the bow. In uttering "I do" one is not describing some other action, rather the utterance itself is the performance of an action. Furthermore, if for any reason the wedding ceremony does not go off successfully it is more appropriate to call the utterance infelicitous than false.

While Austin has undeniably given expression to an idea that seems to correspond strongly with our common sense, namely that some utterances say things while others do them, one of the main points of his book is to show that the distinction between constatives (i.e., descriptive statements) and performatives ultimately breaks down. Constatives are not always so easily distinguished from performatives. In understanding a statement it is important to recognize that the speaker is in fact performing an act of stating, rather than another kind of act (asking, ordering, etc.). Furthermore, certain constative utterances appear to be infelicitous rather than true or false (for example the utterance "All Jack's children are bald" when Jack has no children).[45]

From the side of performatives the distinction also seems to break down. In some cases it appears that for them to be felicitous certain things have to be so, that is, performatives may imply statements that have to be true. (For example, in welcoming you to my home, I do not necessarily imply statements regarding my true feelings as to your being there, but I do imply statements describing my behavior towards you while you are there).[46]

After showing that there are no firm distinctions of grammar or vocabulary by which we might try to sort out constatives and performatives,[47] Austin distinguishes various aspects we can use to analyze any speech act. He proposes three categories. Speech acts may be comprised of locutionary, illocutionary, and perlocutionary aspects.

The first category is that of a locutionary act. A locutionary act is simply the physical act of producing sounds which are words in a specific language with sense and reference.[48]

Second, all locutionary acts are also illocutionary acts (illocutionary because one performs an act *in* making the utterance). The force of a locution is illocution. If, for example, I utter the locution, "Do not open the door," I might be warning, giving advice, ordering, etc., and it is important to your correctly understanding my illocutionary act that you understand my intention in making the utterance.

Third, some illocutionary acts may also be perlocutionary acts, that is, an act performed *by* making the utterance.[49] I may, in fact, prevent you from opening the door with my utterance.[50]

A further refinement is needed to clarify the various speech acts constituting the ritual of baptism. Given that each sentence will have a locutionary, an illocutionary, and perhaps a perlocutionary aspect, we need some way of distinguishing the various forces of utterances. Does the speaker intend to describe some aspect of the world, or does the speaker, in issuing a command for example, intend to produce an action in the hearer? That is, we need to distinguish types of illocution. As we will see, the way speech act theory accounts for illocution bears a striking resemblance to Taylor's model of directed action.[51] Austin offers a tentative classification of possible illocutionary forces.[52] For the actual classificatory schema, however, I turn to the work of John Searle, a student of Austin's, who has tried to offer a more explicitly formulated set of factors to consider than does Austin when analyzing the illocutionary force of an utterance.[53]

Searle tries to isolate more rigorously than does Austin the various "continua" which come into play in analyzing the rather broad concept of illocutionary force. Searle offers twelve such continua, but we need mention only the most important. Searle bases his entire taxonomy of illocutionary acts on the following three: (1) illocutionary point, that is, Is the speaker trying to represent something? get the hearer to do something? undertake an obligation? etc.; (2) direction of fit, that is, some illocutionary acts try to get their words to fit the world (assertions, descriptions), others try to get the world to fit their words (orders, promises); and (3) psychological states, that is, in representing something about the world the speaker expresses a belief, in ordering or requesting the speaker expresses a desire, etc.[54] Based on these three criteria (or continua) for analyzing the illocutionary force of utterances, Searle offers his own classification of speech acts.[55]

I will call Searle's first category of the illocutionary force of utterances descriptives.[56] For each of his classes of illocutions we examine (1) point, (2) direction of fit, and (3) psychological state. For descriptives,

> the point or purpose of the members of [this] class is to commit the speaker (in varying degrees) to something's being the case, to the truth of the expressed proposition. All of the members of the [descriptive] class are assessable on the dimension of assessment which includes *true* and *false*.[57]

The direction of fit is words-to-world, that is, the speaker tries to get his or her words to fit the world, and the psychological state expressed is belief (that something, p, is the case). This corresponds roughly to Austin's original class of constatives, but note that the point, direction of fit, and psychological state account for illocutionary aspects of a constative, the very illocutionary aspects that Austin was the first to point out.

Searle's second class is directives.

> The illocutionary point of these consists in the fact that they are attempts (of varying degrees . . .) by the speaker to get the hearer to do something.[58]

The direction of fit is world-to-words. The speaker tries to get the world to fit his or her words. The psychological state of the speaker is want (or wish or desire).

The last class of illocutionary force described by Searle that is important for us is called declarations.

> It is the defining characteristic of this class that the successful performance of one of its members brings about the correspondence between the proposi-tional content and reality; successful performance guarantees that the propo-sitional content corresponds to the world. . . . Declarations bring about some alternation [sic] in the status or condition of the referred to object or objects solely in virtue of the fact that the declaration has been successfully per-formed.[59]

The direction of fit is both words-to-world and world-to-words, and there is no psychological state.

While Searle's classification schema is not uncontroversial,[60] the rough con-trast between descriptives, directives, and declarations is widely accepted. This contrast is all I require to make my argument that different classes of speech are appropriate in different ecclesiastical speech acts.

Let us turn now to the two 1868 ceremonies of baptism and place the utter-ances important to my analysis in this classification of speech acts.[61] The first thing to note is that the entire ceremony of baptism, in some sense, could be called a declaration, since the point of the whole ceremony is to initiate a child into the community. The end result of the entire ceremony is the baptism of the child, and it is only by virtue of the ceremony, felicitously carried out, that this is accomplished. But we will learn more by adjusting the grain of our analysis to a finer level. Within the ceremony of baptism as a whole there are smaller units of utterances that can be classified.[62] These smaller grained con-stituents in the ritual under consideration divide up in fairly obvious ways.[63]

Both ceremonies of baptism include instances of descriptive utterances, those utterances that commit the speaker to something's being the case. Both ceremonies contain utterances, the propositions of which commit the speakers to the truth of the quoted descriptions of Jesus' institution of baptism. Before quoting Matthew 28: 18-20 Baptism I has the minister say, "[S]o hear and con-sider how our Lord and Savior instituted baptism as a symbol of the covenant of the New Testament," and before quoting Mark 10:14-16, "[U]nderstand fur-ther how Jesus declared the children too to be members of his kingdom, when he spoke to his disciples. . . ."[64] Baptism II quotes the same two passages, con-catenated together, with the preceding utterance: "That is why the Savior said to his disciples. . . ."[65]

Both ceremonies also offer examples of directives. Directives express a wish of the speaker that the hearer perform some future action. Commands, for example, fall into this category. Both ceremonies explicitly label their prayer components as falling into this class. In Baptism I, before leading the congre-gation in a prayer addressed to God, the minister says, "Now let us ask God for faith for this child, and that the baptism occur internally through the Holy

Ghost, and all pray together . . . ."[66] In Baptism II the minister says, "And so let us call upon God for his blessing."[67]

One important difference between the two ceremonies is that Baptism II addresses directives only to God. Baptism I includes directives in which Jesus and the Holy Ghost are intended as the hearer. ("Surround it, O precious Savior, with your grace. Lead it and direct it, O you Spirit of knowledge and life . . . .")[68]

The trinitarian formula of baptism found in both ceremonies ("I baptize you in the name of God the Father, and the Son and the Holy Ghost")[69] is clearly a declaration. While it must take place in the context of the larger ceremony, it is this utterance, spoken by the minister, that effects the baptism. It brings about the correspondence between the words spoken and the world.

Baptism I, as I have noted, also includes the Apostles' Creed. It is clearly identified as a member of the descriptive class of utterances. The Creed itself consists of two sentences, each of which contains a series of dependent clauses following the independent clause beginning "I believe . . . ."[70] The first clause of the minister's utterance introducing the Creed is also a descriptive: "So run the articles of the Christian faith, upon which the child is baptized and in which it should also be instructed."[71]

Further justification for classifying these statements, including the Apostles' Creed, as descriptives is found in the grammatical forms of the statements themselves. Though Austin came to believe that the attempt to distinguish locutionary from illocutionary acts by means of grammar is futile,[72] Searle believes that generative linguistics provides a means for associating a deep grammatical structure with each of his five classes of illocutionary acts.[73] Both of the utterances ("So run the articles of the Christian faith . . . ." and "I believe . . . .") have the deep structure Searle identifies as the paradigm for descriptives.[74]

Speech act theory has given us a system of classification for sorting out the various utterances in the two ceremonies of baptism. We have learned that both ceremonies contain sentences, the illocutionary force of which is directive. These utterances are attempts by the speaker to get the hearer to do something. While Baptism I addresses directives to all three persons of the Trinity, Baptism II does not address directives to Jesus. We have also learned that the Apostles' Creed, found in Baptism I but not in Baptism II, is to be classed as a descriptive. In other words, it is a member of the class of utterances that commits the speaker to "something's being the case, to the truth of the expressed proposition."[75]

Who cares? One of the central questions to address is why Biedermann, who urged the use of representational language in sermons, led a movement that tried to remove just such language from the ceremony of baptism. We are almost in a position to answer these questions, but first we'll have to describe

the structure of the ritual of baptism, and what sets it apart from other contexts in which language is used. This is the task of chapter six.

CHAPTER 6

LITURGY WARS, CULTURE WARS

The most amazing offspring of the human imagination . . . was now . . . definitely stated and expounded to us, so as to enable us, in the spirit of those flights of imagination, to consume a little wine and a bit of bread in the most correct way; and if this was not done, if we did not subject ourselves to this strange and amazing discipline, with or without conviction, then we were of no account in the State, and we couldn't ever get married.

My mother believed that if I had a Sunday suit, I should be more likely to live in harmony with the divine order of the universe.

–Gottfried Keller, *Green Henry*

Speech act theory gives us a taxonomy with which we can analyze the various utterances found in the two ceremonies of baptism in the 1868 Zurich liturgy. But it will also be important to our analysis to locate each utterance in the structure of the ceremony, and to be able to show the significance of the fact that it is certain people at certain times who must say or do these actions. In addition to speech act theory we need some way of analyzing the structure of the ritual.

The approach I use to analyze the ritual structure of the Zurich baptism focuses on the "ritual competence" of the participants. Because this competence approach is closely related to the analysis of language found in linguistics, I will begin with a brief discussion of linguistic competence. I will then show how a similar approach works in ritual studies.

Mapping out the structure of ritual using this approach will have three important consequences. First, we will have a way of noting the fact that a legitimate ritual performance requires that each participant and object have the appropriate properties. Our analysis will include the kind of information that Bell's analysis overlooks. For example, we will be able to include the fact that not just anyone can perform the mass, but only someone with the property of being an ordained priest, and that not any bread and wine can be raised, lowered, and ingested, but only bread and wine that have the property of previously having been blessed are legitimate ritual objects. In my analysis of baptism in Zurich I will be able to account for the fact that not just anyone can legitimately perform a baptism. Only someone who has the property of having been legitimately baptized themselves can perform a baptism.[1] And not just any child can be baptized, but only a child who has the property of having legitimate sponsors is a legitimate ritual object.

Second, the competence approach I use shows that some of these properties which make ritual agents and objects legitimate depend on previous rituals. That is, other rituals may be embedded within a legitimate baptism. A legitimate mass, for example, depends on the previous rituals of the priest's ordination and the blessing of the elements. In Zurich, the property by which the minister is a legitimate ritual agent is that minister's own previous baptism. The minister's legitimate baptism, of course, depends on the legitimate baptism of the minister who baptized him. This chain of baptisms ultimately depends on the institution of baptism by Jesus. The liturgy debate of 1864-1868 is, in part, a debate about the original instituting of baptism by Jesus. What properties of Jesus make him a legitimate institutor, that is, a legitimate ritual agent?

Third, the competence approach helps explain a curious fact. The very language that the liberals demanded be removed from the ritual context was believed by them to be appropriate in other contexts. Biedermann, for example, held that the task of preaching demanded language similar to the language of the Apostles' Creed. Only after we understand the role of different kinds of speech acts in ritual can we explain this paradox.

One convenient way of describing the structure of a cultural-symbolic system is by focusing on the competence of the participants in the ceremony.[2] The success of generative grammar in analyzing language has shown that explanation as well as interpretation (or understanding) of language is possible.[3] Since the cognitive approach to ritual structure I take here is modeled closely after this linguistic work, a brief discussion is in order.

Generative linguistics is based on the competence approach to linguistic theory. This approach distinguishes "what the speaker of a language knows implicitly (what we may call his *competence*) and what he does (his *performance*)."[4] Though most native speakers of a language are unable to state explicitly the rules of grammar of their language (these rules are, in fact, descriptive of their behavior, not generative of it) they are able to produce and understand an indefinite number of sentences which they have never before encountered. It is the implicit knowledge that allows them to perform these tasks. The focus of linguistics in recent decades has been on this intuitive competence.[5]

Another way to state the same point is to say that the object of the discipline of linguistics has become the intuitions of the native speaker.

There are several advantages to this competence approach. At the very least it is a way of systematically organizing a mass of historical material (performances and records of performances). More importantly, it allows us to abstract from the indefinite and overwhelming data of performance (not merely infinite but also corrupt–broken sentences, mispronunciations, memory lapses, changes of mind mid-sentence, etc.) to an object of study that is actually susceptible of explanatory analysis and empirical verification.

The cognitive turn in linguistics was initiated by Noam Chomsky. Chomsky's approach is called generative because he describes the capacity to produce and understand sentences by means of a relatively short list of rules. Application of these rules is said to generate proper sentences. Chomsky's revised standard theory includes several components: (1) It contains a lexicon, which is simply an exhaustive list of all the possible morphemes or words available to speakers. (2) It contains phrase structure rules that describe the generation of simple phrases (or base strings), and (3) It contains transformational rules that transform these base strings into more complex sentences in the form of questions, negatives, etc.[6]

Chomsky describes the competence of an ideal speaker by means of re-writing rules. Re-writing rules take the form of $X \rightarrow Y$, which is read, "replace X with Y." The derivation of sentences is shown by breaking them down into noun phrases and verb phrases ($S \rightarrow NP + VP$), and then further breaking down the noun and verb phrases into their constituents ($NP \rightarrow$ the $+ N$), until finally constituents are replaced with items from the lexicon ($N \rightarrow$ man, ball, etc.).[7] A set of transformational rules can then transform a string into different forms by, for example, changing the word order to create a question, or combining it with a dependent clause.

To a great degree, linguists have been able to formulate a relatively small number of rules that can generate any correct sentence in English. While learning the grammar of a new language constitutes a big challenge to most adults, at one level languages appear to have the same deep grammar. Because native speakers of any language can produce and understand an indefinite number of correct sentences, most of which they have not encountered before, linguists argue that something like this system of rules, this deep grammar, must be present as part of an adult's capacity for language. Exposure to linguistic stimuli at a certain stage of cognitive development triggers the development of this competence.

A competence approach to ritual may be equally as fruitful. Ritual, like language, is a highly constrained activity. The very repetitiveness and emphasis on correct performance that so many have seen as the hallmark of ritual indicates that it is a rule-governed activity. Like language, then, it should be possible to formulate rules which describe ritual action. In other words, we can examine the structure as well as the meaning of rituals. In so doing we can explain as well as interpret them. As in linguistics, the focus is not on performed rituals (not on spoken sentences) but on the representations participants make to themselves of those ritual actions (langue, not parole).

Paul Ricoeur has pointed out the ways in which action can be explained as well as interpreted by considering it on the model of text.[8] He argues that, given the possibility of structural explanation in textual studies, and given certain similarities between text and what he calls "meaningful action," the human sciences can overcome the problem (the gap between understanding and explanation in the human sciences) set by Dilthey.[9]

In what ways, then, is ritual action similar to language such that we are justified in drawing on the linguistic metaphor in explaining the structure of ritual, and the ritual change in Zurich? Ritual, as the manipulation of objects and words with stipulated cultural meanings, falls into the class of cultural-symbolic phenomena (what Ricoeur calls semiotic phenomena) with language. Further, ritual is a highly constrained activity, that is, it is rule governed. The creation of new rituals is not individual, as is the production of sentences in a natural language. We may nevertheless call the system of rules we will use to describe well-formed rituals generative, since they describe the implicit knowledge of ritual participants regarding well-formed rituals.

That ritual participants have such implicit knowledge is clear. One of the characteristics commonly identified with ritual is the care taken by all involved to perform the ritual in precisely the prescribed manner, so as not to perform an infelicitous (ineffective) ritual (what Austin calls a misinvocation or a misexecution). Frits Staal records the fact that, in addition to the great care taken to perform the complex Vedic Agnicayana-Atirâtra ritual correctly, the twelfth and final day of the ceremony includes "expiation rites for errors that were made or might have been made" during the course of the previous eleven days.[10] In Zurich the degree to which baptism was a highly constrained activity is attested to by the fact that many parents in the early nineteenth century considered it a sin when so small a change occurred as schools beginning to teach children to say "die Taufe" instead of "der Tauff." Furthermore, it was common in the seventeenth through the nineteenth centuries to find "baptism books" in many churches, in which pastors described in great detail local baptismal customs for the benefit of their successors, so that the new pastor would be able to perform the ritual correctly to the satisfaction of the community.[11]

J. L. Austin gives several examples of what we might classify as ritual competence. For instance, to utter the phrase "I do" in the context of a Christian marriage normally counts as the performance of a valid ritual act. But under certain circumstances we might say that this ritual fails (in Austin's terms, that it is infelicitous.) If, for example, the speaker of the phrase is already married, with a wife living and undivorced, we would reject this as a valid wedding ritual.[12] Many participants in a wedding may not be able to state explicitly before the ceremony begins that just such a rule about marriage exists, and yet anyone familiar with the most common forms of Christian marriage would make this judgment. The climax of *Jane Eyre*, for example, depends on just such a notion of ritual competence. When the solicitor Mr. Briggs interrupts the wedding ceremony of Jane Eyre and Mr. Rochester to announce that Mr. Rochester already has a living wife whom he never divorced, the reader as well as the characters in the novel know instinctively that the wedding cannot go off, even if they do not know the laws governing marriage in England. The very strong sense of participants that ritual is such a rule governed activity makes ritual acts a strong candidate for a competence approach that focuses on such intuitions of participants.

Among the growing number of scholars of religion who take a cognitivist approach there have been only two full-fledged theoretical treatments of ritual along a generative model: that of Frits Staal and that of E. Thomas Lawson and Robert McCauley. While Staal works at the level of the arrangement of whole rituals in a larger ritual structure (the twelve day Agnicayana ritual), Lawson and McCauley work at a finer grain: the structure of individual ritual acts. It is to their work, then, that I turn to see what a cognitive approach to structure can teach us about the baptism ceremony in Zurich.[13]

Lawson and McCauley on Competence

Lawson and McCauley present their theory at three levels. First, they defend the general approach, called the competence approach, that they use. Second, they offer a set of generative rules to describe ritual competence. Finally, their theory makes several empirically testable predictions about the structure of rituals.

There are advantages to the competence approach, but it does bring them into conflict with other theorists. By narrowing the range of data to be explained to ritual competence, Lawson and McCauley delimit an area that is amenable to explanation and empirical verification. This narrowing is their fundamental move. It is, however, controversial, because they then have no need or occasion to discuss any outside reference for ritual. It is precisely the desire to analyze ritual as referring to something outside itself that Lawson and McCauley criticize in other theorists. Theories that see ritual as a means of communication, they argue, overlook the fact that "the information communicated within ritual systems only incidentally concerns the world."[14]

Intellectualists, in treating religion as roughly analogous to scientific attempts to explain the world, "obscure many of its important features," including the "underlying coherence of ritual systems and the diverse functions of myth."[15] Symbolists cannot offer any explicit principles for "decoding" symbols, for showing how the system of symbols refers to psychological or social systems they supposedly represent.[16] Lawson and McCauley conclude that the only plausible reference for religious systems is self-reference.[17] Their claim about Lévi-Strauss, that for him "symbol systems signify . . . only the human mind which produces them," could just as easily be made about their work.[18]

Lawson and McCauley's Generative Rules

Second, Lawson and McCauley offer a set of rules that generate ritual acts and describe the competence of ritual participants. They call this the "action representation system."[19] It has several components. (1) Their action representation system contains a "religious conceptual scheme," which is analogous to a lexicon in linguistics. It is merely a list of possible things (agents, actions, and objects) that are available to play a role in a ritual. In addition to all the other possible agents and actions conceivable in a given society that can be represented in every day actions, the religious conceptual scheme includes narratives (myths and histories), theologies, commentaries, and sacred texts (scriptures, hagiographies, etc.).

Note two things about this religious conceptual scheme. First, it is important to emphasize that the religious conceptual scheme will vary from religion to religion, and from group to group within one religion. The Buddha or the Pope will not play a role in very many felicitous actions in Reformed Zurich. Second, the religious conceptual scheme will include properties of agents and actions (equivalent to a lexicon's adjectives and adverbs). We must account for these properties, too, in our analysis of ritual. Thus, in certain rituals it is important that the agent have a particular status or occupy a certain office. For example, the Roman Catholic mass will only be felicitous if the agent performing the ritual is a properly ordained priest, and if the elements have been blessed. A baptism in Zurich will be felicitous only if the minister performing the baptism has properly been baptized, and if the child being baptized has legitimate sponsors (God-parents).

(2) Proper rituals are generated by a set of "formation rules," analogous to the phrase structure rules of linguistics. These are the same rules that describe the mental representations of *any* action. In a rare agreement with Bell, Lawson and McCauley argue that ritual action belongs on the same grid with all human action. In linguistics these rules show the structure of sentences by rewriting sentences, breaking them down into noun phrases and verb phrases,

etc. Lawson and McCauley's rules break actions down into agents, actions, and in some cases objects.[20] The ritual action "minister baptizes baby," for example, is analyzed into its constituents:

Action → Participant + Action + Participant.

(baptism) (minister)   (baptizes)(child)

Participants, objects, and actions are further broken down into agents (with the proper properties) and objects (with the proper properties) as follows:

Participant → (Agent + Property), (Object + Property)

(minister,   (minister)(baptized) (child)   (sponsored)
  child)

until specific items from the religious conceptual scheme have been filled in:

Agent → (minister, Jesus, etc.)

Object → (bread, wine, child, etc.)

Action → (baptize, bless, marry, institute, etc.)

Property → (baptized, ordained, sponsored, blessed, divine, etc.)

(3) Lawson and McCauley's action representation system also includes an "object agency filter." This filter is analogous to transformational rules. Its function is to weed out objects that find themselves in inappropriate places in the formation rules (a mere man, for example, instead of a priest). The object agency filter either rejects the entire ritual, or guarantees that the man, in this case, has in fact previously been ordained a priest. In the case of Reformed baptism, the object agency filter guarantees that the minister has been properly baptized. The object agency filter is a formal way of describing the intuitive knowledge of ritual participants that a ritual has or has not come off felicitously.

Lawson and McCauley's complete set of formation rules, and the derivation of a baptism in Zurich generated by these rules, is found in Appendix II. The derivation can be represented in a cognitively more easily digestible form as a tree diagram. This diagram has the advantage of showing graphically embedded rituals. Embedded rituals appear stacked beneath the ritual under consideration, as for example, we see the baptizing minister's own baptism, and Jesus's institution of baptism, in the diagram of the 1868 ceremony of baptism:

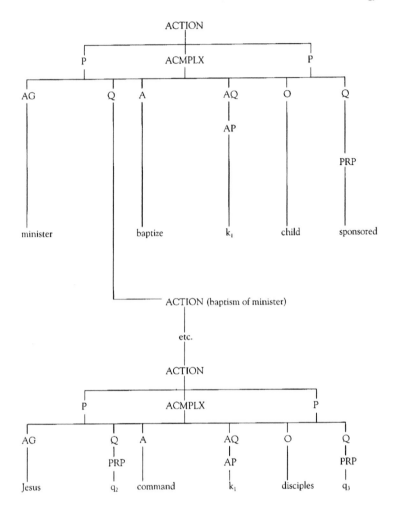

Legend

P	=	Ritual Participant
ACMPLX	=	Action Complex (the act, and whatever quality is necessary to make it legitimate)
AG	=	Agent
O	=	Object
Q	=	Quality (the property of an agent or object that makes them an appropriate ritual participant, or a previous action giving them such a property)

PRP	=	Property (by virtue of which an agent or object is an appropriate ritual participant)
A	=	Act
AQ	=	Action Quality (property, condition, or previous act making an act appropriate)
AP	=	Action Property (property of an act by which it is legitimate in ritual at stake)
AC	=	Action Condition (participant or condition making act valid)
C	=	Condition (by virtue of which an act is valid)

At first, Lawson and McCauley seem to have done little more than to formalize what is common sense (actions can be analyzed into agents, actions, and sometimes objects). But there are some important consequences of charting out the structure of the ritual of baptism according to the categories agent, action, and object. First, Lawson and McCauley's rules allow for the embedding of rituals. The efficacy of many rituals depends on the previous felicitous performance of other rituals. In Zurich, for example, a felicitous baptism required legitimate sponsors who had been confirmed in a Reformed ceremony (a ritual that itself required that the confirmand already be baptized). Baptism, in turn, was required for other religious and civil ceremonies such as marriage rites.

Important for my argument is the fact that the agent performing the baptism is a legitimate agent only by virtue of the fact that he had previously been baptized himself. This requirement, that the agent performing the baptism be previously baptized, sets up something of an regress, since the agent's baptism can only be legitimate by virtue of the legitimate baptism of the person baptizing him. Lawson and McCauley's action representation system allows for the description of this intuitive requirement that certain rituals must be embedded in other rituals, by stacking tree diagrams of the embedded rituals beneath the ritual in question.[21]

Another important consequence of my generative analysis of the structure of baptism is that this embedding, in the case of ritual, is not in fact an infinite regress but reaches a definite original action. Lawson and McCauley claim that reaching such a starting point, rather than regressing infinitely, is a characteristic of religious rather than profane action. Evolutionary accounts of the origin of the human species extend back into the prehistoric genetic mists, but Genesis traces the genealogy back to Adam and Eve. Not surprisingly, the agent initiating such a chain of actions will be superhuman.[22] The chain of baptisms does not stretch back infinitely, but to the instituting of the ritual by Jesus. And indeed, both 1868 ceremonies of baptism cite the institution of baptism by Jesus found in scripture, along with the traditional verses used by the Reformed Church to defend infant baptism.[23]

This immediately raises the important question, By virtue of what quality of the actor Jesus is the institution of baptism a legitimate ritual action?[24] If this question cannot be answered adequately, then the whole house of cards on which contemporary baptisms are based begins to tumble. Jesus belongs to the religious conceptual schemes of both the conservatives and the liberals. But Jesus is a legitimate ritual agent only by virtue of specific properties. Here the conservatives and the liberals part ways. That is to say, their religious conceptual schemes differ in assigning different properties to Jesus, by virtue of which he is a legitimate ritual agent. As we have seen, we gain access to these different religious conceptual schemes by looking at such things as theologies and creeds.

Lawson and McCauley's Predictions

Lawson and McCauley claim that describing the structure of rituals in this way leads to a set of universal principles that explain certain interesting features of ritual. For example, they claim that if the superhuman agent imbedded in a religious ritual is embedded in the agent slot of a ritual action, as opposed to the action or object slot, then the ritual will not be repeated. This is true of baptism. In the end the minister (agent) is a legitimate ritual agent because of the act of Jesus founding the church. Baptism is a one-time affair. Participants will, however, repeat rituals in which the superhuman agent is involved in the action or object slot. The Lord's Supper, for example, involves the superhuman agent in the object slot (the blessed host). If we represent the Lord's Supper as "Participant receives elements," it is because Christ is somehow present in the elements (and just how is very contentious in the history of Christian theology) that this is a legitimate ritual. Participants repeat this ritual periodically.

Further, Lawson and McCauley claim that the more removed the superhuman agent is from the ritual in question, the less central this ritual will be for the religion. For example, because of the Catholic doctrine of transubstantiation, in which the superhuman being is directly present in the ritual, the mass is a central ritual for the Catholic church. The Lord's Supper will not be as central (or at least it will share the stage with other activities such as preaching, for example) for groups with weaker doctrines of the presence of Christ in the elements. Zurich offers empirical support for this assertion as well. Zwingli famously argued that Jesus' statement "This is my body" (Matt. 21:21, 1 Cor. 11:24) means that the bread *signifies* Christ's body, not that the bread *becomes* Christ's body. The fact that the Reformers in Zurich replaced the altar where the Catholic mass had been performed with the stone baptismal font demonstrates that Lawson and McCauley's theory has accurately predicted the relative importance of these rituals in the two traditions.[25]

Already the relationship between the liturgy change (what gets said to and about Jesus, among other things) and the christological controversies of Biedermann and his opponents is becoming clear. The legitimacy of baptism, finally, rests on what kind of action one thinks it is possible for Jesus to have taken. My task now is to bring together these two strategies for explaining the ritual change in Zurich (speech act theory and the generative description of ritual competence), by showing the different roles different kinds of speech act play in the overall structure of baptism.

Explaining the Ritual Change in the 1868 Liturgy

I am now in a position to analyze the two ceremonies of baptism in the 1868 Zurich liturgy, and show that Baptism II (the liberal ceremony) implies a worldview compatible with what I called an immanent sense of history's dynamics. Specifically, we want to know (1) why it was necessary for the liberals to remove the Apostles' Creed from the ceremony of baptism, and (2) why it was necessary for the liberals to remove any direct address to Christ from the ceremony of baptism.

The first thing to note is that both ceremonies of baptism themselves give us some access to the religious conceptual schemes supplying agents, actions, and objects to each ceremony. Because of the speech act analysis of the utterances in the ritual of baptism undertaken above, we are in a position to describe more precisely than Lawson and McCauley in what ways the various utterances give us access to the religious conceptual schemes.

As we have seen, both ceremonies contain speech acts that I have classified as descriptive. Descriptive speech acts commit the speaker to statements about the world analyzable in terms of truth and falsity. Their fit is words-to-world. That is to say, in uttering a descriptive speech act the speaker is offering a description of the speaker's own cognitive representations of the world he or she perceives him- or herself to be living in. These speech acts purport to describe the way the world is. Any agent, action, or object denoted in a descriptive speech act must therefore be a member of the class of agents, actions, and objects available to the speaker in his or her conceptual scheme, in this case his or her religious conceptual scheme. *Descriptive illocutions, therefore, denote items in the religious lexicon, that is, they give us access to the religious conceptual schemes of the ritual participants.*

Both baptism ceremonies, we have seen, include descriptive speech acts. For example, both give descriptions of infant baptism by Jesus.[26] We can conclude from this that both conservatives and liberals include Jesus as a legitimate ritual agent and baptism as a legitimate ritual action in their religious conceptual schemes.

But the descriptives in both ceremonies are not exactly the same. Baptism I includes the Apostles' Creed, which I have classified as a descriptive. This descriptive denotes the properties of Jesus by virtue of which he is a legitimate ritual agent. The Apostles' Creed clearly describes counter-intuitive[27] acts by Jesus: conceived by the Holy Ghost, he descends into hell following his crucifixion, and then ascends into heaven on the third day. As we saw in chapter one, of all the claims made in the Apostles' Creed it is precisely these counter-intuitive acts, when they are described as descriptive speech acts in a ritual context, which most offended the liberals. They are the acts of a mythological God-man, which, for Biedermann means that they would be acts of a contradiction or a non-possible agent, as made clear in chapter four.

References to Jesus in Baptism II, the liberal ceremony, describe him as doing the kinds of acts in theory any mortal human being is capable of performing. He is a religious founder, not a God-man. Jesus instituted baptism (lines 6-8). He reconciled us with God (lines 14-16). This is a somewhat unusual act, but Biedermann's entire christology is directed towards showing that in doing so he in no way transcended the bounds of possible human action.[28] Finally, God is asked to help the children imitate Jesus' life and death (lines 39-42). As my discussion of Biedermann's christology in chapter four shows, all these acts can be performed in history by someone essentially like us without violating the laws of nature or of history. Jesus had a heightened religious self-consciousness, which is available in principle to all humans. Biedermann attributed no trace of counter-intuitive activity to Jesus. Rather, he counted any such activity as a failure of theology to complete its task of critical-speculative processing.

Just as the descriptive illocutions in the two baptism ceremonies give access to the religious conceptual scheme of the ritual participants, so too do the directive illocutions give us access to the kind of community into which the participants represent the child as being initiated. Both ceremonies ask God to make the baptism efficacious. The minister in Baptism I says,

> We ask you [almighty God] in the name of our Lord Jesus Christ, that you would look on this child with grace, according to your infinite compassion, and make this baptism, this sign of the covenant of your grace, efficacious for it.[29]

The minister in Baptism II says, "Through your power let what is portrayed and vouched for for the child in the external deed of this baptism become truth in it."[30] In these two statements the direction of fit is world to words, and the psychological state of the speaker is want. Both speakers try to get the hearer (God) to do something, namely, to make the initiation rite into the Reformed Church efficacious.

But again, not all the directives in the two ceremonies are the same. Baptism I also asks God that the child be given "spiritual treasures and blessings, . . . the power of the blood of Jesus for the forgiveness of sins, and the operation of the Holy Ghost for sanctification."[31] Baptism I initiates the child into a community in which there is the potential for such things as Anselmic satisfaction. To request this of God is plausible given a religious conceptual scheme in which Jesus is the God-man, and in which Jesus' blood creates a spiritual treasure.[32]

Baptism II makes slightly different requests of God. It asks God that the child be able to "live in imitation of Jesus," its soul impressed "with the image of his life and death."[33] This is a plausible request to make of God, not because Jesus is the God-man, but because Jesus is a human precisely like us, and so Jesus' religious self-consciousness (his relationship to God) is available to us. It is a reasonable request to make in a community in which people have faith in their "filial relationship with [God]."[34]

By classifying the illocutionary forces of various speech acts, and by identifying the structure of ritual action, the link between theology and the ritual of baptism becomes clear. Utterances with a descriptive illocutionary force denote agents and objects and their properties in the religious conceptual scheme, or ritual lexicon. Utterances with a directive illocutionary force denote the properties of the community into which the child is baptized.

In the case of the two 1868 ceremonies of baptism in Zurich the properties of Jesus in the religious conceptual scheme of Baptism I are counterintuitive. This is compatible with a view of history in which the ability to act significantly in history is located hierarchically, in special individuals. The properties of Jesus in the religious conceptual scheme found in Baptism II are compatible with what I have called an immanent sense of history's dynamics. In this religious conceptual scheme, Jesus' properties, by virtue of which he is a legitimate ritual agent, are the same properties which, in principle, we all have. All of us act in history the same way. The Jesus of Biedermann's christology also presupposes a view of history in which history's dynamic is located broadly across the human community, in which "the masses enter into public life as a decisive factor." We all share the same filial relationship with God.

Speech Acts in the Context of Preaching

The analysis of ritual that focuses on the intuitive ritual grammar, or ritual competence, of the participants, solves what at first appears to be a vexing contradiction. Why did the Young Hegelians insist on removing descriptive illocutions from the liturgy, but not from other contexts? And why did they insist on removing all direct addresses to Christ? Once again, these questions can be answered once we have understood the structure of ritual action described by Lawson and McCauley's syntactical rules.

Traditional language was not only tolerated but required by Biedermann and the liberals in other contexts. On preaching Biedermann wrote: "It was always my first goal to be orthodox."[35] He also noted that people correctly sensed a "pietistic streak" in his preaching.[36] A scholar of Biedermann's preaching states that, in Biedermann's view, "the sermon must remain bound to the old texts."[37] Biedermann in fact chastised a former student for confusing the proper roles of the language of the lecture room and the language of the pulpit when preaching.[38]

As we saw in chapter three, it was Biedermann's theory of language which allowed him to remain a committed pastor and preacher. Biedermann classified traditional language about God and Jesus as representational, not conceptual. Why is representational language appropriate in the pulpit, but not in the ritual context of baptism?

The first thing to recall is that religion, for Biedermann, is not composed of ideas about the absolute, ideas that might better be expressed in conceptual rather than representational language, as it apparently is for other Young Hegelians. Religion is a relationship of the whole person, thinking, willing, and feeling, to the absolute. Furthermore, for Biedermann, conceptual thinking can never stand alone. Its sole task is to process representations. For both these reasons religion cannot do without representational language. But we still have not addressed the question of why representational language is appropriate in some specific contexts (like preaching), but not in others (certain parts of the baptism ceremony).

The answer lies in the different categories of speech appropriate to each context. For Biedermann, the task of the preacher is to proclaim the religious truth

> as it became his own life-truth, and how he was convinced of it, that he also
> opens up this truth to his congregation . . . as truly, clearly, and therefore as
> effectively as possible, that their remaining spiritual life is in a good position
> to be penetrated by it.[39]

Preaching, for Biedermann, is an attempt to have a certain effect on the hearer, to put him or her in a certain frame of mind. That is, preaching is not a descriptive but a directive act. It is an attempt to effect a change in the hearer, to get the hearer to be open to an additional perlocutionary effect.[40] The "fit" is world-to-words, and the psychological state of the speaker is wish or desire (for a certain state to be achieved in the hearer). In preaching, Biedermann puts the emphasis on what Austin would call the perlocutionary sequel in the hearer. That is, the main point of preaching is not to get the hearer to do something so much as to have a perlocutionary effect on the hearer. *Through an act of speech* the preacher tries to make the congregation's spiritual life be in such a state that they might be penetrated by religious truth. And Biedermann clearly thinks that representational language is appropriate, even necessary to this task.

Such representational language, however, is not appropriate to the kind of speech acts I have classified here as descriptive. Biedermann's argument that the church's representational language must be purified in theology in order to retrieve the conceptual kernel of truth contained in it shows that representational language does not describe the world literally. Every representation, for Biedermann, contains a contradiction, and he goes to great lengths in his *Christliche Dogmatik* to show that the concept of a God-man is a complete contradiction. The entire history of dogma is the history of the increasing obviousness of this contradiction, culminating in what he calls Gess's "absolute kenosis of reason." While it is appropriate to use such contradictory language to achieve a certain effect, it would be inappropriate to describe the world in contradictory terms. The illocutionary force is key. Language that is conceptually contradictory cannot be an adequate descriptive. Representational (but conceptually contradictory) language can work in a directive in which the speaker wishes to effect a psychological state in the hearer. Representational language cannot be literally true, and therefore requires purification or critical speculative processing before it can be said to give us access to the religious conceptual scheme of liberals like Biedermann. If my wish is to scare (perlocutionary effect) my children (directive), it is appropriate to tell stories that include counterintuitive characters (e.g., ghosts). If I am responding to a request for information with a descriptive speech act, this is no longer appropriate because it is a misrepresentation ("It's ghosts that keep the planets in their orbits, kids").

Biedermann's categories of language become critical in the ritual context. For we have seen that the felicity of the baptism ceremony depends on the felicity of the embedded ritual acts. Representational language is not merely inappropriate in this context. To preserve the Apostles' Creed as a descriptive which gives us access to the religious conceptual scheme of the ritual participants would be to posit a logical contradiction, an absurdity, as an agent.

Because Jesus' institution of baptism is embedded in the successful performance of subsequent baptisms, it would be infelicitous to describe Jesus as a God-man. The God-man, for Biedermann, cannot be the agent ultimately embedded in the ritual of baptism, because the God-man is a confusion of principle and man, something which does not belong to the set of things conceivable as agents. To posit an absurdity as a ritual agent would be to posit a non-agent. This would generate an ungrammatical, or infelicitous ritual, one that would violate the ritual intuitions of the liberal participants. Regardless of the perlocutionary benefits, to denote a God-man in a descriptive act would generate an ungrammatical, and therefore infelicitous ritual act.[41]

Turning to the removal of all direct addresses to Christ from Baptism II, we see that the issue is once again one of the grammatical felicity of the ritual act. To put it bluntly, an absurdity (a God-man) cannot serve as the hearer of a directive speech act, nor is it wise to address such requests to someone who is dead. To place such a person as the object of a ritual act would again be to generate an ungrammatical or infelicitous act.[42]

The stance of the liberals may, at first, appear to be odd, if not contradictory: In one and the same ecclesiastical setting, the service of worship, representational language is required at certain points (the sermon), and rejected at other points (the baptism, which usually followed immediately on the heels of the sermon). This apparent contradiction disappears, however, when we uncover the structure of ritual actions. While *representational* (or anthropomorphic) language serves legitimate perlocutionary ends, to insert such language at a point where the structure of ritual demands *descriptive* (or factual) utterances threatens to invalidate the ritual. The fact that these demands for separate kinds of language stand next to one another in the service of worship is all the more evidence for the highly constrained, though implicit, competence of ritual participants.

Once we understand the different kinds of speech and the various uses to which they can be put during a service of worship, and once we understand the special role descriptive utterances play in denoting items in the religious conceptual schemes of ritual participants, we see that behind the explicit debate about church/state relations, the implicit debate in the liturgy battle is about christology. What kind of agent, by virtue of what properties, could institute baptism? For Biedermann and his followers no ritual agent was conceivable who violates their immanent philosophy of history.

Speech act theory and a competence approach to the structure of ritual have helped make explicit the implicit subtext in the controversy over revising the Zurich liturgy. Speech act theory has given us a tool to understand why certain utterances imply commitments about the world, and can be evaluated in terms of their truth and falsity. Other utterances, spoken for other reasons, can (and must) make use of traditional, anthropomorphic, counter-intuitive language (what Biedermann calls representational language). The competence approach to ritual structure has shown why these categories of speech take on such critical importance in the ritual context. To make a mistake of classification here is to risk an ungrammatical, and therefore ineffective ritual performance, with important consequences for the daily lives of the ritual participants.

I began chapter five by noting that the people who took part in the liturgy debate in Zurich framed their arguments in terms of matters of conscience and church/state relations, but never explicitly stated why the Apostles' Creed and direct address to Christ became the focus of the debate. What, precisely, is so conservative about Baptism I, so liberal about Baptism II?

By classifying the different speech acts in the baptism ceremonies and showing the role that these speech acts play in the structure of the baptism, it has been possible to show the relationship between theology and ritual, or theory and praxis. Beneath the christological debates of Biedermann and his conservative opponents lay two different senses of history, or worldviews. Where is significant historical agency located? For Biedermann it is located immanently, in every human by virtue of their essence as a rational being. And this is true for the significant historical action taken by Jesus as much as it is true of anyone else.

Because theology is a component of the religious conceptual scheme of ritual participants, the lexicon of legitimate agents, actions, objects, and properties, such a radical shift in christology must effect a change in ritual. Language that commits a ritual participant to the truth of certain propositions about the world (descriptive speech acts) must be removed, if those descriptive speech acts are inaccurate. The Apostles' Creed and direct address to Christ imply commitments that violate the liberals' views about the way history works, and who acts as a significant agent in history. There may be perlocutionary benefits to such speech, but if these utterances are taken to describe the religious conceptual scheme, then the ritual at stake is infelicitous.

A change in theology entails a change in religious conceptual scheme, and the ritual must change with it. Thus we see that the liturgy debate, like the christological debates, at base is a debate about the philosophy of history. As A. C. Danto points out, philosophies of history like those of both the liberals and the conservatives presuppose knowledge about the way history is going.[43] That is, both worldviews determine historical significance in light of facts not readily at hand in history. For the conservatives, history is oriented towards a life everlasting. For Biedermann and the liberals, history is oriented towards realizing eternal life on earth, that is, living in accord with one's true principle. Both the conservative and liberal philosophies of history, then, are theological. In these last two chapters we have seen that the sense of history's dynamics presupposed by the liberal ceremony of baptism is an immanent one, reflecting Biedermann's immanent christology.

Only at this point has the structural groundwork been laid to focus on our third level of ritual analysis. We are now in a position to discuss with supporting data the negotiations over worldview that take place in ritual, the government's attempts to impress a certain way of taking for granted the way things are on the very bodies, physical and corporate, of Zurich's citizens, and the relationship of this liturgy struggle to other contested sites in Zurich's culture wars.

CONCLUSION

In each phase of my argument I have focused on what I call the sense of history's dynamics presupposed by the various cultural systems under analysis. My claim has been that Biedermann's theology and the ceremony of baptism adopted in 1868 share an immanent sense of history's dynamics, that this sense was contested in Zurich, and that this sense links them to the political, economic, and educational reforms during the Regeneration. We are now in a position to enquire more precisely what is meant by an immanent sense of history.

The political motto of the Regeneration was sovereignty based on the totality of the people. It was at this time that "the masses enter[ed] into political life as a decisive factor."[1] Another way of expressing the same idea is to say that a far broader segment of the populace in Zurich became political actors, agents capable of effecting significant historical action.

This political agency, however, was based neither collectively nor atomistically. The representative democracy crafted by the liberal party in Zurich was designed to represent reason first and foremost. It was by virtue of their human nature as reasonable that each member of the masses exercised political power. Reason, and therefore political agency, is located essentially in all individuals. Thus, while the franchise was increased dramatically, steps were taken to ensure that the government could still represent reason even should the majority demand otherwise. Precisely this issue (expressed in terms of the popular veto and popular petition) separated the liberal democrats (among whom Biedermann was included) from their radical democratic and socialistic successors (who respectively located power more atomistically or more collectively).

This immanent location of political power, based on the essential location of reason, motivated the liberal agenda in both the economic and educational arenas. In replacing the guild system with a free market economy, and again in trying to regulate some of the excesses of that economy, the government based its proposals on the tenet that each individual, as a reasonable, autonomous agent, ought to be free to pursue his or her economic ends freely. The only constraints arose when the unbridled pursuit of these ends threatened the very conditions which allowed the proper development of reason. That is why the factory law of 1859 focused on working conditions for children, guaranteeing that they have the opportunity to receive proper schooling. The very terms of the protests of the factory workers against these regulations demonstrate that the notion of their economic autonomy, based on their essential reasonable natures, was widespread.

The government of Zurich was aware that their new representative democracy required an educated populace, and the man they hired to build a new system of elementary schools, Thomas Scherr, shared this view completely. His pedagogical theories reveal that the basis of the new schools was the belief that each individual child, if tended to carefully, would blossom into a rational (and rationally Christian) adult.

It is at this level of "sense of history," I argue, that the connection between Biedermann's theology and the liberal democrats is to be found. While Biedermann does, in fact, have sophisticated theories of theological history, neither he nor the politicians attempted to formulate explicitly the reasons for their sense of close affinity.

The immanent philosophy of history is immediately apparent in Biedermann's doctrine of God. God is defined as the universal creative essence of humans. God is not external to humans, but encompassed in their essence. Biedermann avoided Feuerbach's conclusion that God is therefore an objectification of humanity itself. Rather, God and humans are two sides of the same coin. The divine side is universal, eternal, ideal; the human side is finite and concrete. Just as Biedermann rejected Feuerbach's "materialism," so too did he reject any kind of Platonic dualism in which humans have real being only insofar as they participate in the divine. Neither side of the coin is independent of the other.

Not only is Biedermann's theology immanent in the sense that God is located within humans, but because God is the essence of humans, God is located across the entire human community. Here we must recall that Biedermann's term of choice for God was absolute spirit, and that the German *Geist* denotes much the same thing as the rational principle which the liberal government claimed to represent.

Biedermann did not shy away from the logical end of these doctrines when he came to the core of his theological system, christology. There could be no more concrete expression of Biedermann's commitment to the idea of the immanent location of God than his argument that there is no essential difference separating Jesus from the rest of humanity. Jesus' relationship to God is filial, by which Biedermann meant that Jesus, as finite spirit, was fully aware that he had absolute spirit as his principle. Biedermann called this awareness Jesus' religious self-consciousness. This filial relationship is the Christian principle.

But this relationship belongs to the essential nature of each and every human as such. Jesus was the redeemer, for Biedermann, not because his relationship to God was any different than anyone else's, but because he was aware of, and lived in accordance with, this principle. Jesus' effect on his followers, which resulted in the records they left, and in the historical Christian community, is available to us. That is, we too are made aware of the possibility of living in accord with our essence. The seriousness with which Biedermann took the immanent location of this principle is indicated by the fact that he claimed that Jesus is the first world-historical person to actualize the Christian principle. That is, Jesus was the first (and only) person we know of, the only one to leave behind a community with this principle as its active spirit. While Biedermann did not stress the point, he left open the possibility that other, non-world historical individuals, prior to Jesus or independently of him, also have had the same religious self-consciousness.

In burning down a factory and in establishing labor laws, in overthrowing the government and in writing a new constitution, in appointing Strauss to a university position and in blocking his appointment, the people of Zurich were fighting over their deepest sense of what made them human, how historical agency was to be constructed. In appointing Biedermann, and in trying to block his Synod membership, the fight continued. Biedermann's christology battles were another contested site in these culture wars. So too, I have shown, were the liturgy wars. Further, I have shown why specific ritual practices entailed certain ontological commitments about how history worked, and therefore why conservative Christians demanded the traditional baptism ceremony, while liberal Christians fought for precisely the changes that they did to the ceremony.

Theology forms one of the components of what Lawson and McCauley call the religious conceptual scheme of a ritual system. Along with scripture, hagiographies, commentaries, etc., theology contributes to the lexicon of possible ritual agents and actions. By examining the structure of the baptism ceremony we learned that embedded within each baptism is the conception of an action taken by Jesus. The felicity of the ceremony depends on this previous action. It is clear, then, that Jesus cannot be represented as a contradiction, an illegitimate agent. The type of historical agent Jesus was, and the kinds of action it was possible for him to take, will have a direct effect, then, on the ritual of baptism. Biedermann's christology has direct implications for ritual.

It is important to note that both Biedermann's theology and the ritual change are influenced by an immanent sense of history's dynamics. We can explain the specific changes in ritual practice by looking at the effect of Biedermann's theology on the religious conceptual scheme of liberal theologians. But the fact of the matter is that the government of Zurich requested the ritual change in the first place. We need not posit theological sophistication and the ability to undertake the kind of analysis between theory and praxis I have undertaken here on the part of Great Council members. For these reforming politicians, the old ceremony of baptism apparently violated their intuitions as competent ritual participants. In other words, they left the specifics up to the theologians, but at some level they wanted a liturgy "more in line with the needs and views of the present."

By turning to the ritual debate, we are able to look at the intersection of theology and society at the broadest possible level. Because every citizen of Zurich participated in the public religious rituals of the Reformed church, their restructuring would have had a direct effect on religious behavior. If we accept Catherine Bell's argument that ritual action constructs ritual environments by imposing itself of the very bodies of ritual participants, we can see that the intuitions of the Zurich government were on target in trying to undertake a religious reform as part of their wider reforms through insisting on a restructuring of the ritual system. What is it that gets imposed on the bodies, physical and corporate, of Zurich's citizens? If it is an environment that comes to be taken for granted as the way things are, and if this environment presupposes an immanent sense of history, then the government would have done a great deal to build popular support for other reforms (political, economic) that presuppose the same immanent philosophy of history. The fact that Biedermann's philosophy of language allowed him to share this modern worldview and remain a Reformed minister offers a beautiful chance to see the links between theology, ritual, and social/political context.

This becomes clear when we pay attention to the illocutionary force of utterances in specific contexts controlled by ritual grammar. This book constitutes one of two attempts I know of in ritual theory to bring together two fields in the philosophy of language that have been used separately with some success: speech act theory and generative linguistics.[2] One important result is to show that certain utterances (descriptives) within the ritual itself give us access to the ritual's religious conceptual scheme, or lexicon. Ritual speech is more constrained here than other types of religious speech (preaching, for example), because a descriptive commits participants to a view of the way the world really is. To utter a descriptive in bad conscience in a ritual context would be to threaten the validity, the felicity, of the ritual. Similarly, we can gain access to participants' view of what kind of religious community they belong to by paying attention to directive illocutions uttered in a ritual context. These claims are susceptible to empirical verification in other religious traditions.

The taxonomy of ritual studies I have provided offers a way to connect the structural work in ritual studies influenced by cognitive science with the interest in social, political, and power relationships that dominates so much of the rest of the field. Again with very few exceptions, analysts tend to focus on one level or the other.[3] I argue that what I have called the second level of ritual analysis provides the necessary underpinnings to the socio-ritual studies being pursued by such leading theorists as Catherine Bell. Given such a structural analysis, along with a complete inventory of the objects and actions available to the ritual participant (the lexicon), Bell's descriptions of the manipulation of this structure in actual ritual will be able to take on far greater subtlety and plausibility than those consisting of such oppositions as inner/outer, male/female, etc., which she currently employs.

I want now to step back from the argument and examine some of its wider implications. The general point made by the taxonomy of ritual studies I propose in chapter five, and by the over all argument of the book, is that the human sciences do appear to be able to overcome the chasm between interpretation and explanation that receives its classic formulation by Dilthey. Just as Saussure and Chomsky have shown in the study of language, a competence approach to cultural phenomena offers the opportunity to construct real structural explanations.

In terms of the contributions of this book to the history of religions, the simple juxtaposition of Protestant theology and ritual theory is critical. Very little history of religions work is done on Protestantism, and the work that is done tends to focus on somewhat marginal traditions, rather than mainstream ones. I believe there are at least two main reasons for this curious lacuna in the history of religions: the discipline's own roots as a branch of nineteenth-century Protestant theology (and its historical desire to move away from explicit theological tasks), and the discipline's historical and continuing fascination with "the other."

While both these motives are understandable, the result has been a paradoxically Barthian position for the history of religions. That is, the Protestant tradition is placed, unjustifiably, in a category separate from other religions. One of my motives in undertaking a study of the role of a theologian in Zurich is the simple fact that there is no more mainstream Protestant tradition than Zurich, one of the three main seats of the Reformation.

In the introduction I framed this issue in terms of Chidester's work on the theorizing about religions that occurred on the "margins," rather than the "center." Typically theoretical work is seen as taking place in universities in the economic and intellectual centers of Europe, where scholars collect data to be explained from other places around the world. I claimed that it would be equally important to take data from the "center" as well as from the "periphery." Why might this be so? Novalis once wrote, "Theories are nets: Only he who casts will catch." Of course, the design of your net, the size of the mesh, will be determined by what you are fishing for. Chidester and Jonathan Z. Smith have both pointed out a fascinating phenomenon, in which travelers first do not recognize indigenous people they meet as having a religion at all.[4] There may be many reasons for this. Chidester points out that at the very least it calls into question the humanity of the indigenous people. Smith claims that it was easy to dismiss myths and beliefs as "antiquities," but when travelers encountered rituals that seemed similar to Christian practice, they were forced to undertake comparative projects.[5] Similar is a relative term.[6] All this is a way of saying that, as a matter of practice, Christianity has served as what Benson Saler calls the prototype for our category of religion. Analysis of Christian rituals will "precise" our theoretical nets, or at least make sure we do not take our net design for granted or as given.

Just as the Reformed tradition has contributions to make to the history of religions, so too I hope that I have demonstrated that the converse is true. One of the major issues facing the study of historical theology today, and in particular the study of nineteenth-century theology, is the need to place theology in its social context. There are various ways to undertake such a task. The way I have pursued here is, I believe, in the tradition of Troeltsch's *Social Teachings of the Christian Churches*. By that I mean that a focus on cult, on practices, etc. can provide a meeting ground for theology and the wider culture. The history of religions has developed great expertise in analyzing public religious behavior. Such behavior is a meeting ground where theology and society intersect, and where their relationship can be laid bare. Such an approach goes even further than the analysis of more strictly intellectual traditions offered by Massey.

While my concern here has been with historical rather than with constructive theology, my belief is that theologians as well as historians ought to make use of ritual studies. The history of religions offers rich resources in particular to those theologians working in the tradition of Schleiermacher. For Schleiermacher, dogmatic theology is "logically ordered reflection upon the immediate utterances of religious self-consciousness."[7] That is why he draws far more from Reformed creeds in his classic systematic theology, *The Christian Faith*, than from scriptural texts. All Christians share the Bible–he was after the peculiar modifications of the religious affections present in the Reformed community. But who writes creeds? If theologians require as much access as possible to the religious self-consciousness of a community, to the peculiar modification of their religious affections, how much more there is to learn from a focus on ritual practice.

I believe this is what Sarah Coakley has in mind when, at the end of her book on Troeltsch's christology, she calls for theologians to turn to the "new methods of the social sciences" in doing christological "fieldwork."[8] It is clear that such fieldwork, to be of any value, must be approached with a high degree of sophistication. Coakley offers no specifics, but I believe that an approach to ritual such as the one I argue for here could provide a useful framework. It offers the opportunity for a fruitful analysis of the rituals a field-worker might find, proposes useful lines of inquiry (for example, it suggests questions researchers might pose to gain access to the religious conceptual schemes of the community being studied), and it proposes one way of tying these inquiries to the underlying worldviews, or philosophies of history, operative in a given community.

CEREMONIES OF BAPTISM FROM THE 1868 ZURICH LITURGY

Translated from *Liturgie für die evangelisch-reformirte Kirche des Kantons Zürich. Von der Synode angenommen am 28. Oktober 1868*. Ceremony I contains two sections which could be abridged in larger congregations with many baptisms. I have not included these abridgements, nor the plural forms for cases in which more than one child was being baptized.

Ceremony I

1   In the name of the Father, the Son, and the Holy Ghost. Amen.

2   Our help is in the name of the Lord, who created heaven and earth.

3   Dearest sponsors [*Taufzeugen*]! Since you have come to this holy place to
4   have this child admitted into the community [*Gemeinde*] of our Lord Jesus
5   Christ through holy baptism, so hear and consider how our Lord and Savior
6   instituted baptism as a symbol of the covenant [*Bundeszeichen*] of the New
7   Testament.

8   Jesus spoke to his disciples: To me is given all authority in heaven and on
9   earth. Go forth and make all peoples into disciples and baptize them in the
10   name of the Father, the Son, and the Holy Ghost, and teach them to observe
11   all that I have commanded you. See, I am with you all days until the end of
12   the world (Matt. 28:18-20).

13   [Abridgement here of above section]

14 Understand further how Jesus declared the children too to be members of
15 his kingdom, when he spoke to his disciples: Let the children come to me
16 and do not prevent them, for such is the kingdom of God. Truly, I say to you,
17 whoever does not accept [*annehmen*] the Kingdom of God as a child, he will
18 not come in. And he took them in his arms, laid his hands on them, and
19 blessed them (Mark 10:14-16).
20   Because the Lord wants to be the Savior of children as well, so let us bring
21 this child to him in so far as we are capable, that is, take it into his commu-
22 nity [*Gemeinschaft*] through baptism, and give him the sign of the covenant
23 of the people of God. May God grant his grace to that end!

24   So run the articles of the Christian faith, upon which the child is baptized
25 and in which it should also be instructed:
26   I believe in one God, the almighty Father, the creator of heaven and earth.
27   And in Jesus Christ, his only begotten son, our Lord.
28   Who was conceived by the Holy Ghost, born from the virgin Mary.
29   Who suffered under Pontius Pilate, was crucified, died and was buried, and
30 descended into hell.
31   [Who] on the third day rose again from the dead.
32   [Who] ascended into heaven, where he sits on the right hand of God, the
33 almighty Father.
34   From thence he shall come to judge the living and the dead.
35   I believe in the Holy Ghost.
36   [I believe in] one holy, universal, Christian church, which is the congre-
37 gation of the saints.
38   [I believe in] forgiveness of sins.
39   Resurrection of the body.
40   And an eternal life. Amen.

41   Let us now ask God for faith for this child, and that the baptism occur
42 internally through the Holy Ghost, and pray all together:
43   Almighty God, loving heavenly Father! We ask you in the name of our
44 Lord Jesus Christ, that you would look on this child with grace, according to
45 your infinite compassion, and make the baptism, this sign of the covenant
46 [*Bundeszeichen*] of your grace, efficacious for it. Give it the spiritual treasures
47 and blessings, through which the power of the blood of Jesus for the forgive-
48 ness of sins and the operation of the Holy Ghost for sanctification are marked
49 and affixed with a seal. Preserve in your love, merciful Father, this child who
50 is passed over to you in faith. Surround it, O precious Savior, with your grace.
51 Lead and direct it, O you spirit of knowledge and life, with your light and
52 your power, that it might grow up in the confession of the truth and the dili-
53 gence of virtue and godliness. Give to the parents and the sponsors, O mer-
54 ciful Father, the grace to the end that they raise this child in fear and knowl-

55 edge of you as a member of the church of Christ, to pious Christian conduct,
56 so that it, mindful of its baptismal vow, might follow Jesus daily and cling to
57 him with true faith, firm hope, and fervent love in joyful as well as unpleasant
58 days, so that it might finally leave behind this feeble life confidently,
59 according to your will, in true penance and under assurance of forgiven sins,
60 and on judgment day come forward unafraid at the universal judgment of
61 your Son and might find eternal blessedness; through our Lord Jesus Christ,
62 who dwells with you and governs in unity of the Holy Ghost, one God in
63 eternity. Amen.

64   [Abridgement here of prayer]

65   Pray further with devotion: Our father, etc.

66   Dearest sponsors! Since you have let the parents prevail on you to bring
67 this child to holy baptism and to testify publicly in their name that it shall be
68 led to our God the Lord and Savior through a Christian upbringing, so you
69 are in this by our Lord admonished, the same where need demands, to
70 remember seriously this your promise and your duty, and according to your
71 circumstances and your capabilities to advise and to help, that this child be
72 raised to the honor of God, to whom we bring it here. If you will do this, say
73 Yes.
74   If you now will that this child be baptized in the baptism of our Lord Jesus
75 Christ, say Yes and name the child.
76   [Child's name], I baptize you in the name of God the Father, the Son, and
77 the Holy Ghost. Amen.
78   God grant you [the child] that, as you now have been washed with pure
79 water in holy baptism, so on Judgment Day you might appear before God,
80 purified of sins, and be eternally blessed.
81   As for us, may God grant us the grace to remember seriously our baptism
82 vow, and to remain true to it in our conduct, that we may be confident of it
83 in life and in death. Amen.

Ceremony II

1   Our help is in the strength of the Lord, who created heaven and earth.
2   Amen.
3   See, what great love the Father shows us, that we should be called chil-
4   dren of God. He has made us into the first-born of his creation through the
5   word of truth, and wants to gather us all into one flock under one shepherd.
6   That is why the Savior said to his disciples: Go forth and make into disciples
7   all people, and baptize them in the name of the Father, the Son, and the Holy
8   Ghost and teach them to observe all that I have commanded you. See, I am
9   with you all days until the end of the world. And also the children he wants

10   to take into his Kingdom according to his word: Let the children come to me
11   and do not prevent them, for such is the Kingdom of God.
12   So we consecrate this child and bear witness that it shall be baptized on
13   faith in God the almighty Creator and Father, who has called us to a filial
14   relationship with him [*seiner Kindschaft*] and to eternal life; in Jesus Christ, the
15   Son of God, in whom we have redemption from our sins and reconciliation
16   with God, and in the Holy Ghost, who brings about faith, love, and hope in
17   us and restores us to true righteousness and holiness according to the image
18   of God. We administer holy baptism to it as a sign, seal, and pledge that it
19   shall be purified inwardly from all sin through the grace of God in Christ.
20   Therefore, dearest sponsors, you have appeared here in a holy place
21   (before the assembled congregation [*Gemeinde*]) to have this child adopted
22   into the bosom of the Christian church, and in the name of the parents to
23   bear witness publicly that it shall be raised to the honor of God and in the
24   discipline and exhortation of the Lord. In so doing you take on yourselves the
25   duty to assist the parents in such an upbringing as you are able, and to give
26   this child Christian aid in advice and deed.
27   To us, who are present at this celebration, may God give the grace to
28   remember and consider our baptism vow, which we, the community
29   [*Gemeinde*] of adults owe to the children, so that we give none of these small
30   ones offence, and have at all times the word of our Lord before our eyes:
31   What you do to the smallest of these, have you done to me! And he who
32   takes up one such child in my name, he takes me up.
33   And so let us call on God for his blessing:
34   Eternal God, you who are the rightful Father over all that are called chil-
35   dren in heaven and on earth, in your hand we lay this child for you to bless.
36   Through your power let what is portrayed and vouched for for the child in
37   the external deed of this baptism become truth in it. Immerse it in the life-
38   stream [*Lebensstrom*] of your grace and sanctify it to your possession. Take it
39   into your Kingdom. Let it be your child in imitation of Jesus and impress the
40   image [*Bild*] of his [Jesus'] life and death from early on in its soul, so that it
41   might not live for himself, but for him [Jesus] who has paid a high price for
42   it [child]. Fill it with your holy spirit, the spirit of truth and of love. Never
43   withdraw from *it* your grace, rather guard and strengthen, purify and sanctify
44   *it* continuously, that it might be and remain a living member in the congre-
45   gation [Gemeinde] of your saints, which is built on the ground of the apos-
46   tles and prophets, and whose cornerstone is Jesus Christ.
47   Eternal, holy God, make the blessing of baptism efficacious among us
48   always, and let the community [Gemeinde] that worships you in spirit and in
49   truth grow with each day, that the earth may be full of your knowledge.
50   Amen.
51   Our Father, etc.
52   If you desire, then, that this child be baptized in the baptism of our Lord
53   Jesus Christ, so say Yes and name the child.

54   [Child's name], I baptize you in the name of God the Father, the Son, and
55   the Holy Ghost. Amen.
56   The God of all grace, who has called you [child] to his eternal glory in
57   Jesus Christ, may he desire fully to prepare, strengthen, firmly establish and
58   through his might guard you, to eternal life.
59   May he desire to grant us all his grace and his peace, that we might be his
60   in life and in death. Amen.

DERIVATION OF THE BAPTISM CEREMONY

Lawson and McCauley's Generative Rules

(1)	ACTION	→	$[(P + ACMPLX), (P + ACMPLX + P)]$
(2)	P	→	$[(AG + Q), (O + Q)]$
(3)	ACMPLX	→	$(A + AQ)$
(4)	AG	→	$(a_1, a_2, a_3, \ldots a_n)$
(5)	O	→	$(o_1, o_2, o_3, \ldots o_n)$
(6)	Q	→	$(PRP, ACTION)$
(7)	PRP	→	$(q_1, q_2, q_3, \ldots q_n)$
(8)	A	→	$(r_1, r_2, r_3, \ldots r_n)$
(9)	AQ	→	$(AP, AC, ACTION)$
(10)	AP	→	$(k_1, k_2, k_3, \ldots k_n)$
(11)	AC	→	$(C + P)$
(12)	C	→	$(c_1, c_2, c_3, \ldots c_n)$

Legend

P	=	Ritual Participant
ACMPLX	=	Action Complex (the act, and whatever quality is necessary to make it legitimate)

AG	=	Agent
O	=	Object
Q	=	Quality (the property of an agent or object that makes them an appropriate ritual participant, or a previous action giving them such a property)
PRP	=	Property (by virtue of which an agent or object is an appropriate ritual participant)
A	=	Act
AQ	=	Action Quality (property, condition, or previous act making an act appropriate)
AP	=	Action Property (property of an act by which it is legitimate in ritual at stake)
AC	=	Action Condition (participant or condition making act valid)
C	=	Condition (by virtue of which an act is valid)

The Baptism Ceremony

ACTION	$\rightarrow$	P + ACMPLX + P (1)
P	$\rightarrow$	AG + Q (2)
AG	$\rightarrow$	minister (4)
Q	$\rightarrow$	ACTION (6)

ACTION	$\rightarrow$	P + ACMPLX + P (1)
P	$\rightarrow$	AG + Q (2)
AG	$\rightarrow$	Jesus (4)
Q	$\rightarrow$	PRP (6)
PRP	$\rightarrow$	q_2 (7)
ACMPLX	$\rightarrow$	(A + AQ) (3)
A	$\rightarrow$	command (8)
AQ	$\rightarrow$	(AP, AC, ACTION) (9)
AP	$\rightarrow$	k_1 (10)
P	$\rightarrow$	[(AG + Q), (O + Q)] (2)

O	→	disciples (5)
Q	→	(PRP, ACTION) (6)
PRP	→	q_3 (7)

ACMPLX	→	(A + AQ) (3)
A	→	baptize (8)
AQ	→	(AP, AC, ACTION) (9)
AP	→	k_1 (10)
P	→	[(AG + Q), (O + Q)] (2)
O	→	child (5)
Q	→	(PRP, ACTION) (6)
PRP	→	sponsored (7)

Notes

1. Numbers in parentheses refer to the specific rule applied at this step.

2. The embedded series of rituals by which the minister's own baptism legitimate is marked off by skipped lines.

3. The same derivation, represented as a tree diagram, can be found on page 98.

NOTES

Introduction

1. Alois Emanuel Biedermann, *Die freie Theologie oder Philosophie und Christenthum in Streit und Frieden* (Tübingen: Ludwig Friedrich Fues, 1844). Hereafter referred to as *Die freie Theologie*. Except as noted, all translations from German and French are my own.

2. G[eorg] Finsler, *Geschichte der theologisch-kirchlichen Entwicklung in der deutsch-reformierten Schweiz seit den dreissiger Jahren* (Zurich: Meyer & Zeller (H. Reimmann), 1881), 7.

3. Those in the academy who would argue that we have moved beyond the modern world of the nineteenth century to a postmodern world should look again at the German Romantics to see how many of today's hot topics in scholarship were already raised in the nineteenth century.

4. The only significant treatments of Biedermann in English are: B. A. Gerrish, "A. E. Biedermann on the Life Everlasting," chap. in *Tradition and the Modern World: Reformed Theology in the Nineteenth Century* (Chicago: University of Chicago Press, 1978); a brief introduction and translation of excerpts from Biedermann's *Christliche Dogmatik* by Claude Welch in, *God and Incarnation in the Mid-Nineteenth-Century German Theology: G. Thomasius, I. A. Dorner, A. E. Biedermann*, ed. and trans. Claude Welch, Library of Protestant Thought (New York: Oxford University Press, 1965); and a brief discussion by Welch in *Protestant Thought in the Nineteenth Century*, Vol. 1, *1799-1870* (New Haven and London: Yale University Press, 1972), 160-67. Biedermann has received far more attention in German. In 1997 Thomas K. Kuhn published an excellent

biography of Biedermann. It covers his life only up to 1844, that is, the year in which he skyrocketed onto the theological scene with *Die freie Theologie*. It has the most complete bibliography on Biedermann available. See Kuhn, *Der junge Alois Emanuel Biedermann: Lebensweg und theologische Entwicklung bis zur "Freien Theologie" 1819-1844*, Beiträge zur historischen Theologie 98 (Tübingen: J.C.B. Mohr, 1997). Karl Barth cited Biedermann's work as the theological path he would follow, were he to pursue a liberal theology, and compared Biedermann's "unshakeable religious faith and incorruptible reasonableness" to that of Zwingli. Emil Brunner recommended Biedermann's *Christliche Dogmatik* to his students as one of the most important works in systematic theology, singling out in particular the first part as "one of the best summaries of Church Dogmatics that I know." Karl Barth, "Liberal Theology: Some Alternatives," *The Hibbert Journal* 59 (October 1960-July 1961): 214; Emil Brunner, "Karl Barth's Alternatives for a Liberal Theology: A Comment," *The Hibbert Journal* 59 (October 1960-July 1961): 319.

5. Lawrence E. Sullivan, "Body Works: Knowledge of the Body in the Study of Religion," *History of Religions* 30 (August, 1990), 87. Theodore Jennings, "On Ritual Knowledge," *The Journal of Religion* 62 (April 1982), 115. Pierre Bourdieu, *Outline of a Theory of Practice*, trans. by Richard Nice (Cambridge: Cambridge University Press, 1977), 118-19. Catherine Bell, *Ritual Theory, Ritual Practice* (New York: Oxford University Press, 1992): 98.

6. Sullivan, 94; Jennings, 115; Bourdieu, 15; Bell, 141 and 170.

7. See Frits Staal, *Rules Without Meaning: Ritual, Mantras, and the Human Sciences* (Toronto: Peter Lang, 1989); Dan Sperber, *Rethinking Symbolism*, trans. Alice L. Morton (Cambridge: Cambridge University Press, 1990); Pascal Boyer, *Tradition as Truth and Communication: A Cognitive Description of Traditional Discourse* (Cambridge: Cambridge University Press, 1990); Pascal Boyer, *Religion Explained: The Evolutionary Origins of Religious Thought* (n.p.: Basic Books, 2001), chap.7; Caroline Humphrey and James Laidlaw, *The Archetypal Actions of Ritual: A Theory of Ritual Illustrated by the Jain Rite of Worship* (Oxford: Oxford University Press, Clarendon Press, 1994); Ilkka Pyysiäinen, *How Religion Works: Towards a New Cognitive Science of Religion*, Culture and Cognition Book Series, vol. 1 (Leiden: Brill, 2001), chap. 5; E. Thomas Lawson and Robert N. McCauley, *Rethinking Religion: Connecting Cognition and Culture* (New York: Cambridge University Press, 1990); Harvey Whitehouse, *Inside the Cult: Religious Innovation and Transmission in Papua New Guinea*, Oxford Studies in Social and Cultural Anthropology (Oxford: Oxford University Press, Clarendon Press, 1995), and Harvey Whitehouse, *Arguments and Icons: Divergent Modes of Religiosity* (Oxford: Oxford University Press, 2000).

8. Jennings, 115.

9. Jonathan Z. Smith, *Drudgery Divine: On the Comparison of Early Christianities and the Religions of Late Antiquity*, (Chicago: University of Chicago Press, 1990), 34.

10. David Chidester, *Savage Systems: Colonialism and Comparative Religion in Southern Africa* (Charlottesville: University of Virginia Press, 1996), xiii. Chidester has in mind histories of the discipline such as Walter H. Capps's *Religious Studies: The Making of a Discipline* (Minneapolis: Fortress Press, 1995) and Eric J. Sharpe's *Comparative Religion: A History*, 2d ed. (La Salle, Ill.: Open Court, 1986).

11. Chidester, *Savage Systems*, xiv.

12. Jonathan Z. Smith has persistently been one of the most astute scholars to point out that objects of academic research can only be understood on the assumption that they are like, not unlike, scholars. Their rituals "provide occasion for reflection and rationalization" (*Imagining Religion: From Babylon to Jonestown* [Chicago: University of Chicago Press, 1982], 63)–which of course is what scholars do. The Ceramese myth of Hainuwele the coconut girl is an "attempt at achieving intelligibility, at achieving rectification of either the data or the model"–in other words, science (101).

13. One might cite as an exception something like James L. Peacock and Ruel W. Tyson, Jr., *Pilgrims of Paradox: Calvinism and Experience among the Primitive Baptists of the Blue Ridge* (Smithsonian, 1989). But the exception proves the rule, since it would be hard to find a more "marginal" (in terms of representation among faculty at European and American universities) Protestant group.

14. By social formation McCutcheon means: "how new social organizations develop[,] . . . how they are institutionalized, maintained over time and place, how they are contested, and, eventually, come to an end." Social formation, describing religion, "refers to a specific and coordinated system of rhetorical acts and institutions that constructs the necessary conditions for shared identities." Russell T. McCutcheon, *Critics Not Caretakers: Redescribing the Public Study of Religion*, Issues in the Study of Religion (Albany: State University of New York Press, 2001), 25. "The construction of 'religion' and 'religions' as global, crosscultural objects of study has been part of a wider historical process of western imperialism, colonialism, and neocolonialism." Timothy Fitzgerald, *The Ideology of Religious Studies* (New York: Oxford University Press, 2000), 8.

15. Benson Saler, *Conceptualizing Religion: Immanent Anthropologists, Transcendent Natives, and Unbounded Categories* (Leiden: E. J. Brill, 1993; reprint with new preface, New York: Berghahn Books, 2000), ix (page references are to reprint edition).

16. Saler, 209.

17. Saler, 206.

18. Alois Emanuel Biedermann, "Erinnerungen," chap. in *Ausgewählte Vorträge und Aufsätze*, ed., with an introduction, by J. Kradolfer (Berlin: Georg Reimer, 1885), 431.

19. Of the relationship of Biedermann himself to the liberal government, Rolf Germann-Gehret writes: "For Biedermann, a deep tie in the development and fate of the liberal rule in Zurich from 1848 to 1866-69 was inevitable. Through his call to the University in 1850 his path joined together with an ecclesiastical and political liberalism, which in Canton Zurich went closely together in many spheres. This meant for a theological thinker the rather rare opportunity, that for many years he could develop and in part realize his ideas in closest context with praxis in a political arena (Biedermann was also a member of the Great Council for a term) as well as in a church-political arena." Rolf Germann-Gehret, *Alois Emanuel Biedermann (1819-1885): Eine Theodicee des gottseligen Optimismus* (Bern: Peter Lang, 1986), 36.

20. This confirms Steven Lukes's argument that we should abandon the "simplistic idea" of those he calls "neo-Durkheimians" (Lloyd Warner is a good example) of ritual "expressing-producing-constituting value integration seen as the essence of social integration. Rather, "ritual should be seen as reinforcing, recreating and organizing *représentations collectives* (to use Durkheim's term), that the symbolism of political ritual *represents, inter alia*, particular models or political paradigms of society and how it functions. . . . [R]ituals can be seen as modes of exercising, or seeking to exercise, power along the cognitive dimension." Lukes, "Political Ritual and Social Integration," *Sociology: Journal of the British Sociological Association* 9 (1975), 301.

21. Gottfried Keller, *Green Henry*, trans. A. M. Holt (New York: Grove Press, 1960). My citations of this novel are as follows: chapter one, 637; chapter two, 230; chapter three, 251; chapter four, 240; chapter five, 65; chapter six, 244, 394.

22. Georg Lukács, *German Realists in the Nineteenth Century*, trans. Jeremy Gaines and Paul Keast, ed. with an Introduction by Rodney Livingstone (Cambridge, Mass.: The MIT Press, 1993), 157.

23. Lukács, *German Realists in the Nineteenth Century*, 169-70.

24. Lukács, *German Realists in the Nineteenth Century*, 174.

25. Friedrich Wilhelm Graf, "Making Sense of the New Empire: Protestant University Theology in Germany, 1870-1918," in *Papers of the Nineteenth-Century Theology Group: AAR Annual Meeting, Philadelphia 1995*, ed. James C. Livingston and Francis Schüssler Fiorenza (Colorado Springs: The Colorado College, 1995), 6.

26. Graf, 16.

27. Claude Welch, "The Problem of a History of Nineteenth-Century

Theology: Welch Reconsidered," *The Journal of Religion*, vol. 70 no. 4 (October 1990), 614.

28. Marilyn Chapin Massey, *Christ Unmasked: The Meaning of* The Life of Jesus *in German Politics* (Chapel Hill: University of North Carolina Press, 1983).

29. Emile Durkheim, *The Elementary Forms of Religious Life*, trans. by Karen E. Fields (New York: The Free Press, 1995).

30. The title of a groundbreaking book by Louise A. Tilly and Joan W. Scott (New York: Holt, Rinehart and Winston, 1978).

31. Men and women were not treated equally in this respect. The first woman was not admitted to the University of Zurich until 1863, and women did not vote in federal elections until 1971. James Murray Luck, *A History of Switzerland: The First 100,000 Years: Before the Beginnings to the Days of the Present* (Palo Alto: Society for the Promotion of Science and Scholarship, 1985), 821.

32. "If, for instance, a man is properly dubbed to knighthood and then proceeds to violate all of the canons of chivalry, or if peace is declared in a properly conducted ritual but soon after one of the parties to the declaration attacks the other, we do not say that the dubbing or peace declaration were faulty, but that the subsequent states of affairs are faulty. *We judge the state of affairs by the degree to which it conforms to the stipulations of the performative act.* Liturgical orders provide criteria in terms of which events–behavior and history–may be judged. As such, liturgical orders are intrinsically correct or moral. Morality is inherent in the structure of liturgical performance prior to whatever its canons explicitly assert about morality in general or whatever in particular may be taken to be moral." Roy A. Rappaport, *Ritual and Religion in the Making of Humanity*, Cambridge Studies in Social and Cultural Anthropology 110 (Cambridge: Cambridge University Press, 1999), 133 (italics in original).

33. This is true not only of individual ritual participants. Rappaport argues that it is ritual that generates the sacred in the first place. See Rappaport, *Ritual and Religion in the Making of Humanity*, 295, 344.

Chapter One: Religious Conflict in Zurich

1. Germaine de Staël, *De l'Allemagne* (1813). German edition (Stuttgart), 68; quoted in Hagen Schulze, *The Course of German Nationalism: From Frederick the Great to Bismarck, 1763-1867*, trans. Sarah Hanbury-Tenison (Cambridge: Cambridge University Press, 1991), 47.

2. Durkheim, *The Elementary Forms of Religious Life*, 44.

3. David Parkin, "Ritual as Spatial Direction and Bodily Division," in

Understanding Rituals, ed. Daniel de Coppet (London: Routledge, 1992).

4. Van Harvey, *The Historian and the Believer: The Morality of Historical Knowledge and Christian Belief*, 2d ed. (Urbana: University of Illinois Press, 1996), 63.

5. Richard S. Cromwell, *David Friedrich Strauss and His Place in Modern Thought* (Fairlawn, NJ: R. E. Burdick, 1974), 15.

6. Cromwell, *David Friedrich Strauss*, 75 and 79.

7. Cromwell, *David Friedrich Strauss*, 197 n. 1.

8. Biedermann was called to the University in 1850, the first appointment to the theological faculty after 1846. For a complete table of appointments to the theological faculty of the University of Zurich, see Zürich Erziehungsrat, *Die Universität Zürich 1833-1933 und ihre Vorläufer. Festschrift zur Jahrhundertfeier*, ed. Ernst Gagliardi, Hans Nabholz, and Jean Strohl (Zurich: Verlag der Erziehungsdirektion, 1938). Reproduced in Paul Schweizer, *Freisinnig–Positiv–Religiössozial: Ein Beitrag zur Geschichte der Richtungen im Schweizerischen Protestantismus* (Zurich: Theologischer Verlag, 1972): 292-95.

9. Biedermann remarks that, in moving to Zurich he found himself transplanted onto the soil of a practical battle of sharp political-ecclesiastical oppositions and factions. He also notes that his call to Zurich was part of the reaction to the conservative backlash of the 1840s. Biedermann, "Erinnerungen," chap. in *Ausgewählte Vorträge und Aufsätze*, ed., with an introduction, by J. Kradolfer (Berlin: Georg Reimer, 1885), 430-31.

10. Biedermann, "Erinnerungen," 431.

11. An excellent brief summary of the liturgy struggle, and the associated battle over efforts by conservatives to have the Church Council censure the minister Friedrich Salomon Vögelin, former student of A. E. Biedermann, for his explicitly Young-Hegelian sermons, is given by G. Schmid, "Die Aufhebung der Verpflichtung auf das Apostolikum in der zürcherischen Kirche," in *Festschrift für Ludwig Köhler zu dessen 70. Geburtstag* (Bern: Büchler & Co. for the Schweizerischen Theologischen Umschau, 1950): 83-92.

12. The Great Council (*Der Grosse Rath*) was the highest legislative body in the Canton of Zurich. The Small Council (*Regierungsrath*) consisted of nineteen members appointed by the Great Council, and was the highest executive body. The Small Council oversaw the Church Council (*Kirchenrath*) and School Board (*Erziehungsrath*), each of which administered its respective state institutions (including hiring and paying ministers and teachers). The Synod of the Canton of Zurich consisted of all Reformed ministers in the Canton. The President of the Synod was called the Antistes, a term of honor originally used as a form of address for Zwingli, which quickly became an official office. Traditionally, the senior minister of the *Grossmünster* served as Antistes. The Synod was responsible for all the internal affairs of the church, including wor-

ship services, liturgies, hymnbooks, religious instruction, etc. All the Synod's decisions were forwarded, with explanations, to the Small Council, which added its own comments and then presented them to the Great Council. The Great Council could either approve the Synod's decisions without alteration, or reject the Synod's decision and return it with an explanation. In addition, as mentioned above, article 10 of the 1861 ecclesiastical law provided for a commission, appointed by the Great Council, to review the annual reports and minutes of the Church Council and the Synod, and alert the Great Council to any problems. Normally a proposal for a liturgy revision would originate with the Synod, and be passed to the Small Council and the Great Council in turn. The 1864 discussion of the liturgy is unusual for originating with the Great Council's commission, which prompted the Great Council to request of the Synod (the request being passed through the Small Council) that they take up the discussion.

13. Zurich, *Gesetz betreffend das Kirchenwesen des Kantons Zürich, in Officielle Sammlung der Seit Annahme der Verfassung vom Jahre 1831 erlassenen Gesetze, Beschlüsse und Verordnungen des Eidgenössischen Standes Zürich*, vol. 12 (Zurich: Orell, Füssli und Comp., 1859), art. 10.

14. Zurich Synod, *Amtlicher Auszug aus den Protokollen der Synode der zürcherischen Geistlichkeit*, vol. 43, *Die Verhandlungen der ordentlichen Versammlung vom 27. und 28 September 1864* (Zurich: Zürcher und Furrer, 1864), 17-18. Hereafter cited as *Protokollen der Synode* (1864).

15. G. Schmid, "Die Aufhebung der Verpflichtung auf das Apostolikum," 89.

16. Zurich Synod, *Protokollen der Synode* (1864), 18.

17. Zurich Synod, *Protokollen der Synode* (1864), 18-19.

18. It does not appear that the Church Council had in mind sacramental formulas for each theological orientation. One of their main reasons for deciding against proposing a church book to the Synod was the feeling that the current theological tensions in the church would make a major revision disruptive, and in particular that in such divided times a "free" liturgy was precisely not what was called for. The Church Council appears, instead, to have had in mind shorter versions of sacraments for use in large churches that performed baptisms every Sunday, or for use in the winter.

19. Zurich Synod, *Protokollen der Synode* (1864), 21-22.

20. G. Schmid, "Die Aufhebung der Verpflichtung auf das Apostolikum," 88.

21. H[einrich] Lang, "Die Herbstsynode in Zürich," *Zeitstimmen aus der reformirten Kirche der Schweiz* 6 (1864), 375. The government persistently denied motives of meddling in church affairs. Several factors, however, indicate that the government's actions may have been, at least in part, motivated

by a desire to prod the Synod into a modernizing reform of the church. During the controversies surrounding the calls of both Strauss and Biedermann to the University, enlisting their help in reforming the church was mentioned as one motive. For the motives behind Strauss's call, see Horton Harris, *David Friedrich Strauss and His Theology* (Cambridge University Press, 1973), 125. For Biedermann's comments on the political motives behind his call, see "Erinnerungen," 430-31. As early as 1859 Jakob Dubs (one of Zurich's representatives in the National Council, whom Largiadèr identifies along with Alfred Escher as one of the two leading figures of the second phase of Zurich liberalism [Largiadèr, 174]), published an article in *Zeitstimmen aus der reformirten Kirche der Schweiz* in which he denied that the Great Council played any roll in church affairs in Zurich beyond ratifying proposals made by the Synod. Dubs's main points in his *Zeitstimmen* article are summarized by G. Schmid, 88-89. Despite explicit claims to the contrary, the following comment of Dubs about the Synod indicates that the Great Council's role in church affairs may not always have been entirely passive: "It [the Synod] has many ideas, many good intentions, but because of sheer striving for the sublime they do not bring forth results. When the good intentions are at the point of passing over to firm decisions and actions, a legion of doubts promptly blocks the departure, and then many think, The world is bad, one cannot, after all, know what consequences the action might have." Quoted in G. Schmid, 88.

22. The other two main issues for discussion on the agenda were a reform of children's religious education, and a revision of the church constitution to create a 'mixed' synod (lay and clergy members). Heinrich Lang reports that most conservatives supported the motion for a mixed synod, and while the majority of liberals opposed it, the liberal camp was split. Lang, "Die Herbstsynode in Zürich," 354. On the one hand some liberals felt that the form of church government ought to reflect the form of state government, that is, it ought to be more representative. But on the other hand, as Lang states, it would be easier for liberal theology to work out its conflict with orthodox theology in a synod composed only of clergy. Lang, "Die Herbstsynode in Zürich," 352.

23. A contributor to the *Evangelisches Wochenblatt* described his reasons for supporting the formation of a commission, though he opposed a revision: (1) The liturgy is used arbitrarily, so it will benefit the church to standardize and enforce its usage. (2) Respect for the Great Council requires considering their proposal. (3) It is better to put to rest the discussion of a church book once and for all. (4) It is impossible not to take seriously the claims of certain ministers that the present liturgy torments their consciences (though their consciences are not to be considered above the needs of the communities they serve). (5) Any conservative who had voted against the motion to form a

liturgy commission could not, in good conscience, have served on that commission, and thus the conservative view would not have been represented. "Rückblicke auf die jüngste Synode," *Evangelische Wochenblatt* 5 (1864), 177.

24. It was Wolfensberger who made the motion, with Salomon Vögelin in mind, that the Synod ask the Church Council to censure certain ministers. Zurich Synod, *Amtlicher Auszug aus den Protokollen der Synode der zürcherischen Geistlichkeit*, vol. 44, *Die Verhandlungen der ordentlichen Versammlung vom 24 October 1865* (Zurich: Zürcher und Furrer, 1865), 20. Hereafter cited as *Protokollen der Synode* (1865).

25. Lang describes these six as the major spokesmen in his report on the 1864 Synod meeting. Lang, "Die Herbstsynode in Zürich," 376-80. G. Schmid's list of the most important members is largely the same as Lang's, though Schmid omits Finsler. G. Schmid, 90. The complete list of the thirteen members of the liturgy committee is found in Zurich Synod, *Protokollen der Synode* (1864), 40.

26. J. Schmid, "Rückblick auf die Synode der zürcherischen Geistlichkeit vom 2. bis 4. Oktober 1866," *Zeitstimmen aus der reformirten Kirche der Schweiz* 8 (1866) 397.

27. J. Schmid, "Rückblick auf die Synode der zürcherischen Geistlichkeit vom 2. bis 4. Oktober 1866," 397.

28. Quoted in G. Schmid, "Die Aufhebung der Verpflichtung auf das Apostolikum," 90.

29. Quoted in G. Schmid, "Die Aufhebung der Verpflichtung auf das Apostolikum," 90-91.

30. J. Schmid, "Rückblick auf die Synode der zürcherischen Geistlichkeit vom 2. bis 4. Oktober 1866," 398.

31. In particular, this revision is in line with Biedermann's emphasis on the christological principle as our filial relationship to God.

32. "Entwurf einer revidirten Liturgie," *Evangelisches Wochenblatt* 7 (1866), 150.

33. Zurich Synod, *Amtlicher Auszug aus den Protokollen der Synode der zürcherischen Geistlichkeit*, vol. 45, *Die Verhandlungen der ordentlichen Versammlung vom 2.-4. Oktober 1866* (Zurich: Zürcher und Furrer, 1866), 33. Hereafter cited as *Protokollen der Synode* (1866). Biedermann commended the commission's work, saying that it found a way to preserve the unity and freedom of the church. But he, too, indicated that they must go further. Against conservative arguments that it was too dangerous to undertake a revision in the current situation he argued: "One should reflect more on the origins of the step onto the precipitous path; the truth, in time, is eternal, and yet it must keep pace with [time] in order to satisfy the latter's deepest needs." "Die Synode," *Evangelisches Wochenblatt* 7 (1866), 179.

34. J. Schmid, "Rückblick auf die Synode der zürcherischen Geistlichkeit vom 2. bis 4. Oktober 1866," 399.

35. Zurich Synod, *Protokollen* (1866), 35, 36.

36. G. Schmid, "Die Aufhebung der Verpflichtung auf das Apostolikum," 92.

37. Zurich Synod, *Amtlicher Auszug aus den Protokollen der Synode der zürcherischen Geistlichkeit*, vol. 48, *Die Verhandlungen der ordentlichen Versammlung vom 27-28. Oktober 1868* (Zurich: Zürcher und Furrer, 1868), 32. Hereafter cited as *Protokollen der Synode* (1868).

38. "Religious freedom of belief is ensured. The Christian religion, in accordance with to the evangelical-reformed doctrines, is the recognized state religion." Zurich, Zurich Constitution (1831), art. 4.

39. "Die zürcherische Synode," *Evangelisches Wochenblatt* 5 (1864), 163. Lang describes these two items as "the two orthodox bulwarks." Lang, "Die Herbstsynode in Zürich," 376.

40. "Die Revision der zürcherische Liturgie," *Evangelisches Wochenblatt* 5 (1864), 148-49. During the discussion of the 1854 revision Biedermann had introduced a motion to remove the Apostles' Creed from the liturgy, but his friends, apparently not convinced that the time was right, persuaded him to withdraw the motion. "Die zürcherische Synode," *Evangelisches Wochenblatt* 9 (1868), 180[?]–page is unnumbered.

41. "Die Revision der zürcherische Liturgie," 148-49.

42. "Die Revision der zürcherische Liturgie," 164.

43. "Die zürcherische Liturgiefrage," *Evangelisches Wochenblatt* 7 (1866), 19.

44. "Die zürcherische Synode," (1864), 164.

45. "Die Synode," *Evangelisches Wochenblatt* 7 (1866), 162.

46. "Moreover, it is not in actuality a question of the confession of faith, but of God's word itself, because though the confession of faith may be of later origin, it is thoroughly in accord with scripture." "Die zürcherische Synode," (1864), 164.

47. "Die Revision der zürcherischen Liturgie," 149.

48. "Bericht über die diesjährige Synode," *Evangelisches Wochenblatt* 6 (1865), 174. This quote refers specifically to the use of the Apostles' Creed in the oath required of ministers on joining the Synod.

49. "There must still be many thousands . . . for whom it would seem to be a step out of the Holy of Holies into the forecourt [of the Gentiles] if the adoration [address] of Christ were abolished." "Die zürcherische Synode," (1864), 164.

50. Lang, "Die Herbstsynode in Zürich," 377.

51. Lang, 379. Traditionally, the Apostles' Creed is seen to have twelve articles. The other eight are those professing belief in (1) God the Father, (2) Christ His son, (3) the Easter resurrection, (4) Christ's judgement, (5) the Holy

Ghost, (6) the universal church (the congregation of saints), (7) the forgiveness of sins, and (8) eternal life.

52. Lang, "Die Herbstsynode in Zürich," 378.

53. Biedermann's comments are recorded in, Schweizerische reformirte Prediger-Gesellschaft, *Verhandlungen der schweizerischen reformirten Prediger-Gesellschaft in ihrer siebenten Jahresversammlung den 22. und 23. Juli 1845, in Zürich* (Zurich: J. J. Ulrich, 1845), 109-110.

54. Biedermann compares the Christian congregation to a body, the external organism of which is the church, and the internal organism or soul of which is "the religious spirit, in the Christian church in particular the spirit of Christ." Biedermann, *Die freie Theologie*, 213.

55. Zurich Synod, *Amtlicher Auszug aus den Protokollen der Synode der zürcherischen Geistlichkeit*, vol. 47, *Die Verhandlungen der ordentlichen Versammlung vom 5.-6. November 1867* (Zurich: Zürcher und Furrer, 1867), 17.

56. Lang, "Die Herbstsynode in Zürich," 383.

57. Kesselring, as quoted in *Evangelisches Wochenblatt*, 7 (1866), 165-66.

58. The themes touched on here are covered by Finsler in *Protokollen der Synode* (1867), 6-17.

Chapter Two: Contesting Humanity and Contesting History

1. Mircea Eliade, *The Myth of the Eternal Return or, Cosmos and History*, trans. Willard R. Trask, Bollingen Series XLVI (Princeton: Princeton University Press, 1954), 3.

2. We can conveniently break the relevant Swiss history into the following periods: prior to 1798 the social and political life of Switzerland, and the Canton of Zurich, were a particular permutation of the *ancien régime*. From 1798 to 1803 Switzerland was under the military protection of France and Napoleon (the Helvetic Republic). From 1803 to 1814 the Cantons of Switzerland administered their own affairs under constitutions designed for them by Napoleon (the Era of Mediation). From the downfall of Napoleon in 1814 to 1830 the Swiss constructed their own loose confederation of Cantons ruled by the same *ancien régime* oligarchies that had controlled the governments before 1798. The period from 1830-1870, during which Zurich and other Cantons modernized under the model of classical liberalism, is the period known as the Regeneration, which forms the context for Biedermann's work.

3. Both self-designations, "*Liberalen*" and "*Freisinnigen*," are best translated into English as "liberal" in the strict or classical sense, as opposed to the sense in which the word is used in contemporary American political discourse. Similarly, "conservative" meant something different in nineteenth-century

Zurich than it does today. The status quo defended by the conservatives in Zurich included a political aristocracy in politics, an economy based on a guild system, an orthodox, or supernaturalist religious commitment, and education primarily for the children of the upper classes.

4. Frederick S. Allen, *Zürich in the 1820s to the 1870s: A Study in Modernization* (Lanham, MD: University Press of America, 1986), vi.

5. The oligarchy controlling the Canton consisted of merchants, financiers, and manufacturers. Allen, 1. Allen estimates that it was made up by about three dozen families, most of whom lived in the city of Zurich. Ibid., 15.

6. Allen, 32.

7. As Anton Largiadèr notes, "the people remained fundamentally liberal, [the overthrow] had merely to do with getting even with some of the leaders," who had demonstrated a certain arrogance in the unrelenting pace with which they pushed through reforms. Anton Largiadèr, *Geschichte von Stadt und Landschaft Zürich*, vol. 2 (Erlenbach-Zurich: Eugen Rentsch Verlag, 1945), 152. On the fast pace of reform as an irritant, see Largiadèr, 140.

8. Rudolf Braun, *Sozialer und kultureller Wandel in einem ländlichen Industriegebiet: (Zürcher Oberland) unter Einwirkung des Maschinen- und Fabrikwesens im 19. und 20. Jahrhundert*, (Erlenbach-Zurich: Eugen Rentsch Verlag, 1965), 120.

9. Emil J. Walter, *Soziologie der Alten Eidgenossenschaft: Eine Analyse ihrer Sozial- und Berufsstruktur von der Reformation bis zur Französischen Revolution* (Bern: Francke Verlag, 1966), 273-74.

10. Basel and Strasbourg, among others, were also free cities.

11. Walter, 14.

12. Thomas A. Brady, Jr., *Turning Swiss: Cities and Empire, 1450-1550* (Cambridge: Cambridge University Press, 1985), 16.

13. Brady, 6.

14. Brady, 32.

15. Walter, 273; Brady, 31.

16. E. Bonjour, H. S. Offler, and G. R. Potter, *A Short History of Switzerland* (Oxford: Clarendon Press, 1952), 200.

17. Brady, 37.

18. Brady, 13. Brady gives three reasons for the development of the councils into ersatz lords: (1) the councils were striving for external recognition in a world in which authority and lordship were nearly synonymous; (2) a series of revolts between 1509 and 1514 seemed to justify greater controls such as censorship, sumptuary laws, and poor laws; and (3) there were external threats to commerce and independence from "bandit nobles" in the countryside and "predatory princes." Brady, 13-14.

19. The Great Council numbered 212 members. Electoral councils were allocated 130 seats in the Great Council, the guilds eighty-two seats.

20. The Small Council had twenty-five members. Its duties included appointing all district and local officials, including teachers and clergy.

21. Largiadèr, 114.

22. Largiadèr, 114-15.

23. Largiadèr, 116-17.

24. Allen, 25.

25. The major efforts of this early period of liberalism were redistricting, establishing popular participation in community government, reforming the judicial system, implementing a progressive income tax, and reforming the schools. Gordon A. Craig, *The Triumph of Liberalism: Zürich in the Golden Age, 1830-1869*, (New York: Charles Scribner's Sons, 1988), 49-50. In connection with establishing a progressive income tax the Great Council sold off state property which had provided income through church tithes and manorial dues. Allen, 30.

26. Largiadèr, 112.

27. *Staatsverfassung für den eidgenössischen Stand Zürich* (1831), art. 1, in *Officielle Sammlung der seit Annahme der Verfassung vom Jahre 1831 erlassenen Gesetze, Beschlüsse und Verordnungen des eidgenössischen Standes Zürich*, vol. 1 (Zurich: Friedrich Schulthess, 1831). Hereafter cited as Zurich Constitution (1831).

28. Unless the "principle" of the Regeneration is identified with greater specificity, it will not be possible to explain the successive period of radical democracy in Zurich's history. This period is marked, in politics, by a new constitution instituting a far more direct democracy, and in religion it is marked by the rise of the religious socialists later associated with Leonard Ragaz. Both the radical democracy and the religious socialism are "mass" movements, but both encountered stiff opposition from the elder generation of liberal statesmen and other leaders, Biedermann included.

29. In the following analysis of the philosophical underpinnings of Swiss liberalism, I rely heavily on Wolfgang von Wartburg, "Zur Weltanschauung und Staatslehre des frühen schweizerischen Liberalismus," *Schweizerische Zeitschrift für Geschichte* (9) 1959: 1-45. Von Wartburg cites as two examples of the common chord struck by Kant among the leaders of early Swiss liberalism correspondence from Philipp Emanuel Fellensberg and Albert Rengger. Fellensberg writes: "Of all the systems that exist, that of the celebrated Kant is perhaps the only one to furnish solid and satisfactory bases in all respects for a good social order." Philipp Emanuel Fellensberg, *Philip Emanuel Fellensbergs Briefwechsel*, ed. A. Rufer (Politische Rundschau, 1945), 75, quoted in von Wartburg, 13. Rengger writes, after advising his correspondent to read Kant: "[T]he attaching of the political relationship to morality was as if taken from my soul, and I maintain that the erection of a constitutional law on the stated grounds is a leading requirement of the times, and that an ever more general

dissemination of a sense of justice is the one means to internal and external peace in our revolutionary days." Ferd. Wydler, *Leben und Briefwechsel Albert Renggers*, vol. 1, 273-74, quoted in von Wartburg, 14.

30. Von Wartburg, 5. Recall Kant's statement that "two things fill the mind with ever new and increasing admiration and awe, the oftener and more steadily we reflect on them: the starry heavens above me and the moral law within me." Immanuel Kant, *Critique of Practical Reason*, trans., with an Introduction by Lewis White Beck (Indianapolis: Bobbs-Merrill Company, 1956), 166.

31. Von Wartburg, 19.

32. Von Wartburg, 26. Kant's influence is again clear. Kant argues from the premise that "rational nature exists as an end in itself," and the fact that "every other rational being thinks of his existence by means of the same rational ground which holds also for myself," to his second formulation of the categorical imperative: "Act so that you treat humanity, whether in your own person or in that of another, always as an end and never as a means only." Immanuel Kant, *Foundations of the Metaphysics of Morals and What Is Enlightenment*, trans., with an introduction by Lewis White Beck (Indianapolis: Bobbs-Merrill Company, 1959), 47.

33. Von Wartburg, 27.

34. This idea is similar to Rousseau's concept of the general will. Rousseau is careful to distinguish the general will, which alone can direct the state towards the common good, from the will of all, which is "merely the sum of particular wills." Jean-Jacques Rousseau, *The Social Contract and Discourse on the Origin of Inequality*, ed., with an introduction by Lester G. Crocker (New York: Simon & Schuster, Washington Square Books, 1967), 27, 30-31. The similarity of Swiss liberalism to Rousseau is noted by Craig, 31.

35. Zurich Constitution (1831). art. 33, par. e.

36. Zurich Constitution (1831), arts. 53 and 61. This view of the mode of representing the masses leads von Wartburg to write that the liberal worldview is comparable to the aristocratic one in terms of patriarchy. Von Wartburg, 30.

37. Biedermann expressed his dislike of radical democrats: "Of all the political orientations of which one can currently speak of seriously in our fatherland, none is so fundamentally detestable to me as . . . the radical democratic, because it is the poorest in spirit, the emptiest of heart, and the most pernicious for 'freedom, education, and prosperity for all.'" Alois Emanuel Biedermann, *Unsere junghegelsche Weltanschauung oder der sogenannte neueste Pantheismus* [Our Young Hegelian World-view or the So-called newest Pantheism] (Zurich: Friedrich Schulthess, 1849), 189-90. Hereafter referred to as *Unsere junghegelsche Weltanschauung*.

38. Biedermann, *Unsere junghegelsche Weltanschauung*, 188-89.

39. Biedermann, *Unsere junghegelsche Weltanschauung*, 187.

40. Biedermann, *Unsere junghegelsche Weltanschauung*, 188.

41. Braun, 11.

42. Walter Bodmer, *Die Entwicklung der schweizerischen Textilwirtschaft im Rahmen der übrigen Industrien und Wirtschaftszweige* (Zurich: Verlag Berichthaus, 1960), 277.

43. Bodmer, 281, 282.

44. By 1852 there were six telegraph lines in Zurich. The first railway line was built in 1847. By 1869 over 200 miles of track had been laid. Allen, 41. Financing for the railroads was originally provided by foreign capital, primarily from two Paris banks, the Péreire brothers' Crédit Mobilier and James Rothschild's Réunion Financière. Bodmer, 423. In 1856 Alfred Escher founded the first of Zurich's great public share banks, the Schweizerische Kreditanstalt. Allen, 50.

45. Allen, 52-53. These figures may be slightly misleading, since before the advent of mechanized factories many families supplemented their agricultural income by participating in the cottage textile trade. Nonetheless, the shift is significant, since it indicates a move away from home based labor to a separation of living and work space. Braun, 185.

46. Bodmer, 402.

47. Braun poses the question as follows: "[T]he old structures of power and order collapsed. But how should the relation, precedence, and subservience of the various spheres–state, economy, society, church, school–be newly integrated? How should rights and duties, powers and dependencies be newly distributed?" Braun, 14.

48. Walter, 17.

49. Walter, 17.

50. Walter calculates that by 1798 there were 256 patricians in Zurich, belonging to only eighty-six families. In contrast, the "middle class" had grown to 60.2% of the population. Walter, 291, 283.

51. Zurich Constitution (1831), art. 7.

52. Allen, 54. At the national level a de facto freedom of trade was guaranteed in the Federal Constitution of 1848 through the decreeing of freedom of settlement. Hans von Greyerz, "Der Bundesstaat seit 1848," in *Handbuch der Schweizer Geschichte*, vol. 2 (Zurich: Verlag Berichthaus Zürich, 1977), 1026.

53. Allen, 33.

54. Allen, 54. The 1831 Constitution stipulates that the countryside receive a total of 141 seats in the Great Council, the City of Zurich seventy-one seats. Zurich Constitution, art. 33.

55. Allen, 33, 54.

56. Allen, 54. In an interesting parallel, Biedermann used the metaphor of

free trade versus the guild system to argue against theologians who condemn philosophy as anti-religious on the basis of hearsay rather than a thorough study of philosophy: "That path [the path of condemning philosophy without studying it] stands open to everyone; but when the philosopher only grants a word on his subject to [another] philosopher, that is not therefore a guild restriction. Everyone is free to practice philosophy; but even in the fullest freedom of trade, one must still have the tools and the practice to know how to handle [the trade] he wants to pursue." Biedermann, *Die freie Theology*, 14.

57. As Braun writes, "[f]reedom calls forth new bonds, and equality new privileges." Braun, 110.

58. The Restoration government had recognized the excesses of the factory system and made some attempt at regulation. In 1815 they passed a regulation outlawing labor by children younger than ten years of age. Children older than ten were required to be able to read, to have begun to write, and have memorized the catechism and certain prayers and religious songs to be eligible to work. Braun, 111. But there was no mechanism in place for inspection by the state, making the factory owners the de facto enforcers of the law. Compliance with these regulations, minimal as they were, was predictably lax. Serious and successful efforts at regulating child labor and working conditions were not undertaken until the liberal government came to power in the 1830s. Braun, 112.

59. Quoted in Largiadèr, 183-84.

60. Bodmer, 395.

61. Bodmer, 397. The factory legislation of 1859 also prescribed a minimum of rest periods for breaks and meals, obligated the factory owners to take precautions for their workers' safety in the work place, and forbid the use of corporal punishment in factories. The Ruling Council took responsibility for regular inspections of factories. The factory legislation of 1859 is reproduced by Braun, 132-34, n. 67.

62. Largiadèr, 180-81.

63. District Representative (*Bezirksrat*) Frei, quoted by Braun, 114.

64. The petition is in the Staatsarchiv Zürich (U 28), and quoted in Braun, 117. Braun hypothesizes that the petition, while doubtless written and submitted by the forty-four heads of households, was in fact instigated by their employers. Braun, 118. Nonetheless, there is ample evidence that factory workers in general did resent the attempts of the government to regulate their working conditions. Braun himself attributes the popular uprising of 1839 to anger stemming from the factory regulations adopted by the Ruling Council in 1837. Braun, 120. A law introduced in 1870 to limit the workday to 12 hours was rejected decisively by a popular vote. Braun, 136.

65. Braun's phrasing, 135.

66. Ernest Gellner, *Nations and Nationalism* (Ithaca: Cornell University Press, 1983), 34.

67. Largiadèr, 143-44.

68. Craig, 127.

69. Zurich Constitution (1831), art. 70.

70. Braun, 298-99.

71. The School Board had already begun its reform in 1831 with the decision to found a university. Towards this end the Great Council dissolved the Carolinum, Zurich's main institution of higher education, in 1832. It had been shaped by Zwingli, and was still associated with the Grossmünster. Zürich Erziehungsrat, *Die Universität Zürich 1833-1933 und ihre Vorläufer. Festschrift zur Jahrhundertfeier*, 3-4. Thus, the only way to study any of the sciences in Zurich (with the exceptions of law, medicine, and politics, for which independent institutes existed) had been to study theology. Largiadèr, 127. In 1833 the University of Zurich was opened, absorbing the faculty of the Carolinum, along with the faculties from the institutes of law, medicine, and politics. Allen, 81-82.

72. Allen, 81-82.

73. Scherr in *Verhandlungsbericht der Helvetischen Gesellschaft 1838*; quoted in Werner Wegmann, *Ignaz Thomas Scherr: Ein Kapitel zürcherischer Schulgeschichte, 1830-1839* (Aarau: H. R. Sauerländer & Co., 1941), 8. Note here Kant's definition of Enlightenment as "man's release from his self-incurred tutelage." "What Is Enlightenment?" in *Foundations of the Metaphysics of Morals and What Is Enlightenment*, 83.

74. When these new materials were delivered to the schoolhouse in the village of Stadel, 200 residents stormed the schoolhouse and burned the new books. Largiadèr, 144. One of the school officials arrested in the aftermath of the book burning stated that he became involved in the disturbance "because they [the educational materials] are instituted by God, and for which our Lord Christ gave up his life." Braun, 298 n. 2

75. Scherr, *Handbuch der Pädagogik*, 120; quoted in Wegmann, 31.

76. Scherr, *Handbuch der Pädagogik*, 122; quoted by Wegmann, 31.

77. "These psychological expositions allow one to recognize Scherr's educational goal more exactly: it was religiosity to which he wanted to raise the people." Wegmann, 31.

78. Henne, *Der Gärtner: Eine schweizerische allgemeine Kirchen- u. Schulzeitung für das Volk* 2 (1833) no. 2; quoted in Wegmann, 47.

79. Ignaz Thomas Scherr, to B. Steinmann, August 12, 1843, Unpublished Papers (*Nachlass*) in the Possession of E. Appenzeller-Frühe, Zurich; quoted in Wegmann, 49.

80. Heinrich Siegried [pseud.], *Grundlinien des Religionsunterrichtes nach den*

Gesetzen der Geistesentwicklung durch die Schule im Gegensatz zur Kirche (Winterthur, 1840); quoted in Wegmann, 44. It should be noted that Scherr called for religious education to be undertaken both by the church and in school, and was not attempting to replace the church in this arena, but merely to include religious instruction as a necessary part of elementary education in general.

81. Biedermann stated that his own goal in studying theology was his desire "to investigate the things of religion, and bring them into harmony with my reason." Biedermann, "Erinnerungen," 382. For Biedermann, the theoretical work of theology was not yet completed, so long as anything "super-reasonable" is left: "The theoretical taking-possession is not yet completely realized so long as the content of faith is accepted as super-reasonable mystery, rather than recognized as the reasonable content of the spirit, from the essence of the spirit." Biedermann, *Die freie Theologie,* 62.

82. In this context it is not difficult to see how, in Bonjour's phrase, the principle of the sovereignty of the people develops into the principle of *vox populi, vox Dei.* Bonjour, 250.

83. Wegmann, 42.

Chapter Three: The Personality of God and Other Contradictions

1. Biedermann's position on the second of these controversies is wonderfully explicated in B. A. Gerrish's "Image and Truth: A. E. Biedermann on the Life Everlasting."

2. There is no satisfactory translation of the German word *Geist* into English. It is often rendered as "mind," but this not only makes translating cognate forms (e.g., *geistlich*) awkward, it also stresses the activity of thought at the expense of other "*geistliche*" activities (e.g., willing, feeling). I have therefore chosen the translation "spirit," with its cognate form "spiritual." In doing so I follow Peter Hodgson's example in his editions of Hegel's *Lectures on the Philosophy of Religion* (see Georg Wilhelm Friedrich Hegel, *Lectures on the Philosophy of Religion,* 1 vol. ed., *The Lectures of 1827,* ed. Peter C. Hodgson, trans. R. F. Brown, P. C. Hodgson, and J. M. Stewart with the assistance of H. S. Harris (Berkeley, Los Angeles, London: University of California Press, 1988). This translation, too, has its dangers, since "spirit" can connote something ghostly to speakers of English, while "spiritual" has vague connotations of religious yearning. For Biedermann, as for Hegel, "*Geist*" denotes the nonphysical aspects of being (including, for humans, all thinking, willing, and feeling), and for this reason the German "*Geisteswissenschaften*" (sciences of the spirit) are translated into English as "the humanities." This is the sense of *Geist* denoted here by the English "spirit."

3. Biedermann, *Die freie Theologie*, 139-40.

4. Biedermann was called to the University of Zurich to fill the position left open when Ebrard left for Erlangen. (Biedermann, as a student in Berlin, had taken over Ebrard's lodgings in Berlin.) Biedermann, "Erinnerungen," 394. Other possibilities for comparison are J. P. Lange, who wrote his own *Life of Jesus* in response to Strauss's, and was called to the University of Zurich to the position which had originally been offered to Strauss; and J. P. Romang, a pastor in Bern who undertook perhaps the most sophisticated attack on Biedermann's theology in print, and in response to whom Biedermann wrote *Unsere junghegelsche Weltanschauung.*

5. A[ugust] Ebrard, "Fünf Artikel christlichen Glaubens und fünf Artikel heglischen Wissens," *Die Zukunft der Kirche* 1 (1845): 31-33. Hereafter referred to as Ebrard, "Fünf Artikel." Biedermann responded in an article entitled, "Fünf Artikel christlichen Glaubens und fünf Artikel heglischen Wissens," *Die Kirche der Gegenwart* 1 (1845): 132-46. Hereafter referred to as Biedermann, "Fünf Artikel." Ebrard then published "Apologie der fünf Artikel christlichen Glaubens und heglischen Wissens," *Die Zukunft der Kirche* 1 (1845): 60, 61-62, 66-68, 71-73, 75-76. Hereafter referred to as Ebrard, "Apologie." Biedermann countered with "Noch einmal die fünf Artikel," *Die Kirche der Gegenwart* 1 (1845): 209-224. Next appeared Ebrard, "Noch einmal die fünf Artikel," *Die Zukunft der Kirche* 1 (1845): 108-110. This exchange resulted in two further articles by Biedermann, which take their starting point from Ebrard's criticisms: "Esoterisch und exoterisch oder die Akkomodation," *Die Kirche der Gegenwart* 1 (1845): 243-259; and "Das Gespenst des Pantheismus und die Vorstellung von der Persönlichkeit Gottes," *Die Kirche der Gegenwart* 1 (1845): 261-280. A helpful discussion of the Biedermann/Ebrard debate can be found in Schweizer, "Der Gegenschlag Ebrards," and "Der Kampf zwischen Biedermann und Ebrard," chaps. in *Freisinnig-Positiv-Religiössozial*, 59-66.

6. Ebrard, "Fünf Artikel," 31.

7. Ebrard, "Fünf Artikel," 31, 32.

8. John Calvin, *Institutes of the Christian Religion*, ed. John T. McNeill, trans. Ford Lewis Battles, vol. 1 (Philadelphia: Westminster Press, 1960), 35.

9. Calvin, *Institutes*, 39.

10. Biedermann, *Unsere junghegelsche Weltanschauung*, 170.

11. "[I]t must be said that the content of philosophy . . . is wholly in common with that of religion." Hegel, *Lectures on the Philosophy of Religion*, 78.

12. On the close identification of religion with representation, Hegel writes: "The fact that the religious content is present primarily in the form of representation is connected to what I said earlier, that religion is the consciousness of absolute truth in the way that it occurs for all human beings. Thus it is found primarily in the form of representation." Hegel, *Lectures on the Philosophy*

of Religion, 144. On the limits of representation: "In the form of representation, however, God is in this simple manner in which we have God on one side and the world on the other." Hegel, *Lectures on the Philosophy of Religion*, 149.

13. Alois Emanuel Biedermann, *Christliche Dogmatik* [Christian Dogmatics] 2d ed., 2 vols. (Berlin: Georg Reimer, 1844), 22 (1:105-106). I cite Biedermann's dogmatics by section, volume, and page in the second edition.

14. See, for example, U. Fleisch, *Die erkenntnistheoretischen und metaphysischen Grundlagen der dogmatischen Systeme von A. E. Biedermann und R. A. Lipsius* (Naumburg, 1901); Axel Gyllenkrok, *Alois Emanuel Biedermanns Grundlegung der Dogmatik* (Uppsala: Almquist & Wiksells, 1943); Valentin Hack, "Das Wesen der Religion nach A. Ritschl und A. E. Biedermann unter besonderer Berücksichtigung der psychologischen Bestimmungen: Darstellung und Beurteilung," *Abhandlungen zur Philosophie und ihrer Geschichte* 19 (1911): 8-57; Max Hennig, *Alois Emanuel Biedermanns Psychologie der religiösen Erkenntnis,* (Leipzig: J. B. Hirschfeld, 1902); Karl Neck, *Das Problem der wissenschaftlichen Grundlegung der Theologie bei A. E. Biedermann,* (Schleitheim: J. G. Stamms Erben, 1944); Oskar Pfister, *Die Genesis der Religionsphilosophie A. E. Biedermanns, untersucht nach Seiten ihres psychologischen Ausbaus,* (Zurich: August Frick, 1898); and H. Lüdemann, "Erkenntnistheorie und Theologie," *Protestantische Monatshefte* 1 (1897): 4-215.

15. Biedermann saved the forms "perception" (*die Wahrnehmung*), "representation," (*die Vorstellung*) and "thought" or "concept" (*das Gedanken*) for the results of these stages in the epistemological process, and uses the words "perceiving" (*das Warhnehmen*), "representing" (*das Vorstellen*), and "thinking" or "conceiving" (*das Denken*) for the activity of the spirit itself. Biedermann, *Christliche Dogmatik*, 22 (1:106).

16. Biedermann defined pure realism in epistemology as "the carrying out of the principle of taking consciousness and its contents purely as it is in fact given to us, without allowing oneself to be led astray to a recasting by a hypothesis one brings along with oneself." Biedermann, *Christliche Dogmatik*, 13 (1:71). Biedermann kept current with the latest research in experimental psychology, a field that was in its infancy during his lifetime. While a student in Berlin he traveled to Göttingen to visit J. F. Herbart, one of the first to conceive of psychology as a science. "Erinnerungen," 396. In addition, Biedermann relied in part on the work of Wilhelm Wundt, founder of the first experimental psychology laboratory, and a colleague at the University of Zurich, in Part 1 of his dogmatics, "The Epistemological Foundation" ("Die erkenntnis-theoretische Grundlage"). Biedermann, *Christliche Dogmatik*, 30 (1:122). For a discussion of Wundt's work in Zurich, see Wolfgang G. Bringmann, Norma J. Bringmann, and Gustav A. Ungerer, "The Establishment of Wundt's Laboratory: An Archival and Documentary Study," chap. in *Wundt*

Studies: A Centennial Collection, ed. Wolfgang G. Bringmann and Ryan D. Tweney (Toronto: C. J. Hogrefe, 1980), 124-25.

17. Biedermann, *Die freie Theologie*, 116. Of course, for absolute spirit, or God, it will not be proper to talk about knowing and willing as such, since these (according to Biedermann) bear essentially the marks of finitude. Absolute spirit has strictly analogous activities to thinking and willing, as we will see.

18. Biedermann, *Christliche Dogmatik*, 23 (1:108).

19. The ego is defined as the subject of the three stages in the process of consciousness. Biedermann, *Christliche Dogmatik*, 22 (1:105). In translating "das Ich" as "ego" I follow Claude Welch, *Protestant Thought in the Nineteenth Century*, vol. 1, *1799-1870* (New Haven and London: Yale University Press, 1972); and *God and Incarnation in the Mid-Nineteenth Century German Theology: G. Thomasius, I. A. Dorner, A. E. Biedermann*, ed. and trans. Claude Welch, Library of Protestant Thought (New York: Oxford University Press, 1965). "Ego" avoids the awkward sentence constructions entailed by translating "das Ich" as "the I." It should be noted, however, that this term refers strictly to the subject of the process of consciousness.

20. Biedermann, *Christliche Dogmatik*, 23 (1:106). "Ideell . . . Seiende" in German means "non-material being." I have translated this as "ideal being."

21. Biedermann judges that Kant's categorical imperative, which is "the objective manifestation of an objective, real, ideal being for the subject" contradicts Kant's own agnostic evaluation of the possibility of ideal knowledge. *Christliche Dogmatik*, 26 (1:118).

22. "Hegel began with pure thought and appeared to want to spin out the entire world of experience from this, whereas to me, in truth the 'pure thought' can only be the final goal that we strive towards from experience and from the form of representation of our consciousness, which is determined by our sensible nature." Biedermann, "Erinnerungen," 390.

23. Biedermann, *Christliche Dogmatik*, 20 (1:103).

24. Biedermann thought that we could distinguish objects that are the products of our own imagination and objects that exist objectively in the world outside the self, and thus avoid complete solipsism, through a process he calls "triangulation." "An isolated perception can leave me unsure whether the object that comes to me in the relationship of being-conscious is really outside [of me] or only in me. But triangulation, which takes place of itself in the continuous perceptions concatenated together instructs us, except for individual cases of hallucination or that of real insanity." Biedermann, *Christliche Dogmatik*, 23 (1:108).

25. *Christliche Dogmatik*, 39 (1:137).

26. One of the reasons that Biedermann's theology is so compelling is that,

based on the psychological theories of Wundt, he does not try to get around the problem of anthropomorphism in religion. He simply assigns it its proper place. Recent trends in cognitive psychology suggest that this is a wise move. Justin Barrett has found that Christians, when asked to answer survey questions, give "theologically correct" (i.e. theologically sophisticated, non-anthropomorphic) answers about the nature of God. But when the cognitive demands are increased and these same Christians are asked to use theological concepts in interpreting a narrative, they inevitably fall back on anthropomorphic descriptions of God. See Justin L. Barrett, "Theological Correctness: Cognitive Constraint and the Study of Religion," *Method & Theory in the Study of Religion* 11 (1999), 325-39. Furthermore, this appears to be pan-cultural, indicating that it is a feature of human cognitive apparatus. Barrett got the same results in India. See "Cognitive Constraints on Hindu Concepts of the Divine," *Journal for the Scientific Study of Religion* 37 (December 1998), 608-19.

27. One of the tasks of the process of representation is to assign words ("heterogenous signs") to the contents of consciousness. Biedermann, *Christliche Dogmatik*, 29 (1:121). This is true even of contents that are the result of conceptual processing. Biedermann, *Christliche Dogmatik*, 37 (1:134).

28. For Biedermann's reference to "kritisch-speculative Verarbeitung," see *Christliche Dogmatik*, 585 (2:395). On returning to representational thinking after undertaking "critical-speculative processing," see *Christliche Dogmatik,,* 716 (2:545-46).

29. Hegel's definition of religion, as formulated by Biedermann, is the "representational view of the philosophical idea of the reconciliation of the finite with the infinite." Biedermann, "Erinnerungen," 406.

30. Biedermann, *Ausgewählte Vorträge und Aufsätze*, 413. Biedermann's definition leads Claude Welch to write: "Biedermann, we may say, tried to take more seriously than Hegel the latter's assertion that in religion the true content is already found." Claude Welch, *Protestant Thought in the Nineteenth Century*, 163-64.

31. Biedermann, *Die freie Theologie*, 13.

32. Biedermann, *Die freie Theologie*, 19.

33. Biedermann, *Ausgewählte Vorträge und Aufsätze*, 390.

34. Biedermann quotes this maxim in *Die freie Theologie*, 15.

35. Terry Pinkard, *German Philosophy 1760-1860: The Legacy of Idealism* (Cambridge: Cambridge University Press, 2002), 41.

36. Biedermann, *Die freie Theologie*, 30-31.

37. Biedermann, *Unsere junghegelsche Weltanschauung*, 101.

38. Biedermann, *Christliche Dogmatik*, 699 (2:516).

39. See Introduction, 2 (n. 4).

40. This formulation of Biedermann's interpretive move is adapted from B. A. Gerrish, "A. E. Biedermann on the Life Everlasting," 169.

41. Biedermann, *Christliche Dogmatik*, 631 (2:457).

42. On the metaphysical attributes of God see Biedermann, *Christliche Dogmatik*, 427-30 (2:262-64), and on the psychological attributes, 431-39 (2:264-68).

43. Biedermann, *Christliche Dogmatik*, 631 (2:457).

44. Biedermann, *Christliche Dogmatik*, 430 (2:264).

45. Alois Emanuel Biedermann, "Das Gespenst des Pantheismus und die Vorstellung von der Persönlichkeit Gottes," *Die Kirche der Gegenwart* 1 (1845): 261-280, esp. 272.

46. Biedermann, *Christliche Dogmatik*, 700 (2:517).

47. Biedermann, *Christliche Dogmatik*, 714 (2:536). For an example of Biedermann's use of the category *actus purus*, traditionally applied only to God, in reference to human actions, see n. 17, p. 57.

48. Ebrard, "Fünf Artikel christlichen Glaubens," 31.

49. Ebrard, "Apologie der fünf Artikel," 61-62.

50. Biedermann, "Das Gespenst des Pantheismus," 270.

51. Biedermann, "Das Gespenst des Pantheismus," 268.

52. See n.18, p. 43.

53. In fact, Biedermann calls the absolute in-itself absolute substance. It is only in relation to another, that is in God's positing of the world, that God can properly be spoken of as absolute spirit. *Unsere junghegelsche Weltanschauung*, 40.

54. Biedermann, *Unsere junghegelsche Weltanschauung*, 63-64.

55. From the human perspective being conscious of absolute spirit as the universal essence, and living in accord with it, constitutes eternal life: "only when the person is what he should be, . . . only then does he have eternal life in temporal existence. For then are moments of existence, that again and again rush by and negate his external existence in their eternal total absolute being for him and in him as they are in God; [the person] himself has therein eternity as his own real determination of existence in time." Biedermann, *Unsere junghegelsche Weltanschauung*, 170. See also Biedermann, *Christliche Dogmatik*, 808 (2:589): "When, however, the absoluteness of the spirit, as the self-opening-up of God for him, becomes the contents of his religious self-consciousness, and he finds therein his own true being as his ego and the absolute goal of his existence, he no longer experiences the natural annulment of his own finite worldly existence outside of God as the negation of his ego itself, which much more is with God, rather [he experiences the annulment] as only of that which is not-spirit, [i.e.] that in him which is worldly existence, belonging wholly to finitude." For a fuller discussion of eternal life in Biedermann's theology, see Gerrish, "A. E. Biedermann on the Life Everlasting."

56. *Die freie Theologie*, 177. Speculative theology knows that the two sides

themselves are unreal, are moments of the one real world.

57. Biedermann, *Die Freie Theologie*, 126.

58. Biedermann, *Die freie Theologie*, 62.

59. David Friedrich Strauss, *The Life of Jesus Critically Examined*, 4th ed., trans. George Eliot, ed. with an introduction by Otto Pfleiderer (London: Swan Sonnenschein & Co., 1898), 80 note 5.

Chapter Four: What Would Jesus Do?

1. Ebrard, "Fünf Artikel," 32.

2. Biedermann, "Erinnerungen," 391. E. Fahlbusch, in his entry in *Die Religion in Geschichte und Gegenwart* identifies Marheineke and Karl Daub as typical representatives of speculative theology. E. Fahlbusch, "Marheineke, Philipp Konrad," in *Die Religion in Geschichte und Gegenwart: Handwörterbuch für Theologie und Religionswissenschaft*, 3rd ed., ed. Hans Frhe. v. Campenhausen et al., vol. 4 (Tübingen: J. C. B. Mohr (Paul Siebeck), 1960). Karl Barth chooses Marheineke as his representative of orthodox Hegelianism in his *Die protestantische Theologie im 19. Jahrhundert*, in part because Marheineke's second edition of *Die Grundlehren der christlichen Dogmatik als Wissenschaft* (Berlin: Duncker und Humblot, 1827) "is unambiguously the dogmatics of the orthodox Hegelians." Karl Barth, *Die protestantische Theologie im 19. Jahrhundert: Ihre Vorgeschichte und ihre Geschichte*, 3d ed. (Zurich: Evangelischer Verlag AG, 1960), 442. On the conservative political implications of Marheineke's theology Robert Bigler writes, "Altenstein [Prussian Minister of Ecclesiastical Affairs and Education, and a supporter of Marheineke's] was apparently convinced that Hegel's philosophy, although too deep for him to grasp personally, provided satisfactory answers to the great historical and contemporary problems of state and church, and that it sanctioned the existing political and social order." Robert Bigler, *The Politics of German Protestantism: The Rise of the Protestant Church Elite in Prussia, 1815-1848* (Berkeley: University of California Press, 1972), 79-80.

3. Biedermann, *Die freie Theologie*, 163.

4. Biedermann, *Christliche Dogmatik*, 619 (2:434).

5. Biedermann, *Christliche Dogmatik*, 791 (2:581).

6. "The Johannine formula is so felicitously set [*bestimmt*] and at the same time indefinite [*unbestimmt*] that it forms the necessary starting point for all further development of the ecclesiastical consciousness of the person of Christ." Biedermann, *Christliche Dogmatik*, 371 (2:176).

7. Biedermann, *Christliche Dogmatik*, 586 (2:395-96).

8. Biedermann, *Christliche Dogmatik*, 407 (2:231).

9. Biedermann, *Christliche Dogmatik*, 407 (2:232).

10. Biedermann, *Christliche Dogmatik*, 618 (2:433).

11. Biedermann, *Christliche Dogmatik*, 619 (2:433).

12. "But he in whom it [Christ's effect] originally is and that which it in itself originally is, and as which it is present as the *causa efficiens* even in him, in whom it originally appears–that is not one thing, but two: the one is the principle, the other is the founder of the community, in whom the principle makes its original historical appearance for the community." Biedermann, *Christliche Dogmatik*, 623 (2:440).

13. "[B]oth [historical and philosophical authorization] are immediately overstepped when one wants to assert more of a specific personality than can be proven from his historical appearance." Biedermann, *Die freie Theologie*, 143.

14. Biedermann, *Christliche Dogmatik*, 793 (2:582).

15. Biedermann, *Christliche Dogmatik*, 794 (2:582).

16. Note here that Biedermann leaves open the possibility that others have had the same religious self-consciousness, but have left no historical record of it. It is important that he not shy away from this possibility, since he argues that Jesus is in no way qualitatively different than any other human being.

17. "The absoluteness of the spirit as such in its pure being-in-self is accordingly in itself already immanent human life-of-the-spirit as its ground, as its effective principle. But it is realized in a human personality as the real contents of its [the human personality's] own subjective life-of-the-spirit. This actualization, objectively, is the self-verification of absolute spirit in creaturely finite spirit. Subjectively it is the finite ego's self-consciousness of its being elevated by God into spiritual fellowship with God in the *actus purus* of its own self-elevation to free being-in-self as spirit. Thus, this human personal self-consciousness of the absoluteness of the spirit is the actual unification of the divine and the human essence in the unity of the personal life-of-the-spirit. It is also the entrance of the principle of God-manhood (which is immanent in each human as finite spirit) into the reality of human life." Biedermann, *Christliche Dogmatik*, 798 (2:584-85). *Actus purus* in scholastic thought is used to denote a quality of being unique to God, absolutely distinct from any human quality or action. Humans possess potentiality (implying change), whereas God is never potential, rather always fully actual. Given Biedermann's definition of God as the creative essence of humans, it is both fitting and significant for him to use this term for human action. Absolute spirit's *actus purus*, for Biedermann, is the positing of *das Andersein*. Finite spirit's *actus purus* is acting in accord with consciousness of the unity with absolute spirit. For a fuller discussion of human *actus purus* see Biedermann, *Christliche Dogmatik*, 706-707 (2:531-32).

18. Biedermann, *Die freie Theologie*, 88.

19. "[S]o we obtain as the relationship of the two members, between which

this movement of the self-consciousness occurs . . . , the relationship and the mediation of the pure eternal creative universal essence and the particular finite existence of the spirit. These are the two moments of the concrete unity of the one real free spirit." Biedermann, *Die freie Theologie*, 98-99.

20. Biedermann, *Christliche Dogmatik*, 797 (2:584).

21. "But now is realized, as the real content of its own subjective spiritual life, that which already is the ground and active principle immanent in each human spiritual life: the absoluteness of the spirit as such in its pure being-in-self in a human personality." Biedermann, *Christliche Dogmatik*, 798 (2:584-85).

22. "Here we have indicated as the theoretical moment in the believing self-consciousness, that in the appearance and in the entire work of Christ it sees the proof of the eternal, reconciling love of God, until this time hidden from humanity, which produces the reconciliation of humans with God. But [the appearance and work of Christ] does not produce the reconciliation of God with humans, rather [it] reveals [the reconciliation] existing in God as love to humanity." Biedermann, *Die freie Theologie*, 101 n. 1.

23. "Biedermann, *Die freie Theologie*, 92.

24. It is consistent with Biedermann's "pure realism" to make the (somewhat) modest claim that Jesus is the redeemer because he is the first world-historical individual with this religious self-consciousness. In principle this religious self-consciousness is a possibility for all humans, including non- or pre-Christians. Biedermann does not rule this out, but claims that, of those individuals about whom history has left a record, Jesus is the first with this religious self-consciousness. Again, this emphasizes the claim that Jesus is a person like all people, not a God-man.

25. Biedermann, *Die freie Theologie*, 98-99.

26. Karl Otfried Müller, *Prolegomena zu einer wissenschaftliche Mythologie* (Göttingen: Vandenhoeck u. Ruprecht, 1825).

27. Massey, *Christ Unmasked*.

28. Hans Frei, *The Eclipse of Biblical Narrative: A Study in Eighteenth- and Nineteenth-Century Hermeneutics* (New Haven: Yale University Press, 1974), 217. Frei's argument adds weight to the argument of Lukács that it is no accident that one of the German language's greatest realist novelists, Gottfried Keller, is a product of Switzerland and not Germany.

29. Welch, *Protestant Thought in the Nineteenth Century*, 147-48.

30. David Friedrich Strauss, *The Christ of Faith and the Jesus of History: A Critique of Schleiermacher's* Life of Jesus, trans. and ed. with an introduction by Leander E. Keck, Lives of Jesus Series, ed. Leander E. Keck (Philadelphia: Fortress Press, 1977).

31. Welch, *Protestant Thought in the Nineteenth Century*, 149.

32. Strauss, *The Life of Jesus Critically Examined*, 779-80.

33. Strauss, *The Life of Jesus Critically Examined*, 780.

34. Biedermann, "Erinnerungen," 406, 411.

35. Strauss responded favorably to Biedermann's dogmatics, in particular to Biedermann's doctrine of God, writing to him towards the end of his life, when Biedermann had sent him a copy, "I hear the good news to be sure; however, faith fails me." Biedermann, "Erinnerungen," 400.

36. Welch, *Protestant Thought in the Nineteenth Century*, 161.

37. Biedermann, *Die freie Theologie*, 128.

38. Biedermann, *Die freie Theologie*, 130.

39. Biedermann, *Christliche Dogmatik*, 815 (2:592).

40. Biedermann, *Christliche Dogmatik*, 815 (2:592-93).

41. Although Biedermann is consistent throughout his career in insisting that Jesus is the historical redeemer, comments such as the following are typical in his earlier work: "The determination of the universal essence of the person of Christ, as it was for the consciousness of his believers, contains the principle of Christianity." Biedermann, *Die freie Theologie*, 81. Also, "This state of affairs [the unresolved scientific research into the self-consciousness of Jesus] . . . could teach us, that we must not turn ourselves directly to Jesus' self-consciousness to find the principle of Christianity, rather [we must direct ourselves] to the self-consciousness of Christ as object of faith, as it was reflected and taken up into the self-consciousness of the faithful." *Die freie Theologie*, 82. Whereas Strauss needed only evidence that the idea of unity is present in history, and feels no need to push behind solid evidence for this idea (the gospel accounts) to the historical cause of that idea, Biedermann's requirement that the idea be concrete led him to draw conclusions about the cause from the effect. He asks rhetorically, "Whence should then this new faith have come—one asks—to the disciples, or any of the first Christians, if it was not communicated to them from him, whose essence and personality forms the contents?" *Die freie Theologie*, 107-108.

42. Biedermann, *Christliche Dogmatik*, 604 (2:417-25).

43. Biedermann, *Christliche Dogmatik*, 811 (2:590-91).

44. Though one must accept a heavy dose of Hegelianism to accept even this.

45. Biedermann, *Die freie Theologie*, 107-108.

46. Paul Wernle, *Der schweizerische Protestantismus im XVIII. Jahrhundert*, vol. 1, *Das reformirte Staatskirchentum und seine Ausläufer (Pietismus und vernünftige Orthodoxie)*, (Tübingen: J. C. B. Mohr (Paul Siebeck), 1923), 90.

47. Ebrard distanced himself from the "old, abstract supernaturalism" which required, as an "external duty" belief in the events related in the Bible. For Ebrard, the authority of the Bible was internal, it is the truth of the reconciliation through Jesus, a truth that cannot be demonstrated, but only experi-

enced. Ebrard, "Noch einmal die fünf Artikel," *Die Zukunft der Kirche* 1 (1845): 109.

48. Wernle, 474.

49. Rudolf Pfister, *Kirchengeschichte der Schweiz*, vol. 3, *Von 1720 bis 1950* (Zurich: Theologischer Verlag Zürich, 1984), 267. Pfister cites these principles as the foundational tenets of the Swiss Evangelical-Church Association [*Der Schweizerische Evangelisch-kirchliche Verein*], an organization founded in 1871 in to defend the Reformed church against the recent liberal changes.

50. Ebrard, "Apologie der fünf Artikel," 71.

51. Ebrard, "Apologie der fünf Artikel," 71.

52. Ebrard, "Apologie der fünf Artikel," 71.

53. Ebrard, "Apologie der fünf Artikel," 71.

54. Ebrard, "Apologie der fünf Artikel," 71. In so arguing Ebrard believes he has again distinguished his position from traditional church doctrine.

55. Ebrard, "Apologie der fünf Artikel," 71.

56. From 1835-36 and 1841-42 Marheineke gave a series of lectures in which he defended Hegel's philosophy as "the best intellectual weapon for sanctioning the existing order in state and church," the Young-Hegelian "aberration" notwithstanding. Bigler, *The Politics of German Protestantism*, 118-19.

57. Marheineke, *Die Grundlehren der christlichen Dogmatik als Wissenschaft*, 181, 192.

58. For Hegel's dictum, see chapter three, note 11, above. Note, however, that Biedermann achieves this by defining religion as the relationship of the whole human spirit to the divine, while Marheineke achieves it by defining religion as concept, as the idea of God: "The idea of God is the essence of religion; concept is the essential and most perfect form of religion." Marheineke, *Grundlehren der christlichen Dogmatik als Wissenschaft*, 5.

59. Philip Konrad Marheineke, *D. Philipp Marheineke's theologische Vorlesungen*, vol. 2, *System der christlichen Dogmatik*, ed. Steph. Matthies and W. Vatke (Berlin: Duncker und Humblot, 1847), 310.

60. Marheineke, *System der christlichen Dogmatik*, 309.

61. Given this idea of a universal personality, it is not surprising that Marheineke thinks it is appropriate to speak of God's personality in conceptual as well as in representational language. See, for example, *Die Grundlehren der christlichen Dogmatik als Wissenschaft*, 113-14. Presumably Biedermann would find the concept of a universal personality as incoherent in the christological context as he does when applied to God.

62. Marheineke maintains a doctrine of vicarious satisfaction, in which those who believe in Christ are redeemed by virtue of his representative sacrifice. See Marheineke, *Die Grundlehren der christlichen Dogmatik als Wissenschaft*, 229.

63. Marheineke, *System der christlichen Dogmatik*, 311.

64. Ernst Troeltsch, "Historical and Dogmatic Method in Theology," trans. James Luther Adams and Walter F. Bense, chap. in *Religion in History*, Fortress Texts in Modern Theology (Minneapolis: Fortress Press, 1991), 13.

65. Troeltsch, "Historical and Dogmatic Method in Theology," 13, 14.

66. Strauss, *Life of Jesus*, 88.

67. Marheineke, *System der christlichen Dogmatik*, 305-306.

68. Marheineke, *System der christlichen Dogmatik*, 314.

69. Marheineke, *System der christlichen Dogmatik*, 312.

70. Marheineke, *System der christlichen Dogmatik*, 312.

Chapter Five: Meta Fights

1. Each ceremony cites the same two scriptural passages: "Jesus spoke to his disciples: To me is given all authority in heaven and on earth. Go forth and make all peoples into disciples and baptize them in the name of the Father, the Son, and the Holy Ghost, and teach them to observe all that I have commanded you. See, I am with you all days until the end of the world." Matt. 28:18-20. Also, "Let the children come unto me and do not prevent them, for such is the Kingdom of God. Truly, I say to you, whoever does not accept the Kingdom of God as a child, he will not come in. And he took them in his arms, laid his hands on them, and blessed them." Mark 10:14-16. I have translated both passages from the German found in the liturgy. Baptism I quotes the passage from Matthew at lines 8-12, the passage from Mark at lines 15-19. Baptism II quotes them together, lines 6-11.

2. For the purposes of this study, I treat baptism I and the baptism ceremony found in the previous liturgy as equivalent.

3. Baptism I, lines 24-25.

4. Baptism I, line 50.

5. Baptism I, lines 53-61.

6. Baptism I, lines 78-80.

7. Baptism I, lines 82-83.

8. Baptism II, lines 27-30.

9. Baptism I, lines 3-5; Baptism II, lines 20-22. While both phrases, "the community of our Lord Jesus Christ" and "the bosom of the Christian church" are ambiguous, the former can more easily be interpreted as referring to the invisible, in addition to the visible church, than can the latter.

10. Baptism II, lines 21.

11. For a description of the development both of the ceremony of baptism itself, and of the customs surrounding baptism in Zurich from the Reformation to the mid-twentieth century, see Erika Welti, *Taufbräuche im Kanton Zürich:*

Eine Studie über ihre Entwicklung bei Angehörigen der Landeskirche seit der Reformation (Zurich: Gotthelf-Verlag, 1967). Welti gives evidence of the primacy of acts of language over other acts in this ceremony in citing historical cases where all participants were prepared to proceed with the ceremony in the absence of water to pour over the child's head. In the eyes of the participants, the ceremony could go forward as long as the proper people were in place to say the proper words (though absence of water was by no means ideal, and in every case great effort was made to obtain some). Welti, 212. This does not constitute a case for the primacy of language in every ritual.

12. This level of analysis would include ethnographies, histories of ritual traditions such as Welti's, emic analyses of the history and current use of ritual such as we find in the field known as liturgics, and descriptions offered by historians and phenomonologists of religion.

13. Examples of this level of analysis include structural accounts such as Claude Lévi-Strauss, *Introduction to a Science of Mythology*, vol. 4, *The Naked Man*, trans. George Weidenfield and Nicolson Ltd. (Chicago: University of Chicago Press, 1966); recent work based on generative linguistics such as Frits Staal, *Rules Without Meaning: Ritual, Mantras, and the Human Sciences* (Toronto: Peter Lang, 1989), Dan Sperber, *Rethinking Symbolism*, trans. Alice L. Morton (Cambridge: Cambridge University Press, 1975), Caroline Humphrey and James Laidlaw, *The Archetypal Actions of Ritual: A Theory of Ritual Illustrated by the Jain Rite of Worship* (Oxford: Oxford University Press, Clarendon Press, 1994), Pascal Boyer, *Religion Explained: The Evolutionary Origins of Religious Thought* (n.p.: Basic Books, 2001), chap.7, Ilkka Pyysiäinen, *How Religion Works: Towards a New Cognitive Science of Religion*, Culture and Cognition Book Series, vol. 1 (Leiden: Brill, 2001), chap. 5, and E. Thomas Lawson and Robert N. McCauley, *Rethinking Religion: Connecting Cognition and Culture* (New York: Cambridge University Press, 1990); and attempts to show the structure of Navajo prayer found in Gladys Reichard, *Prayer: The Compulsive Word* (New York: J. J. Augustin, 1944), and Sam D. Gill, *Sacred Words: A Study of Navajo Religion and Prayer* (Westport, CT: Greenwood Press, 1981).

14. Prominent examples from this level of analysis, which is (at least in part) concerned with the role of ritual in society, include Pierre Bourdieu, *Outline of a Theory of Practice*, trans. Richard Nice (Cambridge: Cambridge University Press, 1977), Clifford Geertz, *The Interpretation of Cultures* (New York: Basic Books, 1973); Victor Turner, *Dramas, Fields, and Metaphors* (Ithaca, N.Y.: Cornell University Press, 1974), and Catherine Bell, *Ritual Theory, Ritual Practice* (New York: Oxford University Press, 1992). In a different vein, analysts who focus on sociopolitical ramifications of ritual structure include Roy A. Rappaport, *Ritual and Religion in the Making of Humanity*, Cambridge Studies in Social and Cultural Anthropology 110 (Cambridge: Cambridge University

Press, 1999), and Harvey Whitehouse, *Inside the Cult: Religious Innovation and Transmission in Papua New Guinea*, Oxford Studies in Social and Cultural Anthropology (Oxford: Oxford University Press, Clarendon Press, 1995), and *Arguments and Icons: Divergent Modes of Religiosity* (Oxford: Oxford University Press, 2000).

15. S. J. Tambiah, "A Performative Approach to Ritual," *Proceedings of the British Academy* 65 (1979): 154. Tambiah has in mind such things as the social status of the child's sponsors, cost and quality of the child's clothing, opulence of the meal traditionally following the service and number of people invited, etc. We could also add the political views of the various participants, as well as their views regarding the theology of the liberal party and the worldview it presupposes.

16. Bell, *Ritual Theory, Ritual Practice*, 170.

17. Pierre Bourdieu, on whose work Bell draws heavily, argues for the importance of what he calls "objectivist" analysis (in which he includes such things as structuralism and linguistics) before moving on to "the *dialectical* relations between the objective structures to which the objectivist mode of knowledge gives access and the structured dispositions within which those structures are actualized and which tend to reproduce them." Bourdieu, *Outline of a Theory of Practice*, 3. For Bourdieu, "epistemological priority is granted to objectivist rupture over subjectivist [dialectical] understanding." Loïc J. D. Wacquant, "The Structure and Logic of Bourdieu's Sociology," chap. in *An Invitation to Reflexive Sociology*, Pierre Bourdieu and Loïc Wacquant (Chicago: University of Chicago Press, 1992), 11.

18. In addition to *Ritual Theory, Ritual Practice*, see Catherine Bell, "Discourse and Dichotomies: The Structure of Ritual Theory," *Religion* 17 (April 1987): 98-118. I have reviewed *Ritual Theory, Ritual Practice* for *The Journal of Religion* (April 1993): 289-91.

19. Bell, *Ritual Theory, Ritual Practice*, 101-102. See also Catherine Bell, "Ritual, Change, and Changing Rituals," *Worship* 63 (January 1989): 31-41, for a slightly fuller discussion of the Roman Catholic eucharist.

20. Bourdieu, *Outline of a Theory of Practice*, 118-19.

21. Jonathan Z. Smith argues that "in the case of man, speech and action are given together. Neither is prior, in fact or in thought." While the influences of Smith on Bell's work are clear, in privileging non-verbal acts over speech, rather than "perceiving action and speech . . . as being coeval modes of human cognition," Bell's theory may contribute to the "mischief" done by one-sided theories. See Jonathan Z. Smith, "The Domestication of Sacrifice," chap. in *Violent Origins: Ritual Killing and Cultural Formation* (Stanford: Stanford University Press, 1987): 191-92.

22. The latter example is taken from Caroline Humphrey and James

Laidlaw, *The Archetypal Actions of Ritual: A Theory of Ritual Illustrated by the Jain Rite of Worship* (Oxford: Clarendon Press, 1994), 95. Humphrey and Laidlaw argue that human action is directed. For Humphrey and Laidlaw the relation between intention and act differs in ritual acts from other every day acts in that a ritual act is stipulated rather than being the agent's own creation. Nonetheless, what makes it an act is the agent's intention to perform that ritual act.

23. Charles Taylor, "Hegel's Philosophy of Mind," chap. in *Human Agency and Language: Philosophical Papers* vol. 1 (Cambridge: Cambridge University Press, 1985), 85. This model is called qualitative because it sees human acts as qualitatively different than other events in the world, rather than seeing them as equivalent to other events in the world except that their cause is some desire or intention.

24. This incident is recounted in George Steiner, *Real Presences* (Chicago: University of Chicago Press, 1989), 20.

25. Lawrence E. Sullivan, "Sound and Senses: Toward a Hermeneutics of Performance," *History of Religions* 26, no. 1 (August 1986): 1-33; Lawrence E. Sullivan, "'Seeking an End to the Primary Text' or 'Putting an End to the Text as Primary,'" chap. in *Beyond the Classics? Essays in Religious Studies and Liberal Education*, ed. Frank E. Reynolds and Sheryl L. Burkhalter, Scholars Press Studies in the Humanities (Atlanta: Scholars Press, 1990), 41-59.

26. Sullivan, "Seeking an End," 46.

27. Sullivan, "Seeking an End," 47-58.

28. Sullivan, "Sound and Senses," 22, n. 61. This is, perhaps, a similar point to one frequently made (both approvingly and disapprovingly) in referring to practitioners of certain modes of analysis as "pathologists." For just one example see Ioan P. Culianu's reference to Jonathan Z. Smith as "the greatest pathologist of the history of religions . . . : he carefully selects his victim, and then dissects with artistic finesse and unequaled acumen." Ioan P. Culianu, review of *Drudgery Divine: On the Comparison of Early Christianities and the Religions of Late Antiquity*, by Jonathan Z. Smith, in *The Journal of Religion* 72, no. 3 (July 1992), 476. Others are less sanguine about the value of analyzing what must first be killed.

29. Sullivan, "Sound and Senses," 22 (note 61).

30. This point is also made by Tambiah in his re-analysis of Bronislaw Malinowski's Trobriand data. S. J. Tambiah, "The Magical Power of Words," *Man* n.s. 3, no. 2 (June 1968): 175-208.

31. Sullivan, "Seeking an End," 56-57, citing Eduardo B. Viveiros de Castro, "A Fabric\ação do corpo na sociedade xinguana," *Boletim do Museu Nacional*, N. S. Anthropologia, no. 32 (May 1979): 40-49.

32. Sullivan, "Seeking an End," 48. Sullivan cites the French text, *La potière*

jalouse, (Paris: Librarie Plon, 1986). My references to the text will be to the English translation: Claude Lévi-Strauss, *The Jealous Potter*, trans. Bénédicte Chorier (Chicago: University of Chicago Press, 1988).

33. Sullivan, "Seeking an End," 49. Of course, it may not be the case that Lévi-Strauss understands pottery "as permutative linguistic codes," as Sullivan seems to claim. Lévi-Strauss's point is not that pottery (or myth, or kinship) is a permutation of language, but that laying out the system of possible relationships between terms in any cultural realm is as important to entering "the world of cultural meaning" of the "consciousness of the potter" as *langue* is to understanding *parole*. In any case, Lévi-Strauss does use the analysis of language as a paradigm for the analysis of other cultural arenas.

34. Robert A. Hinde, *Why Gods Persist: A Scientific Approach to Religion* (London: Routledge, 1999).

35. Again, this point is made by Bourdieu in *Outline of a Theory of Practice* (see note 17 above). Bourdieu's project in some ways is similar to Sullivan's in that he is concerned to show the "dialectical relations" between objective structures, that is, the ways in which individual actors, who do not see themselves as manipulating a pre-set structure, make their choices and perform their actions. Bourdieu, 3. Bourdieu uses the analogy of a musical score: the objectivist mode of knowledge can "decode the 'unwritten musical score according to which the actions of agents, each of whom believes she is improvising her own melody, are organized.'" Pierre Bourdieu, *Questions de sociologie* (Paris: Editions de Minuit, 1980), 89; quoted in Bourdieu and Wacquant, 8.

36. Lévi-Strauss's explicit claims for the importance of the structural level of analysis are perhaps most strikingly exemplified in his "canonic formula," which "can represent any mythic transformation." Lévi-Strauss, *The Jealous Potter*, 57. It is difficult not to read this formula as at least in part tongue-in-cheek in the context of his analysis as a whole.

37. The first chapter of Arnold Van Gennep's *The Rites of Passage* is an attempt to classify rituals on the model of botanical taxonomy. Arnold van Gennep, *The Rites of Passage*, trans. Monika B. Vizedom and Gabrielle L. Caffee, with an introduction by Solon T. Kimball (Chicago: University of Chicago Press, 1960), 1-14. Van Gennep sees classification as the hallmark of science (see p. 1). For his comparison of his project to botany, see p. 11. Anatomy and other branches of biology continue to play a large role in the analyses of scholars seeking a means of understanding structures of cultural systems in addition to individual manifestations of those systems. See, for example, the discussion of monothetic as well as polythetic taxonomies used in the classification of religions in Jonathan Z. Smith, "Fences and Neighbors: Some Contours of Early Judaism," chap. in *Imagining Religion: From Babylon to Jonestown* (Chicago: University of Chicago Press, 1982), 1-18, and the use of

such classifications for purposes of comparison in Jonathan Z. Smith, *Drudgery Divine: On the Comparison of Early Christianities and the Religions of Late Antiquity* (Chicago: University of Chicago Press, 1990) esp. 47-48 n. 15.

38. Jonathan Z. Smith, "A Twice-Told Tale: The History of the History of Religions' History," *Numen* 48 (2001): 143 and 145 (italics in original).

39. From *Traducción: Literatura y Literalidad* (Barcelona: Tusquets, 1971), translated by Irene del Corral and cited in Rainer Schulte and John Biguenet, eds., *Theories of Translation: An Anthology of Essays from Dryden to Derrida* (Chicago: The University of Chicago Press, 1992).

40. Paul Ricoeur argues for a textual model of explanation for other social phenomena in, "The Model of the Text: Meaningful Action Considered as Text," in *Interpretive Social Science: A Reader*, ed. Paul Rabinow and William M. Sullivan (Berkeley: University of California Press, 1979): 73-101.

41. "Utterance" is ambiguous, since it can mean either the thing that is uttered or the act of uttering it. Which of these two meanings is intended should be clear from the context in each case.

42. One influential definition of meaning in the philosophy of language is that the meaning of an utterance is its truth conditions. It is such a definition that is inappropriate to the utterances analyzed by John Austin.

43. J[ohn] L. Austin, *How to Do Things with Words*, ed. J. O. Urmson and Marina Sbisà, 2d ed. (Cambridge, Mass.: Harvard University Press, 1962). Austin prefers the word "constative" to "description," since "not all true or false statements are descriptions." Austin, 3. I will follow his usage.

44. "The issuing of the utterance is the performing of an action—it is not normally thought of as just saying something." Austin, 6-7. Austin's original distinction is between performatives and constatives.

45. Austin, 48.

46. Austin, 44.

47. Failure to note this point is one of the major flaws of an earlier attempt to make use of speech act theory in the analysis of a ritual. See Wade Wheelock, "A Taxonomy of the Mantras in the New- and Full-Moon Sacrifice," *History of Religions* 19, no. 4 (May 1980): 349-69, in which Wheelock classifies sections of part of a Vedic liturgy by grammatical form (utterances in indicative, first person future indicative, etc.).

48. Austin distinguishes three aspects of locutionary acts: To say something is always (a) to perform an act of making certain noises (a "phonetic" act), (b) which are in fact vocables and words (that is they belong to a certain language—a "phatic" act), and (c) to use these vocables and words in ways that have more or less definite sense and reference (meaning—a "rhetic" act). To say something in the full sense of performing a phonetic, phatic, and rhetic act constitutes the performing of a locutionary act.

49. While Austin thinks in general that perlocution is a result of the illocutionary force of an utterance, this is not always the case (though some have assumed that Austin meant that it is always the case. See, e.g., Max Black, "Austin on Performatives," *Philosophy* 38 (1963): 217-26). Ted Cohen offers an example of a locution resulting in a perlocution without doing so via the illocution: I may, in the course of discussing percussion music, attract your attention (perlocution) by uttering your name, if your name happens to be "Glockenspiel." See Ted Cohen, "Illocutions and Perlocutions," *Foundations of Language* 9 (1973): 492-503.

50. This is an example of what Austin calls a direct perlocutionary object. In addition to such a direct consequence of my utterance there may be other, indirect effects, which Austin calls perlocutionary sequels. In warning you not to open the door I may also alarm you, or in ordering you I may anger you.

51. Just as I can (and must) distinguish driving away in a car from stealing a car, or a tic from a hand signal, based on the intention of the actor, so I can and must distinguish the intention that makes your utterance an act of warning from other intentions that could make the identical string of phonemes a completely different speech act. Imagine that we are walking by a baseball diamond and you yell "Duck!" at me. If I were to ask you what you were doing, your response would not be that you were uttering a specific string of phonemes (the speech act's locution), but rather that you were giving a warning (your act's illocutionary force). I could not function as a human agent were I unable to distinguish the intention that makes this act a warning (imagine the same utterance, but now we are bird watching).

52. Austin's categories are: (1) verdictives, (2) exercitives, (3) commissives, (4) behabitives, and (5) expositives.

53. Searle criticizes Austin's locution/illocution distinction in John R. Searle, "Austin on Locutionary and Illocutionary Acts," *The Philosophical Review* 77, no. 4 (October 1968): 413-14. Searle prefers to distinguish the propositional content (p) of an utterance from the illocutionary force: F(p). See also John R. Searle, *Speech Acts* (Cambridge: Cambridge University Press, 1992). For Searle's own five-part classification of illocutionary acts, see John R. Searle, "A Taxonomy of Illocutionary Acts," in *Language, Mind, and Knowledge*, ed. Keith Gunderson, Minnesota Studies in the Philosophy of Science, ed. Herbert Feigle and Grover Maxwell, no. 7 (Minneapolis: University of Minnesota Press, 1975). It is not at all clear that Searle's classification of illocutionary acts is a significant advance over Austin's, as Searle claims. This was pointed out to me in a conversation with Ted Cohen. For my purposes, however, Searle's classification is useful in that he attempts to lay out the principles of classification explicitly.

54. John R. Searle, "A Taxonomy of Illocutionary Acts," 345-48.

55. Like Austin's classification, Searle's has five classes, only three of which we must consider for my purposes here. In addition to "descriptives (representatives)," "directives," and "declarations," discussed here in detail, Searle includes "commissives" (like promising) which commit the speaker to a future course of action and "expressives" (like thanking) that express the psychological state of the speaker.

56. Searle calls this category "representatives," but I have changed the name here to avoid confusion with the category of speech Biedermann calls "representational," which is language corresponding to a certain phase of the epistemological process, and which, for our purposes, corresponds roughly to anthropomorphic language about concepts.

57. Searle, "A Taxonomy of Speech Acts," 354.

58. Searle, "A Taxonomy of Speech Acts," 355.

59. Searle, "A Taxonomy of Speech Acts," 358.

60. See note 53, above.

61. Austin excludes certain kinds of utterances, which he calls "aetiolations of language," from his analysis (Austin, *How to Do Things with Words*, 104). He means that certain performative utterances issued in special circumstances, for example a promise spoken by an actor in the course of a play, are void. It is possible to conceive of utterances spoken in the special context of church rituals as falling into this category. Though Austin never discusses this case explicitly, he does not appear to think so. His very first example of a performative utterance is taken from the marriage ceremony of the Church of England *(How to Do Things with Words*, 3). In any case it is clear that the ritual participants in Zurich would not classify their utterances as "aetiolations of language." Failure to be properly baptized had very real world consequences: ineligibility to be confirmed, to be married, to be recruited into the military, to receive public aid, etc.

62. There is an obvious difficulty here regarding how to determine the size of the constituents to be classified, and where they begin and end. In the philosophical literature on speech acts the unit of utterance is generally one sentence ("I do," "I promise to . . .") or a sentence fragment. But some sentences, which as parts of larger units would clearly be classified one way, might be classified in another way taken in isolation. For example, in quoting scripture both ceremonies of baptism have the minister utter the sentence: "Go forth and make all peoples into disciples and baptize them . . ." (Baptism I, line 9; Baptism II lines 6-7). As presented in the Zurich Bible, this sentence was clearly a directive–Jesus was trying to get his disciples to do something. The minister, however, in saying these words, is citing a historical utterance. That is, in this context the minister's utterance is to be classified as a descriptive. So it appears that the scope of the unit of utterance varies with context. In other

words, when Austin writes, "The total speech act in the total speech situation is the *only actual* phenomenon which, in the last resort, we are engaged in elucidating," he leaves us with several important issues to sort out, not the least of these is what constitutes the "total speech act" and the "total speech situation."

63. Sam Gill offers at least three very rough criteria as a start towards a way of making the kinds of divisions I do: (1) changes in style, rhythm, and phrasing; (2) obvious differences in form and content; and (3) the fact that some passages appear in nearly identical form in other contexts, but surrounded by other passages (for example, the Apostles' Creed). Gill, *Sacred Words*, 10-12.

64. Baptism I, lines 5-7, and Baptism I, lines 14-15. These classifications are not straightforward. There is clearly a descriptive here: that is, the minister is claiming to describe a historical event to his listeners. Yet this descriptive is embedded in a directive, for the minister admonishes his listeners to pay attention to what he says. Situations like this indicate that speech act theory will benefit from more attention to the deep structure of utterances described by generative grammar, which provides a way of separating out constituent strings underlying the final utterance: "understand further," and "Jesus declared."

65. Baptism II, line 6. This is a straightforward descriptive.

66. Baptism I, lines 41-42.

67. Baptism II, line 33.

68. Baptism I, lines 50-51.

69. Baptism I, lines 76-77; baptism II, lines 54-55.

70. Baptism I, lines 26 and 35. In my translation of the Creed I follow the punctuation found in the German of the Zurich liturgy, which punctuates some of the dependent clauses as complete sentences.

71. Baptism I, lines 24-25.

72. See Austin, *How to Do Things with Words*, lecture 5. Though Austin was aware of developments in generative grammar, he never discussed the possibility of using the "deep" grammatical structure of utterances for distinguishing speech acts.

73. "Deep structure" in linguistics refers to the underlying strings of sentences, before transformational (and in some versions of the theory, phonetic) rules have been applied.

74. For "paradigm" descriptives such as "I state that it is raining," and "I predict that he will come," Searle characterizes the deep structure as: I verb (that) + S. Searle, "A Taxonomy of Speech Acts," 362.

75. Searle, "A Taxonomy of Speech Acts," 354.

Chapter Six: Liturgy Wars, Culture Wars

1. The Reformers were torn between two principles, each of which distinguished them from Catholics. On the one hand, in a priesthood of all believers, there should be no need for an ordained minister to be the baptizer–any baptized member of the community could do it. On the other hand, the impetus for non-ordained baptism in Catholicism had always been the belief that baptism was required for salvation, and so (with infant mortality rates high) sometimes there was not time to get a priest. This contradicts the principle of salvation by faith alone, that is, God can save whom God will regardless of the rites (works) performed by humans. In addition there are issues of prestige and control and gender in fights over who may baptize (non-ordained emergency baptizers were almost always mid-wives). In practice in Zurich the baptism was performed by the minister, although there are records of midwives or schoolmasters (both of whom were officials of the state in Zurich) performing baptisms if for some reason the minister could not. Since the time of Zwingli, however, the one absolute requirement for the performing of baptism was that the agent him or herself be a member of the Reformed community, which is to say that the agent be legitimately baptized.

2. This competence can described by means of rewriting rules, just as is done in descriptions of linguistic competence. We must be very clear about the ways in which a ritual system is, and is not, similar to a natural language. Both symbolic-cultural systems are highly structured and formalized. Performers in both systems have implicit knowledge of the set of rules constraining well-formed performance, even if they cannot state these rules explicitly. Natural languages differ from ritual in that the former have what linguists call a dual structure. That is, the relation between the level of the phonemes and morphemes is essentially arbitrary. Ritual signs, by contrast, are largely onomatopoetic, not entirely arbitrary (the bread and wine of the eucharist, for example). Further, the two have different relations to societal institutions. The performance of language is creative at an essentially individual level, while ritual is generally creative at a more social level (though private rituals no doubt exist). Ritual in general is aggressively defended from change by religious elites (or, as in Zurich, the authority to control change is tightly exercised). There may be some analogy in language to something like the French Academy, but such institutions are not the norm in the case of natural languages. Finally, the communicative function of ritual is controversial.

3. Wilhelm Dilthey gives the classic formulation of the split between explanation and interpretation (or understanding), and the impossibility of the former in the human sciences: "[W]e must begin to see methods of investigation which are in no sense analogous to those of the natural sciences. These methods . . . rest on the relations between life expressions and the inner reality

expressed by them." Wilhelm Dilthey, "The Understanding of Other Persons and Their Life-Expressions," in *Theories of History*, ed. Patrick Gardiner (Glencoe, Ill.: Free Press, 1959), 223.

4. Noam Chomsky, *Topics in the Theory of Generative Grammar* (The Hague: Mouton, 1966), 9-10.

5. This approach is called "cognitive" since, as Chomsky notes, a theory that can explain the movement from some initial state (such as infancy) to a state where a speaker-hearer can exhibit linguistic competence "is an explanatory theory of a particular human cognitive faculty. Were such theories available for various cognitive systems, we might proceed to investigate the general structure of human intelligence." Noam Chomsky, *The Logical Structure of Linguistic Theory* (Chicago: University of Chicago Press, 1975), 10.

6. Chomsky's system also includes phonetic rules describing the production of the sounds made by a speaker.

7. This is an example of phrase structure rules. For an example of a complete derivation of the sentence "The man hit the ball," see Noam Chomsky, *Syntactic Structures* (The Hague: Mouton, 1957), 26-27.

8. "The structural model, taken as a paradigm for explanation, may be extended beyond textual entities to all social phenomena because it is not limited in its application to linguistic signs, but applies to all kinds of signs which are analogous to linguistic signs. . . . A linguistic system, from the point of view of semiology, is only a species within the semiotic genre, although this species has the privilege of being a paradigm for the other species of the genre." Paul Ricoeur, "The Model of the Text: Meaningful Action Considered as Text," 98-99. Ricoeur also makes the distinction of structural vs. causal explanation, 99.

9. Ricoeur, 87-88.

10. Frits Staal, *Rules without Meaning: Ritual, Mantras, and the Human Sciences*, 76.

11. Welti, *Taufbräuche im Kanton Zürich*, 27-28.

12. Austin, 8-9, 14.

13. E. Thomas Lawson and Robert N. McCauley, *Rethinking Religion: Connecting Cognition and Culture* (New York: Cambridge University Press, 1990).

14. Lawson and McCauley, 55. Specifically they criticize Benjamin Ray and Edmund Leach.

15. Lawson and McCauley, 37. Lawson and McCauley discuss John Skorupski and Robin Horton in particular.

16. Lawson and McCauley, 38, 39. Victor Turner and Dan Sperber are their targets here.

17. Lawson and McCauley, 148.

18. Lawson and McCauley, 147.

19. Lawson and McCauley, 87.

20. Again, it is important to remember that this theory accounts not for the ontological status of events in the world, but only for the cognitive representations of these events by participants.

21. It is not important that such a regress of felicitous baptisms actually occurred in an unbroken chain in history. It is only important that such a regress be thought necessary (at least implicitly), and be represented in the cognitions of the ritual participants.

22. In Robert N. McCauley and E. Thomas Lawson, *Bringing Ritual to Mind: Psychological Foundations of Cultural Forms* (Cambridge: Cambridge University Press, 2002). Lawson and McCauley have switched from the problematic notion of "superhuman" (which depends on culturally specific constructions of "human") to the less problematic "counter-intuitive." In this they rely on the description of what kinds of ideas about religious agents are likely to be successful in Boyer's *Religion Explained*. Boyer is careful to delimit this category not as a psychological one (agents I may find surprising) but as concepts that have specific features that violate the ontological categories of "naïve" physics, biology, and psychology. See Boyer's *Religion Explained*, chap. 2. A person with six fingers is surprising. One who rises from the dead is counter-intuitive, even if years of Sunday school make it seem obvious.

23. Baptism I, lines 8-19; baptism II, lines 6-11.

24. Note that in the derivation of baptism diagramed above this property of Jesus (which appears as "q_2" in the diagram) is left unspecified.

25. On the importance of preaching in at least Calvin's branch of the Reformed tradition, see Dawn DeVries, *Jesus Christ in the Preaching of Calvin and Schleiermacher*, Columbia Series in Reformed Theology (Louisville: Westminster John Knox Press, 1996). DeVries argues that preaching, for Calvin, is an incarnational event. In Reformed churches the pulpit is often more prominent than the communion table.

26. Baptism I, lines 8-19; baptism II, lines 6-11.

27. See note 22, above, for Boyer's technical definition of "counterintuitive."

28. What is redemptive about Jesus is his religious self-consciousness. Biedermann argues that it is not on behalf of this man or this self-consciousness that we are reconciled with God, in fact, quite the opposite. Biedermann cites Jesus as historical evidence that such a religious self-consciousness, which Biedermann has shown to be in principle available to everyone is in fact (in history) possible, and so is possible for anyone.

29. Baptism I, lines 43-46.

30. Baptism II, lines 36-37.

31. Baptism I, lines 46-48.

32. Baptism I, lines 46-47.

33. Baptism II, lines 39-40.

34. Baptism II, lines 13-14.

35. Biedermann, "Errinerungen," 417. Biedermann quickly adds that the only judge of his orthodoxy is his own theological conscience, but that, in any case, questions of mere theoretical interest have no place in the pulpit (417-18).

36. Biedermann, "Erinnerungen," 418.

37. Klaus Otte, *Durch Gemeinde zur Predigt: Zur Verhältnisbestimmung von Theologie und Predigt bei Alexander Schweizer und Alois Emanuel Biedermann* (Frankfurt am Main: Peter Lang, 1979), 61.

38. In 1864 Friedrich Salomon Vögelin, young minister in the village of Uster and a former student of Biedermann's, published a collection of sermons entitled *Gott ist nicht ein Gott der Toten, sondern der Lebendigen* [God Is Not a God of the Dead, Rather of the Living], (Zurich: David Bürkli, 1864). Many conservative ministers were outraged by his sermons, particularly the sermon on Acts 1:6-12, given on Ascension Day. Vögelin preached that the significance of Ascension Day is that, while Christ personally is separated from us, we still feel connected to him through his spirit. Seventy-eight members of the Zurich Synod signed an "open declaration" in the *Zürcher Tagblatt* accusing Vögelin of violating his ordination oath, and demanding that the Church Council remove him from his post. Biedermann published an article in the March 1, 1865 issue of *Zeitstimmen aus der reformirten Kirche der Schweiz*, in which he discussed the "Vögelin affair." Biedermann stated that the task of scientific theology is to state religious truth as clearly as possible, but that it does not follow that preaching must become philosophical. Further, piety always expresses itself in sensible form, and that therefore preaching must also make use of this form. Biedermann's article is summarized in Schmid, "Die Aufhebung der Verpflichtung auf das Apostolikum in der zürcherischen Kirche," 86.

39. Biedermann, *Heinrich Lang* (1867), 47. Cited in Otte, *Durch Gemeinde zur Predigt*, 61-62.

40. Preaching is an example of what Cohen calls a direct unassociated perlocution. It is direct because the perlocution is the result of the illocution. It is unassociated because the perlocution does not "go with" the illocution as intimidating goes with threatening, alerting with warning, convincing with persuading, etc. Preaching may also be a direct associated perlocution if, for example, in addition to putting the listener in a frame of mind where he or she is open to penetration by religious truth the minister also succeeds in getting the listener to be charitable. Cohen, "Illocutions and Perlocutions," 496-97.

41. In Lawson and McCauley's terms, a baptism containing the Apostles' Creed would be rejected by the object agency filter, because it contains an ille-

gitimate ritual agent.

42. Because Biedermann has defined God as the universal creative essence of humans, that is, as the ideal moment of the really real, God is an appropriate addressee of a directive illocution. The question, of course, remains: Given a strict doctrine of predestination (which Biedermann shares with his orthodox opponents), why does it make sense to address requests to God? Biedermann writes: "Between the representation of the external objective effect of prayer [which is a miraculous view of prayer] and the mere subjective representation, in which the one praying calms and elevates himself through prayer, are the objective-subjective and the subjective-objective views. The former attributes the effect of the prayer in the praying subject not to the subject but to divine love. The latter recognizes that the prayer has consequences also for objectivity in that, through the calm and elevated mood that follows prayer, a man is enabled to lay hold upon objectivity quite differently and better, and to view things from the right perspective. We recognize both of these." Biedermann, *Unsere junghegelsche Weltanschauung*, 142. Biedermann's point is that he and his orthodox opponents share the view that prayer cannot influence God, or alter the path of predestination (or nature). Insofar as prayer is addressed to God, therefore, both groups reach the same conclusion: ultimately one prays to effect changes in oneself.

43. Arthur C. Danto, *Analytical Philosophy of History* (Cambridge: Cambridge University Press, 1965), 11.

Conclusion

1. Largiadèr, 112.

2. The other is Humphrey and Laidlaw's *The Archetypal Actions of Ritual*.

3. Theorists who work on both levels and show their connection include Harvey Whitehouse, *Inside the Cult*, and *Arguments and Icons: Divergent Modes of Religiosity*; and Roy Rappaport, *Ritual and Religion in the Making of Humanity*.

4. See Jonathan Z. Smith, "Religion, Religions, Religious," in *Critical Terms for Religious Studies*, ed. Mark C. Taylor (Chicago: University of Chicago Press, 1998), 269; Chidester, *Savage Systems*, 11-16.

5. Smith, "Religion, Religions, Religious," 271.

6. In *Inside the Cult* and *Arguments and Icons* Harvey Whitehouse has distinguished two ritual modes, doctrinal and imagistic, that organize the transmission of religious knowledge differently. The emphasis on faith and the prevalence of the doctrinal mode of religiosity in Christianity, especially Protestantism, could easily lead some one raised in that tradition not to recognize an imagistic ritual as belonging to the same category.

7. Friedrich Schleiermacher, *The Christian Faith*, 2d ed., English translation

edited by H. R. MacKintosh and J. S. Stewart (Philadelphia: Fortress Press, 1976), 81.

8. Sarah Coakley, *Christ Without Absolutes: A Study of the Christology of Ernst Troeltsch* (New York: Clarendon/Oxford Press, 1988), 195 ff.

BIBLIOGRAPHY

Allen, Frederick S. *Zürich in the 1820s to the 1870s: A Study in Modernization.* Lanham, MD: University Press of America, 1986.

Austin, J[ohn] L. *How to Do Things with Words.* Edited by J. O. Urmson and Marina Sbisà. 2d ed. Cambridge, MA: Harvard University Press, 1962.

Barrett, Justin L. "Cognitive Constraints on Hindu Concepts of the Divine." *Journal for the Scientific Study of Religion* 37 (December 1998): 608-19.

————. "Theological Correctness: Cognitive Constraint and the Study of Religion." *Method and Theory in the Study of Religion* 11 (1999): 325-39.

Barth, Karl. *Die protestantische Theologie im 19. Jahrhundert: Ihre Vorgeschichte und ihre Geschichte.* 3d ed. Zurich: Evangelischer Verlag AG, 1960.

————. "Liberal Theology: Some Alternatives." *The Hibbert Journal* 59 (October 1960-July 1961): 213-15.

Bell, Catherine. "Discourse and Dichotomies: The Structure of Ritual Theory." *Religion* 17 (April 1987): 98-118.

————. "Ritual, Change, and Changing Rituals." *Worship* 63 (January 1989): 31-41.

————. *Ritual Theory, Ritual Practice.* New York: Oxford University Press, 1992.

"Bericht über die diesjährige Synode." *Evangelisches Wochenblatt* 6 (1865): 173-76.

Biedermann, Alois Emanuel. *Die freie Theology oder Philosophie und Christenthum in Streit und Frieden.* [Free Theology or Philosophy and Christianity in Conflict and Peace]. Tübingen: Ludwig Friedrich Fues, 1844.

_____. "Fünf Artikel christlichen Glaubens und fünf Artikel heglischen Wissens." *Die Kirche der Gegenwart* 1 (1845): 132-46.

_____. "Noch einmal die fünf Artikel." *Die Kirche der Gegenwart* 1 (1845): 209-224.

_____. "Esoterisch und exoterisch oder die Akkomodation." *Die Kirche der Gegenwart* 1 (1845): 243-259.

_____. "Das Gespenst des Pantheismus und die Vorstellung von der Persönlichkeit Gottes." *Die Kirche der Gegenwart* 1 (1845): 261-280.

_____. *Unsere junghegelsche Weltanschauung oder der sogenannte neueste Pantheismus.* [Our Young Hegelian Worldview or the So-called newest Pantheism] Zurich: Friedrich Schulthess, 1849.

_____. *Christliche Dogmatik.* 2d edition, 2 volumes. Berlin: Georg Reimer, 1884-85.

_____. "Erinnerungen." Chap. in *Ausgewählte Vorträge und Aufsätze.* Edited, with an introduction, by J. Kradolfer. Berlin: Georg Reimer, 1885.

Bigler, Robert. *The Politics of German Protestantism: The Rise of the Protestant Church Elite in Prussia, 1815-1848.* Berkeley: University of California Press, 1972.

Black, Max. "Austin on Performatives." *Philosophy* 38 (1963): 217-26.

Bodmer, Walter. *Die Entwicklung der schweizerischen Textilwirtschaft im Rahmen der übrigen Industrien und Wirtschaftszweige.* Zurich: Verlag Berichthaus, 1960.

Bonjour, E., H. S. Offler, and G. R. Potter. *A Short History of Switzerland.* Oxford: Clarendon Press, 1952.

Bourdieu, Pierre. *Outline of a Theory of Practice.* Translated by Richard Nice. Cambridge: Cambridge University Press, 1977.

_____. *Questions de sociologie.* Paris: Editions de Minuit, 1980. Quoted in Pierre Bourdieu and Loïc J. D. Wacquant, *An Invitation to Reflexive Sociology.* Chicago: University of Chicago Press, 1992.

Boyer, Pascal. *Tradition as Truth and Communication: A Cognitive Description of Traditional Discourse.* Cambridge: Cambridge University Press, 1990.

_____ *Religion Explained: The Evolutionary Origins of Religious Thought.* N.p.: Basic Books, 2001.

Brady, Thomas A., Jr. *Turning Swiss: Cities and Empire, 1450-1550.* Cambridge: Cambridge University Press, 1985.

Braun, Rudolf. *Sozialer und kultureller Wandel in einem ländlichen Industriegebiet: (Zürcher Oberland) unter Einwirkung des Maschinen- und Fabrikwesens im 19. und 20. Jahrhundert.* Erlenbach-Zurich: Eugen Rentsch Verlag, 1965.

Bringmann, Wolfgang G., Norma J. Bringmann, and Gustav A. Ungerer "The Establishment of Wundt's Laboratory: An Archival and Documentary Study." Chap. in *Wundt Studies: A Centennial Collection*, ed. Wolfgang G. Bringmann and Ryan D. Tweney. Toronto: C. J. Hogrefe, 1980: 123-57.

Brunner, Emil. "Karl Barth's Alternatives for a Liberal Theology: A Comment." *The Hibbert Journal* 59 (October 1960-July 1961): 319.

Calvin, John. *Institutes of the Christian Religion.* Edited by John T. McNeill, translated by Ford Lewis Battles. Vol. 1. Philadelphia: Westminster Press, 1960.

Capps, Walter H. *Religious Studies: The Making of a Discipline.* Minneapolis: Fortress Press, 1995.

Chidester, David. *Savage Systems: Colonialism and Comparative Religion in Southern Africa.* Charlottesville: University of Virginia Press, 1996.

Coakley, Sarah. *Christ without Absolutes: A Study of the Christology of Ernst Troeltsch.* New York: Clarendon/Oxford Press, 1988).

Chomsky, Noam. *Syntactic Structures.* The Hague: Mouton, 1957.

_____. *Topics in the Theory of Generative Grammar.* The Hague: Mouton, 1966.

_____. *The Logical Structure of Linguistic Theory.* Chicago: University of Chicago Press, 1975.

Cohen, Ted. "Illocutions and Perlocutions." *Foundations of Language* 9 (1973): 492-503.

Craig, Gordon A. *The Triumph of Liberalism: Zürich in the Golden Age, 1830-1869.* New York: Charles Scribner's Sons, 1988.

Cromwell, Richard S. *David Friedrich Strauss and His Place in Modern Thought.* Fairlawn, NJ: R. E. Burdick, 1974.

Culianu, Ioan P. Review of *Drudgery Divine: On the Comparison of Early Christianities and the Religions of Late Antiquity* by Jonathan Z. Smith. In *The Journal of Religion* 72, no. 3 (July 1992): 476.

Danto, Arthur C. *Analytical Philosophy of History.* Cambridge: Cambridge University Press, 1965.

de Saussure, Ferdinand. *Course in General Linguistics.* Edited by Charles Bally and Albert Seshehaye, in collaboration with Albert Riedlinger, translated, with an introduction, by Wade Baskin. New York: McGraw-Hill, 1959.

DeVries, Dawn. *Jesus Christ in the Preaching of Calvin and Schleiermacher.* Columbia Series in Reformed Theology. Louisville: Westminster John Knox Press, 1996.

Dilthey, Wilhelm. "The Understanding of Other Persons and Their Life-Expressions." In *Theories of History,* ed. Patrick Gardiner. Glencoe, IL: Free Press, 1959.

Durkheim, Emile. *The Elementary Forms of Religious Life.* Translated by Karen E. Fields. New York: The Free Press, 1995.

Ebrard, [Johannes Heinrich] A[ugust]. "Fünf Artikel christlichen Glaubens und fünf Artikel heglischen Wissens." *Die Zukunft der Kirche* 1 (1845): 31-33.

_____. "Apologie der fünf Artikel christlichen Glaubens und heglischen Wissens." *Die Zukunft der Kirche* 1 (1845): 60, 61-62, 66-68, 71-73, 75-76.

_____. "Noch einmal die fünf Artikel." *Die Zukunft der Kirche* 1 (1845): 108-110.

Eliade, Mircea. *The Myth of the Eternal Return or, Cosmos and History.* Translated by Willard R. Trask. Bollingen Series XLVI. Princeton: Princeton University Press, 1954.

"Entwurf einer revidirten Liturgie." *Evangelisches Wochenblatt* 7 (1866): 146, 149-52, 153-54.

Fahlbusch, E. "Marheineke, Philipp Konrad." In *Die Religion in Geschichte und Gegenwart: Handwörterbuch für Theologie und Religionswissenschaft.* 3rd ed. Edited by Hans Frhe. v. Campenhausen et al. Vol. 4. Tübingen: J. C. B. Mohr (Paul Siebeck), 1960.

Fellensberg, Philipp Emanuel. *Philip Emanuel Fellensbergs Briefwechsel.* Edited by A. Rufer. Politische Rundschau, 1945). Quoted in Wolfgang von Wartburg. "Zur Weltanschauung und Staatslehre des frühen schweizerischen Liberalismus." *Schweizerische Zeitschrift für Geschichte* (9) 1959, 13.

Finsler, G[eorg]. *Geschichte der theologisch-kirchlichen Entwicklung in der deutsch-reformierten Schweiz seit den dreissiger Jahren.* Zurich: Meyer & Zeller (H. Reimmann), 1881.

Fitzgerald, Timothy. *The Ideology of Religious Studies.* New York: Oxford University Press, 2000.

Fleisch, U. *Die erkenntnistheoretischen und metaphysischen Grundlagen der dogmatischen Systeme von A. E. Biedermann und R. A. Lipsius.* Naumburg, 1901.

Frei, Hans. *The Eclipse of Biblical Narrative: A Study in Eighteenth- and Nineteenth-Century Hermeneutics.* New Haven: Yale University Press, 1974.

Geertz, Clifford. *The Interpretation of Cultures.* New York: Basic Books, 1973.

Gellner, Ernest. *Nations and Nationalism.* Ithaca: Cornell University Press, 1983.

Germann-Gehret, Rolf. *Alois Emanuel Biedermann (1819-1885): Eine Theodicee des gottseligen Optimismus.* Bern: Peter Lang, 1986.

Gerrish, B. A. "A. E. Biedermann on the Life Everlasting." Chap. in *Tradition and the Modern World: Reformed Theology in the Nineteenth Century.* Chicago: University of Chicago Press, 1978.

Gill, Sam D. *Sacred Words: A Study of Navajo Religion and Prayer.* Westport, CT: Greenwood Press, 1981.

_____. *Native American Religious Action: A Performance Approach to Religion.* Columbia, SC: University of South Carolina Press. 1987.

Graf, Friedrich Wilhelm. "Making Sense of the New Empire: Protestant University Theology in Germany, 1870-1918." In *Papers of the Nineteenth Century Theology Group: AAR Annual Meeting, Philadelphia 1995*, edited by James C. Livingston and Francis Schüssler Fiorenza, 5-18. Colorado Springs: The Colorado College, 1995.

Gyllenkrok, Axel. *Alois Emanuel Biedermanns Grundlegung der Dogmatik.* Uppsala: Almquist & Wiksells, 1943.

Hack, Valentin. "Das Wesen der Religion nach A. Ritschl und A. E. Biedermann unter besonderer Berücksichtigung der psychologischen Bestimmungen: Darstellung und Beurteilung." *Abhandlungen zur Philosophie und ihrer Geschichte* 19 (1911): 8-57.

Harris, Horton. *David Friedrich Strauss and His Theology.* Cambridge: Cambridge University Press, 1973.

Hegel, Georg Wilhelm Friedrich Hegel. *Lectures on the Philosophy of Religion*, 1 vol. ed., *The Lectures of 1827.* Edited by Peter C. Hodgson, translated by R. F. Brown, P. C. Hodgson, and J. M. Stewart with the assistance of H. S. Harris. Berkeley, Los Angeles, London: University of California Press, 1988.

Helvetische Gesellschaft. *Verhandlungsbericht der Helvetischen Gesellschaft 1838.* Quoted in Werner Wegmann, *Ignaz Thomas Scherr: Ein Kapitel zürcherischer Schulgeschichte, 1830-1839*, 8. Aarau: H. R. Sauerländer & Co., 1941.

Henne. *Der Gärtner: Eine schweizerische allgemeine Kirchen- u. Schulzeitung für das Volk* 2 (1833) no. 2. Quoted in Werner Wegmann, *Ignaz Thomas*

Scherr: Ein Kapitel zürcherischer Schulgeschichte, 1830-1839, 47. Aarau: H. R. Sauerländer & Co., 1941.

Hennig, Max. *Alois Emanuel Biedermanns Psychologie der religiösen Erkenntnis.* Leipzig: J. B. Hirschfeld, 1902.

Hinde, Robert A. *Why Gods Persist: A Scientific Approach to Religion.* London: Routledge, 1999.

Humphrey, Caroline and James Laidlaw. *The Archetypal Actions of Ritual: A Theory of Ritual Illustrated by the Jain Rite of Worship.* Oxford: Oxford University Press, Clarendon Press, 1994.

Kant, Immanuel. *Critique of Practical Reason.* Translated, with an Introduction by Lewis White Beck. Indianapolis: Bobbs-Merrill Company, 1956.

————. *Foundations of the Metaphysics of Morals and What is Enlightenment.* Translated, with an introduction by Lewis White Beck. Indianapolis: Bobbs-Merrill Company, 1959.

Keller, Gottfried. *Green Henry.* Translated by A. M. Holt. New York: Grove Press, 1960.

Kuhn, Thomas K. *Der junge Alois Emanuel Biedermann: Lebensweg und theologische Entwicklung bis zur "Freien Theologie" 1819-1844.* Beiträge zur historischen Theologie 98. Tübingen: J. C. B. Mohr, 1997.

Lang, H[einrich]. "Die Herbstsynode in Zürich." *Zeitstimmen aus der reformirten Kirche der Schweiz* 6 (1864): 349-57, 375-83.

Largiadèr, Anton. *Geschichte von Stadt und Landschaft Zürich.* Vol. 2. Erlenbach-Zurich: Eugen Rentsch Verlag, 1945.

Lawson, E. Thomas and Robert N. McCauley. *Rethinking Religion: Connecting Cognition and Culture.* New York: Cambridge University Press, 1990.

Lévi-Strauss, Claude. *Introduction to a Science of Mythology,* vol. 4, *The Naked Man.* Trans. George Weidenfield and Nicolson Ltd. Chicago: University of Chicago Press, 1966.

————. *La potière jalouse.* Paris: Librarie Plon, 1986. English translation, *The Jealous Potter.* Translated by Bénédicte Chorier. Chicago: University of Chicago Press, 1988.

Luck, James Murray. *A History of Switzerland: The First 100,000 Years: Before the Beginnings to the Days of the Present.* Palo Alto: Society for the Promotion of Science and Scholarship, 1985.

Lüdemann, H. "Erkenntnistheorie und Theologie." *Protestantische Monatshefte* 1 (1897): 4-215.

Lukács, Georg. *German Realists in the Nineteenth Century.* Translated by Jeremy Gaines and Paul Keast. Edited with an Introduction by Rodney

Livingstone. Cambridge, MA: The MIT Press, 1993.

Lukes, Steven. "Political Ritual and Social Integration." *Sociology: Journal of the British Sociological Association* 9 (1975): 289-308.

Marheineke, Philipp Konrad. *Die Grundlehren der christlichen Dogmatik als Wissenschaft.* 2d ed. Berlin: Duncker und Humblot, 1827.

————. *D. Philipp Marheineke's theologische Vorlesungen.* Vol. 2, *System der christlichen Dogmatik.* Edited by Steph. Matthies and W. Vatke. Berlin: Duncker und Humblot, 1847.

Massey, Marilyn Chapin. *Christ Unmasked: The Meaning of* The Life of Jesus *in German Politics.* Chapel Hill: The University of North Carolina Press, 1983.

McCauley, Robert N. and E. Thomas Lawson. *Bringing Ritual to Mind: Psychological Foundations of Cultural Forms.* Cambridge: Cambridge University Press, 2002.

McCutcheon, Russell T. *Critics Not Caretakers: Redescribing the Public Study of Religion.* Issues in the Study of Religion. Albany: State University of New York Press, 2001.

Müller, Karl Otfried. *Prolegomena zu einer wissenschaftliche Mythologie.* Göttingen: Vandenhoeck u. Ruprecht, 1825.

Neck, Karl. *Das Problem der wissenschaftlichen Grundlegung der Theologie bei A. E. Biedermann.* Schleitheim: J. G. Stamms Erben, 1944.

Otte, Klaus. *Durch Gemeinde zur Predigt: Zur Verhältnisbestimmung von Theologie und Predigt bei Alexander Schweizer und Alois Emanuel Biedermann.* Frankfurt am Main: Peter Lang, 1979.

Paz, Octavio. "Translation: Literature and Letters," trans. Irene del Corral and reprinted in Rainer Schulte and John Biguenet, eds. *Theories of Translation: An Anthology of Essays from Dryden to Derrida.* Chicago: The University of Chicago Press, 1992.

Peacock, James L. and Ruel W. Tyson, Jr. *Pilgrims of Paradox: Calvinism and Experience among the Primitive Baptists of the Blue Ridge.* Washington: Smithsonian Institution Press, 1989.

Pfister, Oskar. *Die Genesis der Religionsphilosophie A. E. Biedermanns, untersucht nach Seiten ihres psychologischen Ausbaus.* Zurich: August Frick, 1898.

Pfister, Rudolf. *Kirchengeschichte der Schweiz.* Vol. 3. *Von 1720 bis 1950.* Zurich: Theologischer Verlag Zürich, 1984.

Pinkard, Terry. *German Philosophy, 1760-1860: The Legacy of Idealism.* Cambridge: Cambridge University Press, 2002

Pyysiäinen, Ilkka. *How Religion Works: Towards a New Cognitive Science of*

Religion. Culture and Cognition Book Series, vol. 1. Leiden: Brill, 2001.

Rappaport, Roy A. *Ritual and Religion in the Making of Humanity.* Cambridge Studies in Social and Cultural Anthropology 110. Cambridge: Cambridge University Press, 1999.

Reichard, Gladys. *Prayer: The Compulsive Word.* New York: J. J. Augustin, 1944.

"Die Revision der zürcherische Liturgie." *Evangelisches Wochenblatt* 5 (1864): 148-49.

Ricoeur, Paul. "The Model of the Text: Meaningful Action Considered as Text." In *Interpretive Social Science: A Reader,* ed. Paul Rabinow and William M. Sullivan, 73-101. Berkeley: University of California Press, 1979.

Rousseau, Jean-Jacques. *The Social Contract and Discourse on the Origin of Inequality.* Edited, with an introduction by Lester G. Crocker. New York: Simon & Schuster, Washington Square Books, 1967.

"Rückblicke auf die jüngste Synode." *Evangelische Wochenblatt* 5 (1864), 176-78.

Saler, Benson. *Conceptualizing Religion: Immanent Anthropologists, Transcendent Natives, and Unbounded Categories.* Leiden: E. J. Brill, 1993; reprint with new Preface, New York: Berghahn Books, 2000.

Scherr, Ignaz Thomas. Letter to B. Steinmann, August 12, 1843. Unpublished Papers (*Nachlass*) in the Possession of E. Appenzeller-Frühe, Zurich. Quoted in Werner Wegmann, *Ignaz Thomas Scherr: Ein Kapitel zürcherischer Schulgeschichte, 1830-1839,* 49. Aarau: H. R. Sauerländer & Co., 1941.

————. *Leichtfassliches Handbuch der Pädagogik für Volksschullehrer, gebildete Eltern und Schulfreunde.* Vol. 1. Zurich: Orell, Füssli u, Co. 1839. Quoted in Werner Wegmann, *Ignaz Thomas Scherr: Ein Kapitel zürcherischer Schulgeschichte, 1830-1839,* 30. Aarau: H. R. Sauerländer & Co., 1941.

Schleiermacher, Friedrich. *The Christian Faith.* 2d ed. English translation edited by H. R. MacKintosh and J. S. Stewart. Philadelphia: Fortress Press, 1976.

Schmid, G. "Die Aufhebung der Verpflichtung auf das Apostolikum in der zürcherischen Kirche." In *Festschrift für Ludwig Köhler zu dessen 70. Geburtstag.* Bern: Büchler & Co. for the Schweizerischen Theologischen Umschau, 1950: 83-92.

Schmid, J. "Rückblick auf die Synode der zürcherischen Geistlichkeit vom 2. bis 4. Oktober 1866." *Zeitstimmen aus der reformirten Kirche der Schweiz* 8 (1866): 395-400.

_____. "Rückblick auf die zürcherische Synode vom 27. und 28. October 1868." *Zeitstimmen aus der reformirten Kirche der Schweiz* 10 (1868): 478-480.

Schweizer, Paul. *Freisinnig–Positiv–Religiössozial: Ein Beitrag zur Geschichte der Richtungen im Schweizerischen Protestantismus.* Zurich: Theologischer Verlag, 1972.

Schweizerische reformirte Prediger-Gesellschaft. *Verhandlungen der schweizerischen reformirten Prediger-Gesellschaft in ihrer siebenten Jahresversammlung den 22. und 23. Juli 1845, in Zürich.* Zurich: J. J. Ulrich, 1845.

Searle, John R. "Austin on Locutionary and Illocutionary Acts." *The Philosophical Review* 77, no. 4 (October 1968): 405-424.

_____. "A Taxonomy of Illocutionary Acts." In *Language, Mind, and Knowledge*, ed. Keith Gunderson. Minnesota Studies in the Philosophy of Science, ed. Herbert Feigle and Grover Maxwell, no. 7. Minneapolis: University of Minnesota Press, 1975: 344-369.

_____. *Speech Acts* Cambridge: Cambridge University Press, 1992.

Sharpe, Eric J. *Comparative Religion: A History.* 2d ed. La Salle, IL: Open Court, 1986.

Siegried, Heinrich [Johannes Scherr]. *Grundlinien des Religionsunterrichtes nach den Gesetzen der Geistesentwicklung durch die Schule im Gegensatz zur Kirche.* Winterthur, 1840. Quoted in Werner Wegmann. *Ignaz Thomas Scherr: Ein Kapitel zürcherischer Schulgeschichte, 1830-1839*, 44. Aarau: H. R. Sauerländer & Co., 1941.

Smith, Jonathan Z. *Imagining Religion: From Babylon to Jonestown.* Chicago: University of Chicago Press, 1982.

_____. "The Domestication of Sacrifice." Chap. in *Violent Origins: Ritual Killing and Cultural Formation.* Stanford: Stanford University Press, 1987): 191-205.

_____. *Drudgery Divine: On the Comparison of Early Christianities and the Religions of Late Antiquity.* Chicago: University of Chicago Press, 1990.

_____. "Religion, Religions, Religious." In *Critical Terms for Religious Studies*, ed. Mark C. Taylor. Chicago: University of Chicago Press, 1998, 269-84.

_____. "A Twice-Told Tale: The History of the History of Religions' History." *Numen* 48 (2001).

Sperber, Dan. *Rethinking Symbolism.* Translated by Alice L. Morton. Cambridge: Cambridge University Press, 1975.

Staal, Frits. *Rules Without Meaning: Ritual, Mantras, and the Human Sciences.* Toronto: Peter Lang, 1989.

Staël, Germaine de. *De l'Allemagne* (1813). German edition (Stuttgart), 68. Quoted in Hagen Schulze, *The Course of German Nationalism: From Frederick the Great to Bismarck, 1763-1867*, trans. Sarah Hanbury-Tenison, 47. Cambridge: Cambridge University Press, 1991.

Steiner, George. *Real Presences.* Chicago: University of Chicago Press, 1989.

Strauss, David Friedrich. *The Life of Jesus Critically Examined*, 4th ed. Translated by George Eliot. With an introduction by Otto Pfleiderer. London: Swan Sonnenschein & Co., 1898.

_____. *The Christ of Faith and the Jesus of History: A Critique of Schleiermacher's* Life of Jesus. Translated and edited with an introduction by Leander E. Keck, Lives of Jesus Series, ed. Leander E. Keck. Philadelphia: Fortress Press, 1977.

Sullivan, Lawrence E. "Sound and Senses: Toward a Hermeneutics of Performance." *History of Religions* 26, no. 1 (August 1986): 1-33.

_____. "'Seeking an End to the Primary Text' or 'Putting an End to the Text as Primary.'" Chap. in *Beyond the Classics? Essays in Religious Studies and Liberal Education.* Edited by Frank E. Reynolds and Sheryl L. Burkhalter. Scholars Press Studies in the Humanities. Atlanta: Scholars Press, 1990.

"Die Synode." *Evangelisches Wochenblatt* 7 (1866): 161-62, 165-67, 169-71, 173-76, 178-80, 181-82.

Tambiah, S. J. "The Magical Power of Words," *Man* n.s. 3, no. 2 (June 1968): 175-208.

_____. "A Performative Approach to Ritual," *Proceedings of the British Academy* 65 (1979): 113-69.

Taylor, Charles. "Hegel's Philosophy of Mind." Chap. in *Human Agency and Language: Philosophical Papers.* Vol. 1. Cambridge: Cambridge University Press, 1985.

Tilly, Louise A. and Joan W. Scott, *Women, Work, and Family.* New York: Holt, Rinehart and Winston, 1978.

Troeltsch, Ernst. "Historical and Dogmatic Method in Theology." Trans. James Luther Adams and Walter F. Bense. Chap. in *Religion in History.* Fortress Texts in Modern Theology. Minneapolis: Fortress Press, 1991.

Turner, Victor. *Dramas, Fields, and Metaphors.* Ithaca, NY: Cornell University Press, 1974.

van Gennep, Arnold. *The Rites of Passage.* Trans. Monika B. Vizedom and Gabrielle L. Caffee, with an introduction by Solon T. Kimball. Chicago: University of Chicago Press, 1960.

Vögelin, F. Salomon. *Gott ist nicht ein Gott der Toten, sondern der Lebendigen.* Zurich: David Bürkli, 1864.

von Greyerz, Hans. "Der Bundesstaat seit 1848." In *Handbuchder schweizer Geschichte.* Vol. 2. Zurich: Verlag Berichthaus Zürich, 1977.

von Wartburg, Wolfgang. "Zur Weltanschauung und Staatslehre des frühen schweizerischen Liberalismus." *Schweizerische Zeitschrift für Geschichte* (9) 1959: 1-45.

Wacquant, Loïc J. D. "The Structure and Logic of Bourdieu's Sociology." Chap. in *An Invitation to Reflexive Sociology,* Pierre Bourdieu and Loïc Wacquant. Chicago: University of Chicago Press, 1992.

Walter, Emil J. *Soziologie der Alten Eidgenossenschaft: Eine Analyse ihrer Sozial- und Berufsstruktur von der Reformation bis zur Französischen Revolution.* Bern: Francke Verlag, 1966.

Wegmann, Werner. *Ignaz Thomas Scherr: Ein Kapitel zürcherischer Schulgeschichte, 1830-1839.* Aarau: H. R. Sauerländer & Co., 1941.

Welch, Claude. *God and Incarnation in the Mid-Nineteenth Century German Theology: G. Thomasius, I. A. Dorner, A. E. Biedermann.* Edited and translated by Claude Welch. Library of Protestant Thought. New York: Oxford University Press, 1965.

_____. *Protestant Thought in the Nineteenth Century,* Vol. 1, 1799-1870. New Haven and London: Yale University Press, 1972.

_____. "The Problem of a History of Nineteenth-Century Theology: Welch Reconsidered." *The Journal of Religion,* vol. 70 no. 4 (October 1990): 606-17.

Welti, Erika. *Taufbräuche im Kanton Zürich: Eine Studie über ihre Entwicklung bei Angehörigen der Landeskirche seit der Reformation.* Zurich: Gotthelf-Verlag, 1967.

Wernle, Paul. *Der schweizerische Protestantismus im XVIII. Jahrhundert.* Vol. 1. *Das reformirte Staatskirchentum und seine Ausläufer (Pietismus und vernünftige Orthodoxie).* Tübingen: J. C. B. Mohr (Paul Siebeck), 1923.

Wheelock, Wade. "A Taxonomy of the Mantras in the New- and Full-Moon Sacrifice." *History of Religions* 19, no. 4 (May 1980): 349-69.

Whitehouse, Harvey. *Inside the Cult: Religious Innovation and Transmission in Papua New Guinea.* Oxford Studies in Social and Cultural Anthropology. Oxford: Oxford University Press, Clarendon Press, 1995.

_____. *Arguments and Icons: Divergent Modes of Religiosity.* Oxford: Oxford University Press, 2000.

Wydler, Ferd. *Leben und Briefwechsel Albert Renggers.* Vol. 1, 273-74. Quoted in Wolfgang von Wartburg. "Zur Weltanschauung und Staatslehre des frühen schweizerischen Liberalismus." *Schweizerische Zeitschrift für Geschichte* (9) 1959, 14.

"Die zürcherische Liturgiefrage." Evangelisches Wochenblatt 7 (1866): 19.

"Die zürcherische Synode." *Evangelisches Wochenblatt* 5 (1864): 163-64.

"Die zürcherische Synode." *Evangelisches Wochenblatt* 9 (1868), 178-79, 180[?].

Zurich. *Staatsverfassung für den eidgenössischen Stand Zürich* (1831). In *Officielle Sammlung der seit Annahme der Verfassung vom Jahre 1831 erlassenen Gesetze, Beschlüsse und Verordnungen des eidgenössischen Standes Zürich.* Vol. 1. Zurich: Friedrich Schulthess, 1831: 5-38.

Zurich. *Gesetz betreffend das Kirchenwesen des Kantons Zürich* (1861). In *Officielle Sammlung der Seit Annahme der Verfassung vom Jahre 1831 erlassenen Gesetze, Beschlüsse und Verordnungen des Eidgenössischen Standes Zürich.* Vol. 12. Zurich: Orell, Füssli und Comp., 1859: 475-555.

Zürich Erziehungsrat. *Die Universität Zürich 1833-1933 und ihre Vorläufer. Festschrift zur Jahrhundertfeier.* Edited by Ernst Gagliardi, Hans Nabholz, and Jean Strohl. Zurich: Verlag der Erziehungsdirektion, 1938.

Zurich Synod. *Amtlicher Auszug aus den Protokollen der Synode der zürcherischen Geistlichkeit.* Vol. 43, *Die Verhandlungen der ordentlichen Versammlung vom 27. und 28 September 1864.* Zurich: Zürcher und Furrer, 1864.

_____. *Amtlicher Auszug aus den Protokollen der Synode der zürcherischen Geistlichkeit.* Vol. 44, *Die Verhandlungen der ordentlichen Versammlung vom 24 October 1865.* Zurich: Zürcher und Furrer, 1865.

_____. *Amtlicher Auszug aus den Protokollen der Synode der zürcherischen Geistlichkeit.* Vol. 45, *Die Verhandlungen der ordentlichen Versammlung vom 2.-4. Oktober 1866.* Zurich: Zürcher und Furrer, 1866.

_____. *Amtlicher Auszug aus den Protokollen der Synode der zürcherischen Geistlichkeit.* Vol. 47, *Die Verhandlungen der ordentlichen Versammlung vom 5.-6. November 1867.* Zurich: Zürcher und Furrer, 1867.

_____. *Amtlicher Auszug aus den Protokollen der Synode der zürcherischen Geistlichkeit.* Vol. 48, *Die Verhandlungen der ordentlichen Versammlung vom 27-28. Oktober 1868.* Zurich: Zürcher und Furrer, 1868.

_____. *Liturgie für die evangelisch -reformirte Kirche des Kantons Zürich. Von der Synode angenommen am 28. Oktober 1868.* Zentralbibliothek Zürich call number AB 6522$_2$. Bound together with *Gesangbuch für die evangelisch-reformirte Kirche des Cantons Zürich*. Zurich: Zürcher und Furrer, 1853.

Index